Fritz Lang

Fritz Lang

Genre and Representation
in His American Films

Reynold
Humphries

The Johns Hopkins University Press
Baltimore and London

Originally published as *Fritz Lang: cinéaste américain.* © Editions Albatros, Paris 1982
English translation © 1989 The Johns Hopkins University Press
All rights reserved
Printed in the United States of America

This English–language edition is a revision of the French text; the translation is by the author, Reynold Humphries.

The Johns Hopkins University Press,
701 West 40th Street,
Baltimore, Maryland 21211
The Johns Hopkins Press Ltd.,
London

The paper used in this publication meets the minimum requirements of American National Standard for Information Sciences—Permanence of Paper for Printed Library Materials, ANSI Z39.48-1984.

Library of Congress Cataloging-in-Publication Data

Humphries, Reynold.
  Fritz Lang : genre and representation in his American films.

  Translated from the French.
  Bibliography: p.
  Includes index.
  1. Lang, Fritz, 1890–1976—Criticism and interpretation. I. Title.
PN1998.3.L36H8613   1989   791.43'0233'0924   88-45408
ISBN 0-8018-3699-9 (alk. paper)

No author, who understands the just boundaries of decorum and good-breeding, would presume to think all. The truest respect which you can pay to the reader's understanding, is to halve this matter amicably, and leave him something to imagine, in his turn, as well as yourself.

For my own part, I am eternally paying him compliments of this kind, and do all that lies in my power to keep his imagination as busy as my own.

—Laurence Sterne, *Tristram Shandy*

The would-be specific literary intellectual who wants to work for social change will, in addition, have to fight off two demons of self-doubt: one from the orthodox left, who will tell him that his work is bullshit and that real political work lies in the organization of workers: the other from the ultra left who will tell him that he must connect his work on traditional texts directly to the "real" situation, our contemporary political situation, directly to the front–page news, or risk total apolitical rarefication. My answer to these demons is that genuine political work for the Henry James scholar, as Henry James scholar, becomes possible when contact is made with the activity of James's writing, with all possible emphasis on its act.

—Frank Lentricchia, *Criticism and Social Change*

To raise the question of the nature of narrative is to invite reflection on the very nature of culture and, possibly, on the nature of humanity itself.

—Hayden White, *Tropics of Discourse*

Contents

Preface

Giving this study a title that would seem to bestow on Lang the function of a kind of center, a pole around which all aspects of his films gravitate, will doubtless be seen in certain quarters as an act of provocation, a reactionary turning back of the clock to the good old days of *auteur* theory—which is as good a starting point as any.

Auteur theory's main claim to fame—and its impact here is as incalculable as it is exemplary—was to have launched an onslaught against what masquerades as taste, in this case on a belief that Europe equals Art and Hollywood equals trash, that the European director is an individual and the Hollywood director an anonymous technician. Along with this has always gone a careful eliding of History in favor of the search for themes one can take "seriously," namely, social comment. As a result, any director specializing in Westerns, thrillers, horror films, and so on was doomed to oblivion, for all he was doing was reworking a genre, submitting to the "dream factory." Hence, for a European director to settle in Hollywood was a sign of betrayal (Alfred Hitchcock, Fritz Lang), and to leave Hollywood was hailed as positive (Nicholas Ray, perhaps?). As will be seen in Chapter 1, the attitude is still knocking around, but *auteur* theory succeeded in toppling a number of bastions and, by insisting on the importance of recurring themes and motifs in general, in reevaluating the work of Samuel Fuller, Howard Hawks, Otto Preminger, Ray, Douglas Sirk and others—not to mention the greatest triumph of all: a reappraisal of the American careers of Hitchcock and Lang.

It was perhaps inevitable that the original displacement should lead to a new recentering onto the person of the newly discovered *auteur*, who became as a result a fascinating pole of attraction. Once one has grasped the psychoanalytic dimension of this search for unity (see chapter 1), I fail to see what is wrong with it, provided an attempt is made to widen the frames of reference. Unfortunately, *auteur* theory also fell victim to the pitfalls of traditional criticism by deciding that lack of consistent themes was real rather than apparent. As a result, John Huston was cast into outer darkness, the only way it was possible to champion Hawks. A policy of exclusion was at work that is as reactionary as it is debilitating. In the light of Huston's remarkably subtle and personal approach to his material in films as disparate as *Freud—the Secret Passion* (1962), *Reflections in a Golden Eye* (1967), *The Kremlin Letter* (1969), and *The Man Who Would Be King* (1975), it could be argued that he has become a more interesting director than Hawks, precisely because of a heterogeneity that indicates a greater openness.

It is not a case of trying to turn things upside down and claim that Huston is "better" than Hawks, which would be to fall yet again into the age–old trap of binary oppositions. Rather, it is a case of historicizing the debate by pointing out that the canonizing of Hawks took place at a time when he had all his major achievements behind him (from *Scarface* to *Rio Bravo*), whereas many of Huston's major films were still to come. The idea of evolution tended to be excluded from *auteur* theory because of the need to fix the stakes once and for all, outside History.

A brief look at the case of John Ford will enable me to indicate my dissatisfaction with *auteur* theory and show the direction criticism has taken since the 1970s. Both Jim Kitses (1969, 8–12) and Peter Wollen (1969, 94–102) have stressed the importance of Henry Nash Smith's *Virgin Land* (1950) for explaining the consistent themes and sets of oppositions that can be found in later Ford, both Westerns (*The Searchers, The Man Who Shot Liberty Valance* and non-Westerns (*The Wings of Eagles, The Last Hurrah*). Wollen draws attention in *The Man Who Shot Liberty Valance* to "the image of the cactus rose, which encapsulates the antinomy between desert and garden which pervades the whole film" (96). This is accurate, but inadequate. The cactus rose also comes, through this antinomy, to represent the characters of Tom Doniphon (John Wayne) and Ransom Stoddard (James Stewart), symbols, respectively, of the past and individual action, of the present and individual and communal rights—and also of the future. Think of the exchange on the train at the end when the conductor says to Stewart, "Nothing's too good for the man who shot Liberty Valance." But of course it was Wayne who shot him, Wayne who is now dead, leaving Stewart as the only man who knows the truth (it is clear from the scene on the train that Stewart has kept his wife in ignorance).

What is so important here is that Stewart is, perhaps, heading for a political career as governor (or even president?), despite his talk of a quiet retirement. The cactus rose thus becomes a condensatory signifier, drawing together not only themes but the very modes of the representation of History and of the ideological dimensions of myth. It is certainly no accident that the press plays such a crucial role and that it is far from being a simple question of fighting for the truth. As the journalist points out to the idealistic young lawyer that Ransom Stoddard was: "Son, this is the West. When the facts contradict the legend, print the legend!"

An insistence on the roles of the signifier and representation, genre, myth, and history—in a film directed by a "conservative"—has been the touchstone for modern film theory, and the insights brought by the writings of Roland Barthes and Jacques Lacan (the two most consistently influential sources in the 1970s) have led to staggering gains, thanks to Christian Metz and the *Screen* group in England in particular.

Unfortunately, just as *auteur* theory was accompanied by a need to exclude, so a desire to be materialist was accompanied, in certain circles, by a guilt complex about finding pleasure in Hollywood movies, as though pleasure were something nasty in the woodshed to be repressed, as though it were bourgeois. I see here the disastrous influence of the so-called cultural revolution, with its repressive denial of sexual difference and its paranoid, Stalinist attitude toward intellectuals and dissent. It is no surprise that the most extreme and fervent advocates of these tendencies, the *Tel Quel* group, should convert their positive anti-Soviet stance into a negative anti-Marxist stance as an imaginary resolution of their total lack of contact with the proletariat they wanted to represent, call their new journal *L'Infini,* and end up as lackeys of everything they once denounced (thus, as I write this, Sollers has gone on the radio to advertise a right-wing weekly).

Fortunately, the situation in Paris does not seem to have found echoes in Britain and the United States as far as a shift to the right goes, but one can discern traces of it in the enthusiasm for the avant-garde.[1] Despite the patent Marxist concerns of Jean-Marie Straub and Danièle

Huillet in their interviews, the subject matter of their films, their approach to representation—indeed, the very articulation of their lives and their aesthetic preoccupations—there is something suspect in their search for purity to counter dominant modes of representation.[2] The same could be said of the dogmatic assertions of the Dziga Vertov Group: one has only to compare *Man with a Movie Camera* and *Vent d'Est* to see how research can turn into repression. This regrettable situation stems, I would suggest, from an inability to understand that concentrating on the films of one particular director does *not* mean fetishizing him as an *auteur*. Let me try to explain through a particular example.

An insignificant little gangster film, *Young Dillinger* (Terry Morse, 1965), includes a sequence lifted frame by frame from Lang's *You Only Live Once:* the actual footage is incorporated into the later film. In *Young Dillinger* the sequence makes no impression: it is just there, meaning nothing beyond the banal storyline of the film; it could have been left out or replaced by something else, and it would have made no real difference, for nothing in the film counts beyond the incompetent telling of a story in order to come up with a film at the end of the process. In the Lang the sequence in question—the bank robbery, during which the gangsters, wearing gas masks, overcome the police with tear gas bombs—is an integral part of a larger sequence where Lang prolongs and refines the elements put gradually into place from the very outset (notably the hero's criminal past and his continued links with his old gang) in order to place the spectators in a very special way: how we interpret the bank robbery, its implications for what follows and, especially, for the status of the hero, which cannot be understood without reference to framing, to cutting, to camera movements, and therefore to the interactions of looking and identifying.[3]

The last point concerns not only the spectators but also the characters in the film and situates the film and Lang's American period in general within an overall framework of vision, point of view, identification, and the camera that it is the aim of this book to analyse and elucidate.[4] I wish to make it clear that the space—or lack of it—devoted to a particular film is determined partly by its importance for the theses developed here, partly by the neglect from which certain films have suffered, partly also by a desire to de-center the dominant discussions of Lang and to recenter them elsewhere. If I would call myself a reconstructed auteurist, it is because I do see Lang as an *auteur,* but in a very special way: precisely because *Fury* is not "about" lynching, *Beyond a Reasonable Doubt* not "about" capital punishment, the anti-Nazi films not "about" Nazism, but because they are analyses of how characters and spectators come to see (that is, interpret) the way they do because of the way they are led to see (that is, look).[5]

This problematic is certainly not particular to Lang. It is central to Hitchcock's American period[6] and can be traced in various forms in films by directors as different as Cukor and Mankiewicz, Welles and von Sternberg, Sirk and Tourneur, Tashlin and Lewis, a list that could doubtless be extended. Much of Preminger from *Laura* to *The Cardinal* falls into this category, as a brief sequence from *Angel Face* will show. Robert Mitchum, a nurse, has been summoned to the home of a woman who may have tried to gas herself or who may have been the victim of attempted murder. The ambiguity is necessary in order that the spectator be faced with and placed by the polysemy of representation and the disarray of the Mitchum character. Mitchum descends the stairs in the background and starts to move toward the front door—and the camera. He glances, very briefly, offscreen left while continuing to advance, then, having taken only another step. stops and stares in the same direction. His look is one of intrigued fascination—the film's intrigue is centered on this fascination—and the spectators are caught up in it because they do not know what the object of this look is. Cut to a shot from Mitchum's point of view. We see, in the background, a young woman playing the piano. She is framed in a doorway in such a way that the image of her in the context of Mitchum's look becomes a metaphor for audience captivation (a word that is anything but innocent). *Angel Face* is a reflection on the place of the spectator in the cinematic machine, and it is not surprising that it should be a thriller, given the symbolic role of enigmas and investigations. It is also a mise en scène of the pleasure principle and the death wish, given that Mitchum's role of willing victim leads to his death. In the first chapter I attempt to clarify these issues.

Some words are in order about the history of the work presented here, which has gone through several versions over the years. It began as a doctoral dissertation prepared under the direction of Christian Metz between 1975 and 1979. The emphasis was on a limited corpus of Lang's American films, approached as a self-contained unity within the Hollywood system. I expanded the original theses of the study for my French book by analyzing all but four of the director's American films (see below). The emphasis was on a semio-psychoanalytical approach to the spectator and to problems of representation.

The present book stresses genre in a way that was only implicit in the French edition. The approach remains the same, but I have tried to be far more explicit about theoretical sources, references, and influences. The years that have intervened between the publication of the French edition (1982) and the writing of the present book (1987) made such a choice inevitable. It has entailed writing a long and completely new first chapter, and questions pertaining to the critical background have largely dictated this Preface. I have also been led to recast the chapter on *The Woman in the Window* until it bears little resemblance to that of the French edition. Chapter 8 and the Conclusion have also undergone substantial changes.

Although aspects of the other chapters have either been eliminated in an attempt to reduce excessive repetition or added in an attempt to highlight the displacement of the center of interest onto genre as a means of coding the spectators, I feel that the main difference between the French and the American editions lies in the dimension of language. This may seem a truism, but it is not. Anyone concerned with enunciative strategies in any artistic medium cannot but become sensitive to one's own enunciation, hence the deliberately self-conscious punning that pervades this book. Translating from the French has led me to grasp just to what extent a translation is a *re-writing*.

One problem of language that I have not been able to solve is that of how to refer to the spectator: *he* or *she?* In most cases, as the reader will see, I have found solutions or have had solutions suggested to me. That it has not always been possible to avoid saying "he" stems from the nature of language itself and the entire question of desire; it is therefore a social problem. Hence—to take an example from the body of the text—I would suggest that a female spectator watching *Laura* will tend (unless a conscious feminist) to share the male spectator's fascination with Laura-as-image and Laura-as-Woman, for the "simple" reason that society's values code all subjects, male and female, to function along the lines of male desire. One only has to think of advertising today to see that at work. To put it schematically, heroes are to be *admired*, heroines to be *contemplated*, which brings us back to the eternal problem of active versus passive.

Saying "he" or "she" is no solution, for a male subject is no more totally male than a female subject is totally female: the mirror-stage and the Law show that we cannot apply such simplistic physiological criteria. I prefer, then, to run the risk of being accused of sexism on this score than that of proposing an imaginary solution as though it were a real one. Marxists will never get anywhere unless they can recognize the contradictions within themselves, hence certain remarks I make in chapter 1.

Certain films are absent from this study. I have never been able to obtain prints to view of *The Return of Frank James* and *Western Union.* A recent viewing of *Clash by Night* revealed it to be a grotesque and unintentionally funny submelodrama with nothing to recommend it. *An American Guerrilla in the Philippines* is best forgotten. In the case of *Human Desire,* I felt that nothing I had to say concerning suture (chapter 8) added anything to my analysis of *Scarlet Street* and the conclusions drawn there.

Acknowledgments

I wish to thank the director, staff, and technicians of the British Film Institute in London for providing me with the working conditions without which my work on Lang over the years would not have been possible. By lending me copies of the films, furnishing me with viewing tables, and giving me all the help and technical advice necessary, the staff ensured that things went smoothly. My debt to the institute is incalculable. No less deserving of my gratitude are the following, who have been, in their own particular and important way, instrumental in my work on Lang coming to fruition: Richard Macksey, of the Johns Hopkins University, whose enthusiasm helped get this project off the ground; Eric Halpern, of the Johns Hopkins University Press, who, despite the problems involved in transatlantic communication, was able to provide useful guidelines and advice; Irma F. Garlick, for reading the manuscript with an eye for eliminating the inevitable Gallicisms; Maxime Arm, who let me use his videotape recorder to see a number of examples of *film noir*, notably *Mildred Pierce;* Réda Bensmaïa, who, by inviting me to give a talk to the students of the Paris Center for Critical Studies, allowed me to elaborate some of the theories underpinning chapter 1; Yves and Nicole Jean, for giving me the opportunity to view a print of *Man Hunt;* Michel Marie, of the University of Paris—III (Censier) for lending me prints of *Man Hunt* and *House by the River* and giving me the facilities to view the latter; Christian Metz, whose research on the cinema, selfless help, and exceptional pedagogical capabilities have been crucial for my own intellectual evolution; Sam Weber, who suggested I contact Richard Macksey and has encouraged this enterprise from the very beginning; last, but not least, my wife, Martine Lannaud, who has now endured three bouts with Lang in French and English. Her help and advice on the material production of the manuscript were indispensable, her patience supererogatory and beyond praise.

Stills of *You Only Live Once* courtesy of the British Film Institute; all others courtesy of La Cinémathèque Française.

Fritz Lang

1   Preliminaries and Polemics

There is a sequence in Blake Edwards's *Pink Panther Strikes Again* (1976) where that intrepid investigator Inspector Clouseau stops off at a hotel in Austria. Having succeeded in procuring a room for the night from the manager, who communicates by nodding or shaking his head, Clouseau spots a tiny dog sitting looking up at him and puts the question, "Does your dog bite?" Reassured by a shake of the head, he bends down to caress the animal, which promptly bites him. Nursing his hand, an enraged Clouseau rounds on the manager. "I thought you said your dog didn't bite!" To which the manager replies, "That's not my dog."

As has been pointed out, a conversation, the very fact of saying something, implies a set of rules to which the various parties involved are expected to adhere and which each expects the other(s) to respect (Récanati 1979, 193–94). Clearly Clouseau was referring to the dog present in the room and was within his rights to assume that the reply, even if only a shaking of the head, was a reply to a question based on an understandable presupposition: the symmetry between discourse and referent, the sign *your dog* and the little creature eyeing Clouseau as he spoke.[1] For the manager, however, another symmetry was at work: that between "your dog" and his own pet, absent from the scene—and therefore inexistent *referentially* for both the unfortunate Clouseau and, crucially, the spectator—but present *discursively*. In other words, the presuppositions and implications involved function only if the sub-

ject positions occupied by the speakers coincide, which can happen
only if they both receive language from the same place—that of the
Other—in the same way. In such circumstances as those just described,
people will normally receive language and the attendant message in
identical ways, which is what enables them to communicate with one
another on a daily basis in a non problematic, non ambiguous fashion.
Given, however, that ambiguity is inherent in language and that any
linguistic system is, first and foremost, a question of the signifier and not
of signification,[2] it is clear that misunderstandings are frequent and that
a whole series of jokes can be based on such a disconcerting, but
elementary, state of affairs.

Another example, as simple as it is effective, is one in which A asks B
if he has taken a bath, to which B replies, "No: is one missing?" Clearly—but how clearly is precisely the point—A is making an insidious
reference to B's (lack of) cleanliness, a reference that, being included
not in the discourse but in the overall context in which the discourse
and the speakers are inscribed, allows B to turn the tables on A by
"misinterpreting" the meaning of "to take a bath." In this way the
figurative dimension of the *énoncé* disappears behind the literal dimension, which is possible only because of the nonsymmetry of the subject
positions adopted, filled, and carried through to their differing conclusions by A and B. A dialogue always involves the absent Other, which
means that, in any and every case of genuine intersubjectivity, the subject is always under the sway of the signifier (Lacan 1986, 124). What is
at stake here, in both the examples quoted and the pages that follow, is
the subject of the enunciation.

Analyzing Freud's position on the question of subject positions,
Samuel Weber has pointed out that "the situation of the subject in the
primal scene is characterized by a constitutive disunity: the child is
impelled by its desire in two different and mutually exclusive directions.
The point of departure is a conflictual position, to which the ego will
attempt to respond. But its identity and unity will, for Freud, always be
marked and structured by the disunity it seeks to organize" (Weber
1982, 18).

This succinct summary is of great importance for my undertaking. It
shows that the disunity in question goes back to earliest childhood and
is a constant factor in adult life. It stresses the role of disavowal inherent
in vision and links it to the castration complex. It highlights the radical
non symmetry between ego and subject, which Lacan designates in just
those terms (1986, 274) and which he sums up elsewhere in the observa-

tion, "If someone perhaps knows he is, he knows, alas! nothing of what he is" (Lacan 1978, 262). Let us take this as a starting point.

In the course of one of his *Introductory Lectures on Psychoanalysis,* Freud cites the case of a lady "well-known for her energy" who once made the remark, "My husband asked his doctor what diet he ought to follow; but the doctor told him he had no need to diet: he could eat and drink what I want." Freud adds as brief commentary that "the slip of the tongue . . . was giving expression to a consistently planned programme" (SE 15:35).

Commenting on the so-called paradox involved in saying "I am lying," Lacan points out that the apparent vicious circle instituted by such a remark can be broken only if one realizes the simple truth that the speaking "I" and the linguistic "I" are not the same (Lacan 1973, 127–28). The former may have lied or may be intending to lie but *is not lying at the time he speaks,* in other words: at the very moment he wants to lead his interlocutor astray, he reveals the Truth, the same Truth—or Truth belonging to the same dimension—as that unwittingly revealed by the lady in Freud's example just quoted. This dimension is that of the enunciation, the subject of which is the subject of the unconscious, which is the locus of desire, that which remains radically unknown to the conscious ego.

Lacan has described desire as a metonymic leftover, absolute and unobtainable, forever unsatisfied, impossible and misunderstood (Lacan 1973, 141), and insists that the subject is de-centered vis-á-vis the individual (Lacan 1978, 17, 244) inasmuch as the Truth the subject reveals, as distinct from what the ego wants to say, is expressed through language, the locus of the Other. It does not mean, of course, that, once the Truth is revealed, the ego adopts a subject position in keeping with the new situation. When Lacan talks of desire being misunderstood, he is referring to a situation of miscognition, which is a fundamental part of the psychic make-up of each and every person. Lacan is anxious to stress that this miscognition is not ignorance but a certain way of organizing affirmations and denials. It cannot be conceived without knowledge, a knowledge of what it is that cannot be recognized (Lacan 1975, 190). Such knowledge is seen as a crystalization of symbolic activity, which is promptly forgotten once the information has been duly constituted as knowledge (Lacan 1978, 29).

Such an act of forgetting enables the subject to deny the social and unconscious dimension of language, the concept of subjectivity, which constitutes the subject in relation to the Other, but which leads individuals to believe they can, by such snares as introspection, understand themselves (Lacan 1975, 9). This delusion, of a basically narcissistic nature, is an integral part of the Imaginary. The human subject, which identifies with its own image (the ideal ego), is also perforce led to constitute itself in relation to those with whom it enters into contact and who function as so many ego ideals, a situation that inevitably leads to a recognition of dependence on others and on language of which the subject is an effect through having no control over it. If this is inherent to the Symbolic Order, it also leads to a vigorous attempt to recapture that primal narcissism that is the locus of unity, self-knowledge, presence, and the satisfaction of desire (Lacan 1975, 156). Harmony and order being the essential components of the imaginary state so defined, "the struggle for order entails the reduction of alterity and the subordination of difference to identity." Such narcissism must be seen as an "effort to keep the other in its (proper) place, to subordinate alterity to an economy of the same" (Weber 1982, 127, 157).

A most striking filmic manifestation of the link between order and narcissism as regards the ego's desire for harmony and non contradiction can be found in Oshima's *Merry Christmas, Mr. Lawrence* (1982). Readers will remember the sequence where the Japanese officer, seeing his rigid, ordered system suddenly threatened, loses control and is about to behead a British army officer. The David Bowie character, the object of the Japanese officer's unconscious homosexual desire, steps in to stop the killing. Faced with the refusal of the other officer to back down, Bowie takes him in his arms and kisses him. Oshima chooses to film the Japanese officer falling backward in extreme slow motion, so slowly in fact that several images of him are simultaneously present on the screen. This jerky, disjointed movement translates remarkably in cinematographic terms the idea of multiple subject positions, as well as the literal shattering of the man's ego as his true subject-ivity is revealed to him in all its horror. That the Bowie character is then buried alive and left to die means not only that he takes the place of the British officer but that the Japanese officer is, literally, striving to keep the other in its place by reducing the incident to a case of insubordination. By preventing Bowie from moving, the Japanese hopes to reconstitute his own ego through an artificial and (re)enforced order that disavows what it has just lost.

The vocabulary Lacan uses in his ceaseless reformulations of the status and function of the ego and the subject is revealing. Identification with the ego ideal is "exalting" since the latter is a system of defense put into place to prolong the subject's "satisfaction," which is also part and parcel of the "closed world" of the narcissistic type (Lacan 1975, 118, 9, 152). I take this line of argument as destined to buttress Lacan's concept of the imbrication of Imaginary and Symbolic, of the ceaseless shuttle operated by the subject between the two. It being out of the question to make all these different identifications merge into a single fixed presence, the ego—the sum of all the subject's identifications (Lacan 1978, 187)—must be seen as a series of mechanisms of defense, negation, inhibition, and fantasy destined to orient the subject, to keep desire going (Lacan 1975, 24).

The purpose of the subject's desire is to satisfy the primal relation to the mother (Lacan 1981, 98), a doomed search for unity and presence. As such, any object—real or fantasized—can be pressed into play as an *objet petit a,* a displaced maternal breast. Given that such an object can never be grasped save as a mirage, each object relation is at once invested with a basic uncertainty (Lacan 1978, 201), a key term in Lacan and of prime concern for any study concerning the nature of the spectator's relation to the filmic image. Since the self is constituted in relation to the other and meaning is located in the Other, the relation between the subject and the people and objects on the screen cannot but be mediated through another subject, which entails at any given moment problems of identification and negative or violent reactions stemming from the unpleasure generated by the nonsatisfaction of a narcissistic object relation.

Again, this is inevitable, the subject being constituted in and by heterogeneity, which it is the task of classical narrative to reduce, mask, and contain: it can never eliminate it except in death, the locus of stasis and noncontradiction. The task can best be seen as one of restoring balance in the sense given by Lacan when he points out that, when we are led to see things in a new perspective that de-centers us in relation to our prior experiences, we try to find again the habitual center of our standard viewpoint (Lacan 1978, 56). Stephen Heath has summed things up neatly in the context of film as "the unbroken alignment of desire and subject" (Heath 1976c, 38), but the question goes far beyond that of going to the cinema and, in view of the tone of some writing on the cinema, it would be prudent to try to assess here what is at stake in the act of narration.

Lacan once asked if we ever reflected on the significance of myths and legends in our lives, on the way we can be taken over by storytelling (Lacan 1975, 60). His constant references at the time in several seminars to the exemplary nature of "the Wolfman" case in the context of memory and narrative as constituting the subject have found an echo more recently in the two remarkable studies of narrative made by Peter Brooks, "Freud's Masterplot: Questions of Narrative" (1977) and "Fictions of the Wolfman: Freud and Narrative Understanding" (1979).[3] At the risk of being reductive, I would sum up the thrust of Brooks's arguments by stating that he is particularly interested in the pleasure we obtain from linearity, the importance of memory in the (re)constitution of the subject through the reading process, and the way each reader uses the text's resolution as an attempt to represent the self as a central, omniscient ego. Since these discoveries are crucial for grasping the positions accorded to the viewing subject, it is essential to look at the issue in some detail.

Referring to an original observation made by Roman Jakobson (1956), Brooks stresses the metonymic nature of the nineteenth-century realist novel. The use of narrative blocks creates, through simple contiguity, the impression of linearity allowing the reader to move from start to finish and hence, by reaching the end, to give a meaning to the tale, thus assuaging desire, which is the desire to complete: to make the end—or "The End"—coincide with knowledge and a sense of plenitude.

Lacan has always stressed the link between metonymy and desire. Because of a false recognition of the real nature of language, the subject speaks in the erroneous belief that the meaning he wishes to attribute to his discourse preexists its enunciation, whereas the meaning will become clear to his interlocutors only when he has finished speaking. At any moment things can go wrong: the speaker can change in mid-sentence, can be misinterpreted, can be victim of a slip of the tongue. Freud has stressed the role of impatience in slips of the tongue, the desire to complete what one has to say as quickly as possible. It can lead the speaker unconsciously to skip over part of the discourse in order to reach more quickly that word or remark toward which it is heading, which then "slides back" along the signifying chain and contaminates the discourse by emerging at the "wrong" place (Freud, SE 15:68).

The speaker is an effect of language and subject-ed to desire. This is crucial for Brooks's argument: reading enables one to find the end(ing) one was looking for all the time and, *retroactively,* to impose a fixed meaning on what has just been read, to return to the beginning and to reconstitute a total presence through meaning. This inevitability means that a strict chronology need not be adhered to, for the end—psychically—precedes the beginning, and starting at the beginning enables one, whatever the detours, to find the solution one desired all along (the signifying chain). Starting to read is thus always already to have found a certain end.

A number of conclusions can be drawn here. Creating links by contiguity between successive and initially heterogeneous elements instills a feeling of reassuring homogeneity and also leads to the fabrication of the referential illusion where the subjects repress the discursive dimension of the text and their real place in its enunciative strategies in favor of a network of fixed meanings anchored in the real world.[4] Moreover, this "sense of an ending" is structured by the enigma of origins that follows the human subject from the cradle to the grave. Following Sartre and Benjamin, Brooks affirms that fiction gives one knowledge about death that is denied in life. Given that to end is to want to begin again, one finds oneself faced with the repetition compulsion to which death is intimately linked.

Things, of course, are not that simple: if the aim of an organism is death, then why should death not intervene at once? Death's inevitablility must be accepted, but on the mode of disavowal, and a whole panoply of narrative devices is there to satisfy desire: enigmas, clues, the sudden introduction of new characters, long descriptions, parentheses, recalling the past or cinematic flashbacks, and so on. What is not accepted, in the context of a work of suspense, in which an investigation is central to the plot—and I do not choose this example by chance—is the "premature" revelation of the real situation. One has only to evoke the negative critical comments on Hitchcock's *Vertigo* (1958), in which the solution of the enigma is revealed in the middle of the film, to see what is at stake in the need for an organism to follow a certain road before reaching the end. The way Hitchcock's use of point of view involves the spectator in James Stewart's scopophilic and necrophilic fascination with the enigmatic heroine(s) means that critics were faced with the return of their own repressed, hence the unpleasure caused by this violation of narcissistic identification and its attendant desire for unity and closure, but only at a precise point: the end.[5]

Lacan has insisted on the role of fascination in the constitution of the ego (Lacan 1978, 67), which, as I have pointed out, has as its basic function that of miscognition. The example of *Vertigo* and critical hostility is a useful condensation of a number of elements raised here. Spectators are forced to recognize an unpalatable truth: they have no control over the ending (or death). They displace such knowledge by accusing Hitchcock of not playing the game, which consists of revealing the truth at the end and hence of lending plenitude and meaning retroactively to what has gone before. Critical disappointment here is conditioned by the metonymy of desire analyzed above. Hitchcock's film being a work of genre, the dimension of repetition is brought into play, but in a very particular way: its being linked to the realization that one does not control a story, its ending—and, hence, one's destiny—gives rise to unpleasure. Instead of perpetuating the cycle—beginning, ending, beginning, ad infinitum—it introduces a gap that breaks the cycle and shows the ending for what it really is: a return to one's origins, the Oedipus complex, castration, and death.

A most effective realization in filmic terms of the link between memory, narrative, and death is to be found in Coppola's *Peggy Sue Got Married* (1986). Readers will remember that Peggy Sue, a married woman in her early forties with a grown-up daughter, faints and, on recovering, finds she has gone back in time to her senior year of high school, when she was eighteen. One brief scene interests me here. At one point Peggy Sue—who retains in 1960 all her knowledge of what life was to reserve for her up to 1985—answers the phone. It is her grandmother. On hearing her voice, Peggy Sue breaks down and runs away, sobbing. What she has heard, of course, is a voice from the grave, her grandmother being long dead by 1985. Peggy Sue is face to face with her own future death, which she can in no way put off by being eighteen again, for she remains a woman of over forty with a daughter older than she is— was in 1960. The scene puts the spectators fairly and squarely in front of their own situation as the consumers of a narrative that seems to be enabling them to turn the clock back, to hold back the inevitable, with the result that its return is all the more devastating.

The case of "the Wolfman" adds another dimension to an already complex tale. Freud tails, so to speak, the clues in the best tradition of the sleuth, only to realize that the primal scene may be a primal fantasy, with his patient reconstituting his past in order to make sense of it in the light of later knowledge; in other words, creating a fiction where he originally saw fact. "We have at this crucial moment of the case history an apparent evacuation of the problem of origins, substituting for a founding event a phantasy or fiction on which is conferred all the authority and force of prime mover, and the evocation of a possible infinite regress in the unconscious of the race" (Brooks 1979, 77).

Freud realized that the question was not one of replacing the account of the primal scene with a revised version, but rather one of creating "a layered text which offers different versions of the same story" (Brooks 1979, 78). The effect of this daring ploy is "to displace the whole question of origins, to suggest another kind of referentiality, in that all tales may lead back not so much to events as to other tales, to man as a structure of the fictions he tells about himself" (78).

Brooks's conclusion is of the utmost importance for any research into narrative and representation:

> Narrative sequences and scenarios must accord with the complex, twisting, subversive patternings of desire. As well as form, plots must have force: the force that makes the connection of incident powerful, that shapes the confused material of a life into an intentional structure which in turn generates new insights about how life can be told. . . . But if plot has become an object of suspicion, it remains nonetheless necessary: telling the story's story remains the indispensable thread in the labyrinth of unauthored temporality. It is of overwhelming importance to us that life remain narratable, which means finding those provisional and fictional plots that capture the force of a desire that cannot speak its name but continues to manifest its drive toward meaning. (Brooks 1979, 80, 81)

The implications of these remarks are far-reaching and far from easy to assume as far as film theory today goes, since theory now depends on theory elaborated in the past, particularly a decade or so ago. If I have no intention of attempting to answer all the questions raised up to now, it is not only because theory is open ended and ongoing but also, and especially, because my book is conceived as an unfolding of a certain number of problems pertaining to narration and representation and how they place the viewing subject. There can be no question of tying up the loose ends in an opening chapter: here I trace out a number of avenues of approach, of paths to follow in an attempt to grasp the matter in its complexity. I have been struck, in preparing this English version of my book (Humphries 1982), by the way I have constantly returned to a certain number of concepts—to my "original" starting point—in order to move off in another direction by elaborating one aspect rather than the others. This book has the very narrative form elucidated and commented on above, which is hardly surprising given the role of enigmas and surprises, ambiguous events and characters, mistaken or problematic identities. One forgets at one's peril that "the mechanism of repetition that structures the drives, and hence the psyche, does not conform to the laws of identity and non-contradiction, which are the laws of consciousness" (Weber 1982, 141).

Remembering, then, that the subject is an effect of the signifier, let us look at at least some of the implications as far as the classical Hollywood cinema is concerned.

Perhaps the most precise and succinct summary of the general thrust of what I have attempted to explicate in the preceding pages is to be found in a passage from an article by Stephen Heath.

> *On the one hand,* the film opens up a flow and circulation, is a symbolic production in which unity and position are ever slipping away, lacking. . . . *On the other hand,* the film is figured out by its narrative as a totality, the imaginary relation of the spectator to an undivided present full of images of the accomplishment of desire (liking a film, the people in it, the things seen), of fictions of wholeness (including that of "the film," the object mastered by the spectator); exactly a memory-spectacle in which the elements of production are bound up and resolved; the representation of unity and the unity of representation. The first is at the loss of the subject of the enounced, retraced in the tensions of desire, put into process; the second is the negation of the subject of the enunciation, the stasis of reflection. (Heath 1977a, 10)

Such striving for "the negation of the subject of the enunciation" in an attempt to achieve and master "the representation of unity and the unity of representation" is, of course, what cinema is "about"—and when I say "cinema" I mean all but a handful of films, not just Hollywood. What matters in the overwhelming majority of films is what is at work in the exegeses of Freud proposed by Peter Brooks: the story and the telling thereof in order to satisfy desire. That desire can never be satisfied changes nothing: it is the belief that it can that takes precedence, which means that secondary revision exists to contain, mask, disavow, paper over the gaps that are the result of the primary processes (Metz 1977b, 324). In order to make it possible, the film must pass the story off as natural, something that just "happens," for it is only in this way that the spectator can disavow those psychic drives that I have pinpointed when discussing Brooks's undertaking.

Psychoanalytic theory has, from the outset, insisted on discursive and enunciative strategies and hence on the subject positions accorded to spectators by the interaction of codes of narration and representation. The achievements of film theory over a period of a decade or so were quite staggering, and it would be impossible to overestimate the importance of the contributions of writers such as Heath and Metz. However, the concern with the Symbolic has had an unfortunate side effect: it has tended not only to underestimate the importance of the Imaginary for everyone but also, implicitly, to lead to a widespread belief that the Imaginary is not very nice and should be overcome. It is as if it could be left behind, as if Imaginary and Symbolic were not interdependent, an attitude that is profoundly ideological, part and parcel of the Imaginary and a resolute refusal of the Symbolic. This attitude, let it be said at once, is also a negation of the Marxist philosophy that has always been the concern of the major film theorists in France, Britain, and the United States period under discussion (roughly the 1970s).

An articulation of Marxism and Freudian psychoanalysis has occupied key twentieth-century thinkers since the 1930s. It seems to me that Lacan's insistence on language and the discourse of the Other, given the social and historical dimension of the former, can be of the greatest help (see Jameson 1977, 1981). Although Lacan strikes me as being very wary about using the word *ideology,* one can surely see links between Marx's theory of ideology and Lacan's analysis of the Other. What Frank Lentricchia has to say about "hegemony" (in the context of Gramsci and Kenneth Burke) can be applied to the ego's search for unity and stability, in an attempt to misrecognize its subject positions, which can only be historical. "Hegemonic rule is therefore the mark of the stable, "mature" society whose ideological apparatus is so deeply set in place, so well buried, so unexamined a basis of our judgment and feeling that it is taken for truth with a capital letter" (Lentricchia 1983, 76).[6]

One should therefore be on one's guard against statements like the following:

> The films which this great German director [Lang] produced in Hollywood seem to us to constitute an especially fertile field for a "specialist" attitude, which, in our view, is particularly suspect in that it conceals, behind the mask of a pseudo "textual" analysis (which, in fact, concerns itself exclusively with the signified) the latest incarnation of the universalist theories of the cinema—whose ultimate aim is to validate linear discourse in film (Burch and Dana 1974, 48).

Clearly, I am one of those under attack here, and I leave it to the reader to decide whether I am concerned "exclusively with the signified" or, as I claim, with the signifier. What strikes me in this passage is its unspoken paranoid content: linear narrative is nothing but a dark, sinister plot hatched by the bourgeoisie to dupe the proletariat. References to "false consciousness" and to the early, militant work of *Tel Quel* make it clear where Burch and Dana stand: as imaginary (and failed) revolutionaries.

This is a perfect manifestation of a belief dear to certain self-proclaimed Marxists that it is only by refusing classical narrative that one can be Marxist; even that a capitalist society can only produce bourgeois culture, which is a highly mechanistic way of approaching the base versus superstructure dialectic. Metz has rightly stressed the idealist content, the desire to be original at all costs, of a discourse that claims that the only cinema is that which does not tell a story (Metz 1977b, 172). What Burch and Dana are doing, in fact, is searching desperately for the lost object in the shape of the cinema they love, which, of course, is always already elsewhere. Lacan has observed that claiming what you have lost is "the best" is a way of not looking at what you possess, which is perhaps something worthwhile (Lacan 1981, 134).

Burch has clearly looked at a lot of Hollywood films, but he does not seem to have *seen* them, nor has he taken much account of the semio-psychoanalytical theories he is anxious to refine in favor of a Marxist definition of culture. To talk of "the non-films of Vincente Minnelli" is a nonsense and nontheoretical (Burch 1969, 242). It is amusing, to say the least, that a materialist should denounce the "collective" nature of Hollywood (246), but since Burch has decided that this anonymity has produced only the occasional success—*Baby-Face Nelson, Vera Cruz, Lady in a Cage*—it is clear that he has not the foggiest notion of what Hollywood is. Colin McArthur has rightly insisted on the stimulating influence of genre and studio constraints on certain directors, citing as an example Nicholas Ray (McArthur 1972, 16). Burch, of course, sees Ray as an example of those stifled by the Hollywood machine and a director who never did anything as good as his first film, *They Live by Night* (Burch 1969, 246). The myth of "origin-ality" at its worst.

A refreshing antidote to the "Burch syndrome" is the following:

> The critics who yesterday argued in the name of a cultural elitism, and the ideologues of today on the extreme left have one thing in common: neither group has ever been unduly concerned with trying to understand Hollywood as an aesthetic phenomenon in its own right. . . . Perhaps as little as one per cent of its total output deserves serious critical discussion, but this leaves anything between 200 and 300 great films, which is more than one could claim about the production of all other countries taken together, and is a single achievement in any art. (Elsaesser 1971, 5,6)

Precisely. It is vitally urgent to return to this down-to-earth stance, to rid oneself of what I would see as a guilt-ridden *gauchisme* over secretly finding pleasure in Westerns, thrillers, and melodramas,[7] to realize that a personal approach is possible within a collective framework, that "working in Hollywood has for most directors meant that instead of expressing individuality through personal themes, they could express personality through universal themes" (Elsaesser 1971, 8).

Which brings me to a critical stance and an aesthetic state of affairs that need to be articulated and set off one against the other: *auteur* theory and the place of genre.

Auteur theory has always tended to insist on consistent elements of a director's work, be they visual or thematic, in an attempt to find a fixed point—the creative genius—enabling *auteur* critics to arrest that "flow" and "circulation" mentioned by Stephen Heath. The ahistorical and individualistic bent of this approach led critics influenced by semiology to displace the accent onto the question of codes and genre. In *Underworld USA,* devoted to American *film noir,* Colin McArthur stressed the importance of clothes and the city (1972, 26, 27), whereas Stephen Neale, following Heath, tended to put the accent on narrative. For him, genre is a question of "balancing . . . points of advance in ceaselessly pushing the flow of text and subject forward, and . . . points of recall in ceaselessly containing that process in figures of repetition, folding it back on itself into the retrospective coherence of memory" (Neale 1980, 27).

There is no doubt that there tended to be far more of an accent on narrative in film theory in the second half of the 1970s, and Stephen Heath insisted on the need to work "much less on 'codes' than on the operations of narrativisation" (Heath 1976a, 109). While agreeing that there was a distinct danger of work on codes becoming purely formal, like so much early semiology, and running the risk of a fetishism that could only be a variant of the fixed, imaginary center sought by *auteur* theory, I would suggest that a concern with narrative has tended to concentrate on the overall thrust and movement of filmic texts at the expense of apparently isolated elements, such as the use of shadows and oppressive camera angles in *film noir.* It is a question not of privileging codes over narrative but of drawing attention to the fact that codes of representation and apparently isolated elements functioning as signifiers are an integral part of narrative. Rather than make of narrative a clarion call for the destruction of classical modes of representation, one should show an interest in *all* narrative devices and, perhaps, shift the center of emphasis—especially now, in the wake of Brooks's studies—onto narrative as a realization of phantasms.[8] Thus an interest in classical narrative must be an attempt not to rehabilitate it but to draw out those elements that criticize such narrative's tendency to be self-effacing and to contain its excesses.

Despite all the emphasis on Lacanian psychoanalysis in modern Anglo-American film theory, I would go so far as to say that the role of the signifier has been seriously neglected precisely because of an insufficient attention to detail in favor of overall narrative strategies. In the light of the central role of *film noir* to Lang's work and the amount of important research done on it, I would like to propose the following remarks on Lang's place within the genre.[9]

By the time Lang settled in Hollywood in 1936, there was a solid tradition of gangster films that had exploited the theme of the city— and its concomitant fear of anonymity, loneliness, and violence—to the point of having created an iconographical system involving cars, dark streets, rain, speakeasies, and shootings in heavily coded settings (steps leading up to apartment buildings, stairs inside these buildings), even down to the use of lampposts and items such as hats.[10] Despite the veneer of social comment eagerly seized on by those who cannot envisage any other dimension to a text, *Fury, You Only Live Once,* and *You and Me* are first and foremost gangster films or part and parcel of the tradition of *film noir.*[11] *The Woman in the Window* and *Scarlet Street* cannot be fully understood outside this framework, and even such melodramas as *Secret beyond the Door* and *House by the River* show clearly the influence of the genre in the use of shadows. The films of the 1950s—*The Blue Gardenia, The Big Heat, While the City Sleeps, Beyond a Reasonable Doubt*—belong explicitly to the genre.

Things are, however, somewhat more complex when one comes to the anti-Nazi films of the 1940s, in which Lang exploits the codes in a way that is, to say the least, unexpected. As I shall show in chapters 2, 3, and 4, these films have as much to do with Nazism as *Fury* has to do with lynching: only on the most superficial and misleading level of a theme within the general story line. Take *Hangmen Also Die.* What is one to make, for example, of the Gestapo thugs who follow Czaka the double agent for his protection like the FBI following an important witness or tailing a suspect (as in Fuller's *Pickup on South Street),* who resemble hoodlums from a gangster film, and who refuse to leave their charge for as much as a moment, saying "Orders is orders"? Or of Czaka dying on the steps of a church, shot down by the Gestapo just as James Cagney was shot by the police at the end of Raoul Walsh's *Roaring Twenties* (1939)? Or of Gruber, the policeman working for the Gestapo, telling Dr. Svoboka that, if he makes a move, he will get a "a slug in the gut"?

This last observation recalls for me an exchange between the hired gun and Sam Spade in Huston's *Maltese Falcon* (1941): "If you keep riding me, they'll be picking iron out of your liver". The link is clear, the only problem being that the Huston is a classic example of *film noir,* whereas the Lang is supposed to be an anti-Nazi film. It is this "obvious" fact that is overlooked, precisely because it is too obvious. Which explains why some audiences prefer to laugh. Poor old Lang: he doesn't even understand genre![12]

What is happening is that the Langian textual system is juxtaposing signifiers in such a way that the expected—read: desired—message no longer comes over loud and clear. The viewing subject is placed in a position of *uncertainty,* of *hesitation,* for reasons going far beyond a simple aesthetic desire or economic need to exploit one genre in the hope of making another more accessible (if this were all, the film would be a flop). In the case of *Man Hunt,* the textual system refuses to submit itself to a cut-and-dried genre in order to elaborate the dimension of the double (Captain Thorndike equals the Nazi Quive-Smith). Instead, Thorndike looks forward to Dave Bannion in *The Big Heat,* a very different genre film. Both men set out on an apparently noble mission— to rid society of an evil force—but the use of a whole battery of sig- nifiers—clothes, lighting, and so forth—shows the two characters have much in common with their enemies.

What Lang's films do in such cases is to show that no fixed meaning preexists the textual articulation of signifiers, which, in the best Laca- nian tradition, are cut free from a given signified, indeed from any signified whatsoever: it is rather the place of a signifier within the signifying chain of images that counts and the reverberations it sets up within the textual system. Needless to say, given the exigencies of genre and Hollywood, these reverberations create meanings that fold back over what has gone before to suture it—very much like Lacan's *points de capiton,* signifiers that ultimately bestow meaning on heterogeneous material (Lacan 1981, 293–306, esp. 303–4). What is important is *how* they trigger the metonymy of desire in spectators leading them to antici- pate the ultimate signified—and to be mistaken, for the signifier is always elsewhere, given the system's refusal to accept the codes as fixed in advance.

Let us look at the signifier at work. I shall start by moving outside Lang's films to the cartoons of Tex Avery, a deliberate displacement of the center of interest whose significance will become clear later. Avery's favorite tactic was the visualization of idiomatic expressions by giving them (back) their literal meaning. His films are full of jaws dropping to the ground with a resounding clang or of eyes popping from heads (*Droopy's Double Trouble, Red Hot Riding Hood*). He even has one astonishing cartoon, *Symphony in Slang,* that is the putting together of sequences to form a narrative by rendering in images idiomatic expressions, puns, or even expressions that are taken literally. Thus the *énoncé* "The boss drew a gun on me" shows a character taking out a pen and drawing a gun on the hero's shirt front. "I had a cocktail" is accompanied by the shot of a waiter producing a cock, plucking off its tail feathers, and popping them into a glass. In this case *cocktail* is a signifier whose function depends on an illogical breaking down of the word into its component parts on a purely phonological basis. As such, it is a perfect illustration of how the unconscious uses the signifier to serve its own logic.

If one turns now to Lang, one can find examples of the signifier circulating freely, not only intratextually but, crucially for genre, intertextually, both within the Langian textual system and between this system and that of films by other directors. In a quite remarkable study of *Scarlet Street,* Tom Conley has pinpointed these functions of the signifier (Conley 1983). The neon light flashing outside the seedy hotel where Chris Cross tries to kill himself is taken up by Orson Welles in *Touch of Evil* (1958) when Quinlan murders an accomplice (1088). When Cross and his fellow workers admire their boss's blond girl friend, they look at her through a window and she becomes "the woman in the window" (1089). The film's title refers to Hawthorne's *Scarlet Letter* and to *Scarface* (1105); one remembers the role of Edward G. Robinson (who plays Cross) in the contemporary *Little Caesar* (Mervyn LeRoy, 1932) and the presence in *You and Me* of one of the stars of *Scarface,* George Raft. Moreover, the word *letter* explicit in the novel title, is also present as an anagram in *Scarlet Street.* One can also point out that the three main actors of this film, Robinson, Joan Bennett, and Dan Duryea, had just appeared in a similar film the previous year, *The Woman in the Window;* that Bennett was in *Man Hunt* and was to appear in *Secret beyond the Door;* and that Duryea appeared—as a Nazi—in *The Ministry of Fear.*

The theme of repetition via the signifier makes *Scarlet Street* a literal companion piece to *The Woman in the Window* through an observation and a play on words. Chris Cross says of his relationship with Kitty, "Why, it's just like a dream!" which refers back clearly to Wanley and the portrait (see the opening of chapter 5 for a summary of *The Woman in the Window*). On top of that, Cross's painting can be seen as a literal realization of Wanley's fantasy, which must be compared to a hallucination, given the status of the image in a dream (Freud, SE 5:565–66; Weber 1982, 126–27). Stephen Jenkins has pointed out that Kitty says to Cross that she will allow him to paint her, then offers her foot—so that he can paint her toenails (Jenkins 1981, 100). I would suggest that one can interpret this as a metaphor for the dreamwork, in which words are represented as images and the literal meaning of the verbal signifier is chosen over the figurative one as a way of realizing desire. Thus *Scarlet Street* becomes an unconscious remake of *The Woman in the Window*, condensing the themes of repetition and the double on the one hand, the economic and aesthetic thrust of genre on the other.[13] As Freud put it succinctly, "in the unconscious nothing can be brought to an end, nothing is past or forgotten" (SE 5:577).

The "full" significance of Freud's remark for the Langian textual system is what I attempt to show in detail in the following chapters, especially chapters 5, 6, and 7. Here I am concerned only with elaborating a question of principle and method. A final example will be *The Woman in the Window*. Professor Wanley puts the body of the murder victim in the back of his car and drives off to dump it in a secluded spot. It is night. As he drives along, he is stopped by a police officer: he has forgotten to put on his headlights. Further on, such is his impatience that he nearly runs a traffic light. Cut to a motorcycle policeman eyeing him mockingly. At a toll bridge, instead of stopping to pay, Wanley tosses a coin through the window at the collector. Of course the man fails to see it and forces Wanley to back up his car. He then takes a flashlight to search for the coin. Every time the car is stopped, Lang cuts to a shot of the victim, his dead eyes staring. Here repetition is used as a narrative ploy, both to advance the story and to create suspense. There is nothing moral about the latter: even if it is in Wanley's interest to be caught before it is too late, as the hero he cannot be caught, for that would mean the premature end of the film and cause audience unpleasure. The suspense is therefore psychic: to allow the pleasure principle to function for the duration of a standard movie, while at the same time functioning as the superego in order to punish Wanley and the spectator for their socially unacceptable acts and desires.

A link, crucial for the overall process of the Langian textual system, is created between narrative and a specific signifier, light. Headlights, traffic lights, flashlights, all variants of a master signifier: the use of light (and dark) in Lang, the element exploited the most systematically to accentuate the dimension of vision and everything that flows from it—the presentation of characters who are not what they seem and the use of mistaken identities; the search for the truth that seems so obvious but is never where it is expected. In short: how we see. If this element is now recognized as central to the Langian textual system, things have not always been that way. A lengthy detour through Lang criticism is essential to highlight—so to speak—what is at stake and to enable me to propose an alternative path to follow.

In his analysis of Lang's German period, Noël Burch bemoans the fate—I use this last word deliberately—that befell Lang in the United States. "He seemingly accepted all the (essentially regressive) inferences which the American sound film had drawn in particular from his best work in Germany; whether consciously or not, he identified himself with that anonymous being who was always much of a muchness, the all-purpose Hollywood director" (Burch 1980, 583). As a result, Lang retreated into "a silence lasting some thirty years" (599).

Thomas Elsaesser (see above) has made the best reply to this sort of criticism, in which, if directors are not denounced for "giving in" to commercialism, they will be castigated for their indifference to social problems, an attitude overdetermined by the myth of originality, itself overdetermined by the role of memory. "Whereas Lang's American work is generally accessible, his German films are extremely difficult to get to see and most criticism is based on opinions formed years ago; the German films therefore are enriched by the tricks of memory and the more 'common' American ones simply don't stand a chance. That something made *now* could possibly be better than something made *then* also seems inconceivable to most 'liberal' critics (Bogdanovich 1967, 6).

These observations can in no way be applied to Burch, whose knowledge of German Lang is second to none, but they still sum up nicely certain trends in Anglo-American criticism, concerning the cinema in general and Lang in particular. Paul M. Jensen's thoroughly disreputable book *The Cinema of Fritz Lang* (1969) symbolizes everything negative in this domain. Take the following comments on *You Only Live Once* and *Scarlet Street* respectively: "an exciting crime melodrama that is raised to full dramatic stature by skillful staging and the inclusion of social criticism" (Jensen 1969, 120); "Renoir's film [*La Chienne,* 1931] was shot in real settings and his characters were alive" (159).

A perfect condensation of journalistic inanities. I presume that *alive* is a synonym for *credible* but Jensen everywhere refuses to take seriously the figurative use of film language—despite his own figurative use of verbal language—because of his obsession with a literal-minded approach to "realism." To talk of the superiority of "real settings" as opposed to the studio when discussing a film like *Scarlet Street* is to show a crass ignorance of Hollywood and to repress the genre aspects obvious to anyone with only a rudimentary knowledge of the cinema of the 1930s and 1940s, given the central role played by what the late Robert Warshow defined somewhere as "the dangerous, sad city of the imagination."[14]

The presupposition at work in Jensen's writing is, apart from the petit-bourgeois contempt for Hollywood, an idealist belief in the ability to grasp reality better if one shoots on location, an ideology that is intimately tied up with its bed partner, social comment. Just as there have been critics and film makers who denounced sound as a perversion of the only true cinema, the silent period, who claimed that black-and-white photography is more aesthetic and realistic than color photography; so there are critics who consider that art is not "Art" unless it approaches what Claude Chabrol once referred to as "Big Themes." This, of course, always refers to what "liberal" critics—I endorse entirely Bogdanovich's irony here—mean by "social comment," "social revelance," "realistic protrayal," and so on. In other words, being vague and general to the point of saying nothing at all. As a result it has always been possible in Britain to repress the lucid and rigorous Marxist analyses of society offered by certain Joseph Losey films such as *Blind Date* (1959) and *The Criminal* (1960) on the grounds that they are variants of the *film noir* transposed into a British setting. Their realism is far too realistic, light-years ahead of the superficial naturalism—shots of grinding poverty, bigoted bourgeois—that passes for "social comment."[15]

Returning then to Jensen's observation on *You Only Live Once,* one finds at work the various ideological and discursive ploys used to validate a certain kind of cinema. Calling the film a crime melodrama enables Jensen to pigeonhole it without having to ask questions about genre: the problem is evoked and repressed at the same time in the best traditions of disavowal. The repressed immediately returns, however, in "raised to full dramatic stature," which indicates that assimilating a film to a genre is to debase it, while "the inclusion of social comment" displaces the question again. The entire *énoncé* is constituted by the placing side by side of signifiers called on to function as fixed signifieds, constituted therefore by the metonymy of desire. As usual in such cases, desire is for "a single harmonious and unified whole" (Jensen 1969, 183), Jensen's inspired description of *The Big Heat*, always high on the list of "the best Lang" because of its apparent commitment to social themes. It ranks therefore with *Fury* and *You Only Live Once*, about the only American Lang to be generally admired. It seems these films are all considered as "progressive," the only way they can possibly enjoy kudos amongst those who make and break taste (and the careers of those who do not conform). I have always wondered what is progressive about *Fury*, in which at one point the sheriff says to the ringleader that if he continues to stir up trouble, "I'll take you and your relatives off the dole." It would surely be much easier to find *Scarlet Street* progressive and subversive, for it shows how many examples of *film noir* can produce "seeds of counter-ideologies" through the "destruction or ab- sence of romantic love and the family (Harvey 1978, 33, 25).[16]

You Only Live Once is one of the very rare Lang that could be called "progressive."[17] Superficially, the same epithet could also be attached to *You and Me,* given its subject matter and narrative codes. I propose to analyze the film at once to show that this is not the case and to open the way for a presentation of the kind of approach to the Langian textual system that I am defending here.

The two main characters in the film, Helen Roberts and Joe Dennis (played by Sylvia Sidney and George Raft) are employed in a New York department store whose managing director offers work to former crimi- nals in order to help them return to a normal life, a point he makes in a discussion with his wife who is scandalized, for these people are born criminals. This is a favorite tactic: desocialize every situation in order to make people forget its economic aspects. The managing director's insis- tence on everyone's right to have a job rather than depend on charity, however progressive it is, must not be allowed to hide the naturalization of social relations between employer and employees, which, as will be seen, is important for the film's presentation of the role of money.

When Helen learns that Joe and his gangster friends intend robbing the store, she tips off the managing director. He catches them red- handed and makes a most interesting little speech: rather than send them to prison to be fed at the expense of the community, he will force them to work, just as he does. Hence, from being a right, work becomes a duty, and unemployment, by extension, becomes a purely individual matter, a personal failing. Reagan and Thatcher are already hovering in the wings.

Ideologically the film has shifted sharply to the right, especially when

one remembers the opening sequence, a memory of which later sequences are there to displace and disavow. A song, sung off, tells us that
everything can be bought and that only a fool believes something can be
had for nothing. There follows a montage sequence of a vast variety of
objects, then a single shot of a cash register, symbolizing the omnipre-
sence of money. Then, to the accompaniment of a reminder that there is
nothing money cannot buy, we are treated to a montage sequence
showing us that vacations and leisure are to be bought, as are education
and beauty. By insisting on money in the context of elements not normally seen as commodities—education, beauty— the film's discourse
makes explicit the notion that money is not natural, something everyone
has, but must be created by labor. The Marxist dimension of such an
approach and its Brechtian aspects are not exactly insisted upon but are
nevertheless remarkable in a Hollywood film.

The managing director's first discourse on work as a right now
intervenes, only to be disavowed in favor of work as a duty, as I have just
shown. Helen now takes over from her employer to convince the gangsters that crime does not pay. With the help of a blackboard and a few
figures, she shows them the robbery would have netted them very little,
given their expenses, such as the need to find someone to get rid of the
cash. A change in the camera set-up places the spectators with the
gangsters, like so many schoolchildren being taught a lesson. The moral
is clear: it is best to be honest, especially when one has such a decent,
understanding boss. As Robin Wood has pointed out, Sylvia Sidney is
here "delivering a Brechtian lesson in social conformity (one of the
cinema's most curious anomalies!)" (Wood 1980, 608).

That it should be the heroine who delivers the lesson is part of the
film's overall ideological project: through her love for Joe she forces him
to submit to the Law, both legal and patriarchal. His "job" is to work
and be a father (at the end a child is born). This social and narrative
function has been in place from early in the film, in a sequence where
Helen and Joe discover they love each other during a night out. The
sequence follows the opening montage sequence already analyzed,
where we see that perfume is one of the myriad objects money can buy.
Who says "perfume" says "beauty," and who says "beauty" says "love."
If a woman buys perfume with the intention of making herself desirable
and seducing the man she loves, it is not because she needs the perfume
but because she desires it—and desires it for what it represents, a
representation that comes to her from the discourse of the Other. The
woman's desire is subject-ed to the "good" economic functioning of

capitalist society. When Helen spies the perfume in a store window, she wonders who could possibly afford such a luxury, which momentarily highlights money and class (she is poor). However, this is at once displaced by her remark that there is nothing like perfume to give a woman self-confidence! Joe fails to understand, but he has "learned his lesson" by the end of the film and buys her the perfume. Given that work is now a duty, working to earn money to buy perfume underlines the need to keep the system going, to conform to the Law. The woman "belongs" to the man via the consumer goods he buys her, just as the worker "belongs" to the capitalist via the money the latter pays him. "In Joe's case, his acquisition of knowledge is made clear. His Oedipal journey is inextricably bound up with the maintenance of the economic order of things" (Jenkins 1981, 96).

The ending of *You and Me* is presented as inevitable, which reinforces the essentially conservative message of the film, given the other possibilities presented, then displaced. The concept of forces drawing characters inexorably to a preordained end—usually death—is rife in Lang and has been given a name, fate. The term has had catastrophic consequences for appraisals of the director's work, as I shall now demonstrate.

It all goes back, as Paul Jensen has pointed out (1969, 28), to *Der müde Tod* (1921), translated as *Destiny*—in other words, fate. In the light of critical tendencies to see a natural link, based on a preexisting referent, between title and subject matter, the theme of Lang's film must be destiny. The theme of the film, rendered explicit in the German title, being death, then death equals destiny or fate. The best example of what has happened to Lang criticism as a result can be found in Lotte Eisner. "*You Only Live Once* is Lang's Song of Songs, his American equivalent, so to speak, of *Destiny*. Man is trapped by fate: the loving woman cannot halt her lover's inexorable destiny; her involvement makes things worse and she must finally perish with him" (Eisner 1976, 177).

In the course of her comments on the film, Eisner makes it clear how fate or destiny is to be interpreted: as social injustice. Since the main characters die, there is henceforth an indissoluble link between death, fate, and social injustice functioning as privileged signifier in the critical unconscious. Such a link enables critics to operate a phantasmatic shuttle service between various concepts, present perhaps in certain films but always linked in an imaginary fashion, to impose a fixed meaning stemming from an original error—taking the sign for the referent—and to demand that each film correspond to a reality that has never existed.

The situation has been summed up cogently by Stephen Jenkins.

> *All* narrative is fatalistic, because all narrative consists of described and depicted events, scenes and characters arranged in a certain sequence. To see the weakness of the notion of Fate as a governing principle one need only consider that Lang's characters are always described as being "trapped" by something. But when has a character within a narrative ever been "free" (i.e., not trapped) within the sequence–pattern– arrangement which is that narrative? The terms, and therefore the question, are essentially meaningless. (Jenkins 1981, 63).

There are two positions to contend with: the "Burch syndrome," basically shared by Jensen, which rejects the American period, albeit for radically different reasons (Burch at least bases his stance on a careful analysis of Lang's German films); and the "Eisner syndrome," which sees Lang as a genius transporting his style around with him from Germany to Hollywood, without any modification (Eisner 1947, 3). Lang is "a born painter" with a "natural sense of rhythm" (5), blessed with "an infallible instinct" for capturing the atmosphere of the country in which he is working (Eisner 1976, 149). One wonders how the "Indian" films, shot in German studios, fit in here. . . Whichever way one turns, the signifier is passed over in favor of the signified, for style equals the man and can never be grasped in the context of discursive strategies, that is of the *énonciation.*

Christian Metz stressed long ago how important it is for film-going to avoid unpleasure or anguish in favor of satisfaction, and he insisted on the role of disavowal (the simultaneous presence of belief and knowledge) to that end (Metz 1972, 187). Jensen obliges here with a perfect example dealing with precisely what Metz had in mind: the use of trick effects. Modern fantasy films, Jensen claims (1969, 55), are more realistic than films such as *Die Niebelungen* (1923–24) because it is now no longer necessary to construct a model 60 feet long on the set: a tiny model and refined photography do the trick (so to speak). I would reformulate this as follows. In 1924,

$$\underset{\text{A}}{\frac{\text{the dragon}}{\text{Siegfried}}} = \underset{\text{B}}{\frac{\text{the model}}{\text{the actor}}}$$

There is a sort of harmony between B *(énonciation)* and A *(énoncé).* With the passing of time, however, all this has been rendered superfluous: now there are even more, and more elaborate, trick effects than before. So, by the 1960s,

$$\begin{array}{cc} \text{A} & \text{B} \\ \dfrac{\text{the dragon}}{\text{Siegfried}} = & \dfrac{\text{the model} + \text{modern trick effects}}{\text{the actor}} \end{array}$$

There is, in this case, a lack of harmony, as a result of which also, apparently, there is greater "realism," a way of saying that Jensen can pass off the *énoncé* as natural while at the same time knowing that far more elaborate trick effects have been used to obtain that brand of realism.

In other words, the *énonciation* is more and more massively disavowed in an attempt to pass straight through to some supposedly preexisting reality endowed with a miraculous referential status. What is ultimately being disavowed—repressed, even, when it is a question not of trick effects but of traditional realist films—is the camera and all the enunciative strategies it puts into place: movement, cutting, framing, shot–reverse shot, the offscreen, and so on. What cannot be allowed to intervene in our pleasure is that which points up its scopophilic nature: the (f)act of looking.

It was, of course, Raymond Bellour who, in a justly celebrated article, first highlighted the look in the context of American Lang:

> He accords pride of place to viewpoint; and it is no accident that, from *Fury* onwards, both in his images and in the implications of his scripts, the focus of Lang's *mise en scéne* is so often vision itself, articulated in various ways among which the most obvious is the presence of the investigator, the reporter or the photographer, the man who sees and seizes appearances within the rectangular frame of his camera. . . . Every film-maker, in a sense, defines the essence of cinema, but is there another for whom it is so nakedly, and so unequivocaly, as with Lang, the ultimate metaphor? . . . What else can one say but a vision of vision? (Bellour 1981, 28).

Let us take a look at two concrete examples, *You and Me* and *Hangmen Also Die*. Near the beginning of the former there is a big close-up of the George Raft character looking offscreen right and saying: "Listen, this is a good racket and I ought to know. There isn't a racket I haven't tried." At this point in the film we do not have all the information on the Raft character, but we do have some. The previous scene has shown a friend of his, a former criminal, receiving a visit from the leader of a gang anxious to get in touch with Raft. The setting is therefore one of potential criminality, massively overdetermined by Raft's status as a player in gangster films and by the linking of the sequence in question to the close-up of Raft speaking by a fade, which, as Metz has suggested, can be seen as a form of displacement, functioning to enable the spectator to disavow the enunciation in favor of a "natural" link invested with a referential—and, hence, nondiscursive—value (Metz 1977b, 336). Thus a complex articulation of the cinematic signifier, a verbal signifier—*racket*—and genre creates audience expectation in the form of a natural(ized) signified: Raft is involved in a criminal act. There now follows a backtrack and a brief pan to the right: Raft is in the department store trying to sell a tennis racket to a female customer.

Rather than see the scene as just a cheap trick on Lang's part—the reaction of critics to a film like *The Woman in the Window*—I would suggest that it takes one to the heart of the Langian textual system. Its apparent frivolity is just that, apparent and that is why I have chosen it. Its simplicity leads one to dismiss it as a gag at best and hence to overlook the obvious: that an entire cinematic tradition of representation is behind our misreading of the shot where Raft speaks his line. As Mae West once said, "It's better to be looked over than overlooked." Keeping that eminently sane advice in mind—especially in the context of desire—let us look over a sequence in *Hangmen Also Die.*

The opening five shots of the film are as follows:

Shot 1: A general view of Prague

Shot 2: A general view of one part of the town

Shot 3: A general view of another part of the town

Shot 4: Close-up of the Czech emblem, *Truth.* The camera tracks back to reveal the German eagle and a portrait of Hitler. A further backtrack reveals stained-glass windows representing biblical scenes.

Shot 5: A general view of the Nazi headquarters. All the elements described in shot 4 are present.

Toward the end of the film, the Gestapo shoot down the double agent Czaka, who dies on the steps of a church. Cut. Close-up of a stained-glass window representing a scene from the Bible. Since Czaka has died in front of the church, we can assume the shot is of the church. Not a bit: a backtrack shows we are in the Nazi headquarters. We would be justified in seeing such an articulation of shots as creating a link between religion and Nazism, but it surely goes much farther. The very nature of vision, interpretation (representation as interpretation on the spectator's part) and memory is involved. A so-called naturalistic detail, supposedly necessary for the film to be considered as "realistic," returns some two hours later (time of the enunciation, of course) to show that no detail is insignificant and that one forgets or overlooks such details at one's own risk, that of failing to grasp the link between looking and seeing, representing and interpreting.[18]

Hardly surprising then that Jensen should find the film artificial precisely because of the opening shots, obviously newsreel footage incorporated into the film (Jensen 1969, 146): the desired homogeneity is missing, but the whole question of representation, of how and what we see and why, is displaced, once again in favor of the referential illusion.[19] The return of the stained-glass windows via a backtrack is a case of what Philippe Demonsablon has nicely referred to as "acts . . . being attracted to the channels dug for them" (Demonsablon 1981, 20), although it is necessary to go beyond the vocabulary of cause and effect to place the question on the terrain of the signifier and its implacable logic.[20] This, I would suggest, is how one can interpret a remark by Michel Mourlet. "An organisation of what is possible as *inevitable,* in such a way that the film ineluctably assaults the spectator's expectations, leads us to the heart of Lang's problem. The elimination of chance, the constant domination of forms by an architecture in which each part determines and is answerable to the others, result in a fascination or an inability in the spectator to escape the discipline of the film (Mourlet 1981, 12).

Demonsablon has made an observation that prefigures remarkably modern theory, even if he lacked the conceptual system to draw the full conclusions. "Lang often delights in endowing even the most natural gesture with repercussions so weighty that the mind, powerless to deny the patent fact, finds itself questioning the logical system behind it" (Demonsablon 1981, 20).

One of his examples, taken from *Rancho Notorious*— "Marlene Dietrich being mortally wounded precisely where she wore the jewel which was torn from" the hero's murdered wife—is particularly pertinent. The hero, Vern Haskell, spends the film looking for his wife's murderers, who also took the jewels he had given her. His quest is based on the look and its attendant misinterpretations in the form of mistaken identities (see chapter 4, section 2). His obsession leads to everyone, guilty and innocent, getting killed and to the "second death" of his wife via the Dietrich character. I shall examine this link between the look and the investigation, death, and knowledge, as well as the way the enunciative strategies that put them into place also place the spectator, in chapters 2, 3, and 4.

Aspects of Looking: 2
On with the Show

A most concise and useful summary of the various kinds of look functioning within the cinematic machine has been proposed by Stephen Heath.

> Classically, cinema turns on a series of "looks" which join, cross through, and relay one another. Thus: 1) the camera looks (a metaphor assumed by this cinema) . . . at someone, something: the profilmic; 2) the spectator looks . . . at—or on—the film; 3) each of the characters in the film looks . . . at other characters, things: the intradiegetic. This series possesses a certain reversibility: on the one hand, the camera looks, the spectator looks at what the camera looks at and thereby sees characters in the film looking; on the other, the spectator sees characters in the film looking, which is to look at the film, which is to find the camera's looking, its "having looked" (the presence in absence). The first and second looks, moreover, are in a perpetual interchange of "priority," of "origination": the camera's look is found only by looking at the film but the former is the condition—one of the conditions—of the latter. (Heath 1977a, 11)

Although much of this chapter is concerned with formal descriptions of certain films—especially *You Only Live Once* and *The Ministry of Fear*—my main objective is to show in what way the films cited fail, at some crucial point, to reproduce exactly the classical articulations of the looks involved. Several preliminary remarks are therefore in order.

The scopophilic thrust of the look and its undertones of castration can be seen at work in numerous films, the most far-reaching of which are arguably Alfred Hitckcock's *Vertigo* (1958), Michael Powell's *Peeping Tom* (1960), and David Lynch's *Blue Velvet* (1986).[1] The theoretical background to this central element in modern film theory has been provided by Jacques Lacan with his concept of the look as *objet petit a,* something the subject has had to separate itself from on the road to constitution as a subject in the Symbolic Order (which implies, of course, the never-ending dialectic of Symbolic and Imaginary). The *objet petit a* that is the look is therefore the symbolic lack of castration, a lack that the subject's desire must try to repair (Lacan 1973, 96, 73). Given that desire is always desire of the Other inasmuch as language (without which there is no demand and no desire) comes to the subject from the field of the Other, our desire to see, which prompts us to go to the cinema, cannot be dissociated from the other looks involved, such as looks into the camera, looks offscreen, or, most frequently, looks between characters. Our desire to identify with these characters of the diegetic world and to lend meaning and coherence to that world through our look leads to our look becoming articulated with the various looks within the text, which means in turn that the look of the other can disorganize the spectator's perceptive field through the dialectic of desire (Lacan 1973, 83). The alienated nature of the ego and the nature of desire entail the following conclusion: the subject is not what he represents himself as, and what is offered to his gaze is not what he wants to see (16).

In such a context of fragile subject-ivity, it is clear that any deviation from a "norm" destined to keep going the state of alienated miscognition that defines the ego risks upsetting the delicate balance: the moment something goes amiss, unpleasure can result, even if the overall flow of the film reorders things again. Hence the need to ensure that looks are especially between characters and to avoid introducing those elements likely to give prominence to the real status of the spectator. In the light of Lacan's insisting on the need not to confuse the eyes (a simple bodily organ) and the look (which introduces the dimension of desire, the lack, and the Other), I wish to look first at a film whose textual system insists on eyes in order to involve the spectators with the look, notably their own: *You Only Live Once.*

You Only Live Once
The hat, the look, and
the bank robbery.

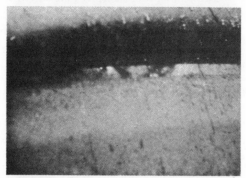

1.The Eyes and the Look

I propose to analyze a single sequence of the film and its textual implications (strictly speaking, I am dealing with three sequences, each comprising several shots, but they are articulated so as to appear as one sequence, which is precisely the point). Eddie Taylor has just been released from prison and, supported by his fiancée, is determined to lead an exemplary life. But he finds himself constantly reminded of his past, both by the members of his former gang and by those he asks for a job. Following a banal incident, Taylor's employer fires him, refusing to listen to his explanations (and the audience is left in no doubt that Taylor has committed no offence and is simply being blamed for his past). It is in this context that we must "see" what follows:

> Shot 1: Close-up of a hat on a table, with the initials E. T. showing. The camera tracks left and frames a photograph of Taylor's fiancée, then continues tracking left and frames a man stretched out on a bed. The man, who is not Taylor and who is wearing a cap, is looking offscreen left. Cut.

> Shot 2: Taylor stands looking out of the window. Given the spatial coordinates of shot 1, it is clear that the man on the bed is looking at Taylor. The two shots are therefore articulated in a classical fashion.

> Shot 3: A general shot of the man on the bed and Taylor standing in the background, making explicit what was obvious from the articulation of the first two shots.

> Shot 4: Someone comes in and tells Taylor a woman is asking for him on the phone. The man on the bed gets up and says he is going to Tony's.

> Shot 5: The conversation between Taylor and his fiancée is shown by crosscutting. She informs him she has just settled into the house they are buying. Taylor is desperate: no longer having a job, he does not have the money necessary for the final payment, but he lies to his fiancée (there are, of course, several shots involved, but I have grouped them together since there is no change in the point of view).

> Shot 6: Taylor goes back to the room and looks at the picture of his fiancée.

> Shot 7: Close-up of the photograph again.

> Shot 8: Taylor looks away from the photograph in the direction of the bed. He moves over to it and throws back the covers.

Shot 9: General shot of a revolver, which was under the pillow.

Shot 10: Taylor stands motionless by the bed and the revolver.

Shot 11: Taylor puts the revolver back under the pillow, picks up the hat, and leaves. Fade to

Shot 12: The interior of an office. Present are Taylor, hat in hand, and his employer.

Shot 13: Close-up of the employer, from behind. His hat, which is very like Taylor's, fills half the screen.

Shot 14: Because he cannot find work, Taylor asks the man to give him his job back, adding: "I've tried to get a job every place. The only people who'll give me one are my old gang." They are thinking of robbing a bank and Taylor is not interested. His former employer refuses to listen.

Shot 15: Taylor knocks him down. "And I wanted to go straight!" Cut.

Shot 16: General shot of the Fifth National Bank. It is raining. Cut.

Shot 17: General shot of a car parked opposite the bank. Forward tracking shot to give a close-up of one of the windows, so steamed up that nothing can be seen. The window is lowered very slightly to reveal a pair of eyes looking right and left, then offscreen right. Cut.

Shot 18: An employee comes out of the bank, takes a look around and checks the time. Cut.

Shot 19: Close-up of the pair of eyes in the car; this is still all that can be seen. Suddenly they look offscreen left. Cut.

Shot 20: An armored truck draws up in front of the bank. An armed guard alights and knocks on the back of the truck. Other men alight and, with the help of policemen, start unloading sacks of money. Cut.

Shot 21: The eyes in the car are now looking offscreen right. Then the window of the car is closed. Cut.

Shot 22: The interior of the car. A gloved hand opens a case containing gas masks and tear gas bombs. The same hand places in the case a hat bearing the initials E. T. The camera tracks back and sideways to frame the owner of the hand, who is already wearing a mask so that his face cannot be seen.

Shot 23: The man wearing the mask throws the bombs, and the police and guards collapse. The man climbs into the armored car and drives off. Cut.

Shot 24: Close-up of a diversion sign. The armored car stops, then leaves the highway and disappears. The camera does not move. Then a loud crash can be heard. Cut.

Shot 25: A road sign: ROAD UNDER CONSTRUCTION: DANGER

A lot is going on in this sequence. It is constructed along classical lines: precise spatial coordinates, homogenization of space by the looks and the camera movements. At the same time it exploits all the narrative codes in order to pinpoint better their artificiality and the ways in which the spectator can be led astray. Let us see how this is achieved.

The close-up of the hat in shot 1 draws our attention to it and hence encourages us to find it important, given our knowledge that any close-up serves to lend value to the object thus seized by the camera's gaze. The initials E. T. allow us to conclude that the hat belongs to Eddie Taylor, a conclusion reinforced by the shot of the picture of his fiancée. Doubt is introduced by the shot of the man on the bed, whom we expect to be Taylor. Why the shot of the hat and the track to the photograph if this tracking shot does not end up by showing us Taylor?[2] Lang could have presented the man on the bed *after* showing us Taylor. The fact that the man is wearing a cap is used to indicate that the hat is not his and encourages us even further to grant some special significance to it. The camera kills two birds with one stone: it emphasizes the hat as signifier and key element, while at the same time showing that such a movement linking A (the hat) and B (the man) need not necessarily create the link "the hat belongs to the man." This undermining of the imaginary referent by an insistence on discursive contiguity will be exploited later in shots 15 and 16. The telephone call (shot 5), the presence of the gun (shots 9, 10, and 11), and Taylor's look at his fiancée's picture (shot 6) allow us to draw a conclusion from what we are seeing: Taylor is going to commit a crime in order to get the money he needs. His failure to get his old job back and his bitter remark about wanting to go straight (shots 12, 13, 14, and 15) all reinforce this reading. These presuppositions on the part of the spectators stem from the classical articulation of the various shots and the codes, both narrative and thematic, of the gangster film.

The cut at one and the same time separating and linking shots 15 and 16 creates the imaginary referent: Taylor is there and about to rob the bank. The presence in shot 22 of the hat bearing his initials helps this process along. A fade would have weakened the essential ambiguity of the situation, whereas a cut—especially in the light of what we have seen in shots 1–14—encourages the spectator's desire to complete what is not *clear* by what is clearly *expected*. What is happening?

The importance given to the hat makes any other reading improbable. The hat belongs to Taylor, so it must be Taylor who is in the car wearing a mask. So far, so good, except for one detail: how do we know that the hat we see in shot 1 is the same hat Taylor picks up as he leaves (shot 11)? The film is here skillfully playing with the spectators: having insisted on the hat in the first shot so that we cannot help but find it important, the film then carefully avoids insisting on it at the very moment when it really is important to know if it is Taylor's hat or not. And, indeed, we learn in due course that it was *not* his own hat that Taylor picked up but one that looked like it. The way the film insists on the resemblance between Taylor's hat (which is not his) and the hat of his former employer shows just to what extent the Langian textual system exploits the spectators' being coded by expectation and their tendency to forget what they are shown. After all, the close-up of the hat in shot 13 is redundant from the point of view of the story but quite crucial as a narrative strategy.[3]

However, it is the eyes in particular that lead the spectator astray. The importance of looking is central to the shots preceding the bank robbery, and the film consistently plays on furtive looks—including Taylor's—to create a pattern throughout, a tactic that is overdetermined not only by the codes of the genre, always carefully exploited and played on by Lang, but also by the necessity for the spectator to look in order to see. The textual system uses this unconscious knowledge of ours to encourage us to see what is not there. Even the end of the sequence— the accident—is not necessarily what it seems, for one of the codes of the genre consists of getting rid of the getaway vehicle so that its occupants cannot be traced. Once again, of course, vision is played on: this time we quite simply are not shown anything but are given a sound to interpret. Taylor could have robbed the bank, just as he could have dumped the armored truck and made good his escape.

The textual system plays on ambiguity in a quite remarkable fashion in the sequences following on from shot 25 of the sequence just analyzed. Shots 25 and the one following it are articulated by a fade, which sets up in the spectator's unconscious a link between them. We see a swing, the same swing Taylor pushed when he and his fiancée were visiting the house they were contemplating buying. Moreover, it is raining, just as it was during the robbery. A classical example of suture that functions to undermine the very code it seems to be exploiting.

Seldom can the imaginary referent have functioned so strongly: the fade plus the rain lead the spectator to displace discursive contiguity onto the diegetic world and assume the existence of a temporal continuity; all of which serves the logic of the text against the logic of genre and expectation, the logic of the signifier as opposed to the logic of fixed signs and codes.

Cut. Taylor, crouching low, is seen making his way through bushes toward the house. He looks in through the window. Cut. We see his fiancée busy putting their belongings away. Cut to a medium shot of Taylor's eyes. He is looking offscreen right, just as the eyes were at one point during the robbery. Moreover, the eyes look alike. Anguish is written all over Taylor's face, which can only encourage one particular reading: having organized the robbery, he made his getaway, dumped the truck, and continued on foot through the rain. Taylor continues to look through the window, which enables the film to exploit the nature of his look: furtive and desperate, a device taken up elsewhere in the film. The first occasion is when the fiancée visits Taylor in prison, the second when he tries to commit suicide. Each time he is seen looking offscreen right and left, exactly as the eyes in shots 17 and 19.

Eyes are used to look at something and hence to determine the spectators' vision. If eyes look offscreen right, they become a look that calls for a change in point of view on the camera's part so that the spectator too can see—that is, look at—the person or object fixed by the gaze of the character. Far from allowing the spectator to disavow the enunciative strategy at work, this insists on it by placing it at the center of the film. Eyes are there to record things, the look to show what is being recorded, the camera to fulfill the two functions. To insist on eyes and looks as central to what is going on in the film, and then to reveal that our interpretation is either partial or downright inaccurate, is to stress the active nature of *our* look, to underline the process by which our look is taken up and inscribed into the textual activity. Henceforth the spectator will be unable to put the errors of justice down to simple bigotry or social injustice, but will have to account for them by the very (f)act of looking and either not seeing what is there or seeing what is not there.

Such a situation becomes one of the prime concerns of the Langian textual system.

2. The Look into the Camera

One of the cardinal rules of film making, rarely broken, is that the actor should not look directly into the camera, so that the spectator may continue to "enjoy" the film without being "distracted" by such frivolities as technique.[4] The spectators must be allowed to identify with the characters and events without ever being aware of it, which puts them immediately in a dual position, a duality that the cinematic machine is there to disavow. For the spectators are both aggressors and aggressed: aggressors because they indulge their scopophilia, albeit in blithe ignorance of its implications, indeed of its very existence;[5] aggressed because they fail to recognize the way the machine is manipulating them.[6] Pascal Bonitzer has pointed out that the look into the camera, a sort of "counter-look", threatens pleasure, becoming an "evil eye" (Bonitzer 1977, 44). For this to function effectively, however, such a look must not be isolated, a gimmick (as in *Tom Jones*), but inscribed into the text as an integral part without which the text would not be the same. A look into the camera must question the look it meets—that of the spectator—and not be seen as something peculiar to the character looking.

Fury is most revealing here. Believed dead by everyone, Joe Wilson returns home to his brothers and unburdens himself of his bitterness through a violent tirade against those responsible for burning the prison and, in the eyes of all America, guilty of his murder. As he speaks he looks menacingly into the camera; his speech lasts for only thirty seconds, but its aggressiveness and the very special circumstances make it seem longer. Joe's look constitutes the spectator as an object, which can only cause unpleasure because the viewing subject is placed unconsciously in the very position that the ego wishes to remain repressed: that of being constituted in and by a lack that the subject desires to fill with precisely some *objet petit a* it is in the process of being turned into at the moment of viewing. It also means the spectator is inscribed into the diegesis as occupying the place of Joe's brothers and, more especially, the absent lynch mob.

The film proposes two other manifestations of this identification. As the crowd advances on the jail, the sheriff stands before the door, daring them to come too close. The camera adopts the point of view of the crowd—and so therefore do we—and tracks forward slowly while the sheriff looks implacably into the lens, that is, at the mob, at us. At the end of the film, the ringleader of the mob tries to flee the courtroom.

Suddenly he stops and stares in horror into the camera. He starts to retreat and the camera moves slowly forward. Cut to the man's point of view from within the courtroom: we see Joe Wilson, who has just opened the door and is now advancing with determination.

When the spectators become the object of Joe's gaze, their superior all-knowing status as consumers of images collapses, but their ability to imagine Joe addressing his brothers enables a displacement from enunciation to enounced to take place and hence a repression of this disquieting new status, with all its knowledge, suddenly forced upon them. Likewise the fact that they know, by seeing the horrified features of the mob leader, what it means to undergo such a murderous gaze is displaced by the cut to Joe, which enables the spectators to assume again their role as consumers of suspenseful images. By looking at Joe without being looked at, the spectators can keep their distance and watch the protagonists fight it out without being too involved. Each situation described certainly functions as a *mise en abyme* of the real status of the spectators, but the need and capacity to identify with characters to undercut the sort of alienation introduced by Joe's thirty second look and speech allows them to maintain the desired presence of both belief and knowledge.

However, another look into the camera functions differently. Once again, only the spectators and Joe's brothers know he is alive. Although everyone assumes he is dead, the prosecution is in a delicate position: it must prove Joe was in the prison at the time it was burned down. Joe's brothers question his fiancée, Katherine, on the matter, and when one of them strikes a match, she remembers seeing Joe's face behind bars. "I saw him," she cries, and the spectators of the film saw him too. We thus identify with Katherine, but we have the advantage of knowing Joe is alive. Katherine's look into the camera of the enunciation—at us— must therefore be assimilated, as far as her knowledge is concerned, to the camera of the diegesis that films the burning of the prison (see chapter 3, section 1). That this camera does not reveal the truth stresses for the spectators that, despite identifying with Katherine, they are *not* part of the diegesis and hence in a special and privileged position through the look of the camera of the enunciation. The real status of the enunciation and the place of the spectator are thus maintained.

3. The Offscreen

The offscreen can be qualified as both diegetic (the space of the film, the enounced) and extradiegetic (the space of the shooting of the film, the enunciation). In the former case it is an absent space summoned up by the looks of the characters; in the latter case, an absent space summoned up by the spectator's gaze via the look of the camera. In both cases, therefore, the common factor is an absence and, more particularly, the role of the camera inasmuch as, without it, there would be no offscreen to talk about. Once again, we have the sort of self-evident Truth that even our friend M. la Palice would blush to announce, which explains, once again, why it causes such embarrassment to film theoreticians such as Jean Mitry, obsessed with hiding the obvious, with creating a spatial unity that does not exist but must be made to appear to (Mitry 1963, 363, 389). Nothing must be allowed to interfere with that harmony—technical and psychical—that reigns supreme when onscreen and offscreen replace each other smoothly and invisibly, as with the classical shot–reverse shot.

If Noël Burch had already provided the formal bases for grasping the phenomenon of the off screen (Burch 1969), it was Jean-Pierre Oudart who first tackled the psychoanalytical implications as far as the cinema was concerned (Oudart 1969). He asked the pertinent question: How and why does the spectator represent the absent offscreen in order to create, through an articulation of that absence and the onscreen, an imaginary totality? Hence the term *suture* came to designate the unconscious element that represses all textual and spectatorial activity, masks the fundamental discontinuity of the chain of images, and thus allows the spectators to fail to recognize their real status as subject of the enunciation constituted in and by absence.[7]

Now the desired continuity cannot be established unless the articulation of the onscreen and the offscreen takes place quickly, smoothly, and without drawing attention to itself. Let us take an example. A general shot of a room shows two people sitting talking over a drink. One of them gets up to replenish his glass and disappears offscreen, leaving the other alone before the camera. Even if the camera follows the person who gets up and "abandons" the other, the spectators will have no trouble in representing the scene as a spatial unity containing two people. In other words, in no way is the real nature of the spectators' gaze brought into play. If the person who has remained seated looks

Man Hunt   Light and dark, onscreen and offscreen, Quive-Smith and (the shadow of) Thorndike.

offscreen and there follows a shot–reverse shot, then the process of identification will enable the spectators to represent as a presence the person, now absent from view, whose gaze they have been inscribed into.

It is here, however, that things can start "going wrong" if a director chooses to exploit the situation. Should the character's gaze offscreen not be followed by a shot–reverse shot but quite simply held in order to insist on it as a look, then the offscreen is emphasized as an absence, with all that can mean for the spectator. Prolonging such absence can create suspense and, in extreme cases, anguish, an element frequently found in horror films, where the offscreen can hide nameless terrors (Vernet 1976). It is a favorite tactic in the films of directors as different as Jacques Tourneur and Jack Arnold, the crucial difference being that

The Ministry of Fear   Mrs. Penteel, Stephen Neale, and Mr. Newby at the séance.

Tourneur often exploits the offscreen in order to hint that there may be nothing there at all and that it is all in our imagination. What returns in such cases is the very (f)act of looking, as an activity in its own right, and not just as a way of seeing something. It is precisely this aspect that is central to the Langian textual system.

At the beginning of *Hangmen Also Die,* someone (later we learn that it was Dr. Svoboda, who had just assassinated Heydrich) runs onscreen from offscreen, exchanges his worker's cap for a bourgeois homburg, then rushes offscreen again. Clearly a man with something to hide, a man being pursued. There follows a shot of a young woman (who, we later learn, is Mascha Novotny) looking offscreen, shocked and horrified; German soldiers appear and she sends them in the wrong direction.

It is enough that she saw and that we saw her see: admirable and terrifying logic of the Langian *découpage,* which sutures the character's viewpoint to that of the spectator and makes us recipients of the trap to which they are predestined by the fiction. For the fiction here starts and functions as a trap, and it is they, the resistants and their accomplices, who are caught in it at the beginning, while we spectators—as we shall see—end as its victims. (Comolli and Géré 1981)

The lie here is the repressed. Miss Novotny has looked offscreen and has seen, but she denies it whenever the Gestapo questions her. Her denial is a form of disavowal, for she believes that she can thus be neutral, whereas she has made her choice, like it or not. This disavowal, which is the disavowal of the look, the fact of having seen (something), makes of Miss Novotny the perfect, typical spectator whose desire, purely imaginary, is akin to that of the three wise monkeys. As usual, the repressed is not long in returning.

It returns, in fact, almost at once. Forced to seek cover because of the curfew imposed by the Nazis, Svoboda heads for the apartment of the Novotnys and rings. Thinking it is her fiancé, Miss Novotny opens the door. There follows a shot of her, horrified, looking offscreen right, a look taken up and repeated in a scene at Nazi headquarters where she realizes that Mrs. Dvorak (who, like Miss Novotny, can identify Svoboda, and who knows the young woman) has been tortured. Miss Novotny's initial denial of what she has seen, a disavowal of the look, is a displacement from her real subject position onto an imaginary innocence, which leads her to believe she can lie without becoming involved in its implications. The displacement is now repeated. Mrs. Dvorak is tortured because she knows Miss Novotny is lying: she takes the young woman's place. Hence Miss Novotny's horror: horror at someone suffering because of her, horror at her discovery of the repressed—multiple subject positions.

The repetition is now taken up in the case of Svoboda. After the assassination and in order to appear as inconspicuous as possible, he retires to a café. Suddenly he looks offscreen left, horrified, as German troops rush onscreen and impose the curfew. His look here prefigures his absent look in front of the Novotnys' apartment. In other words, if Miss Novotny's horrified look when she opened the door had been followed by a reverse shot, we would have seen Svoboda looking offscreen left in order to maintain spatial unity. As a result, given that there is an identical repetition of looks offscreen in the case of the two characters, we can say that each is the offscreen of the other, hence the return of the repressed of the other. The offscreen creates an imaginary space that undermines the spectatorial imaginary inasmuch as the true status of the look and its attendant subject positions insist. The spectators, who have been put in the position of identifying with the looks of the two characters, are now in a position to judge the articulation of a certain kind of look and a lie. Such an articulation places spectators before the real nature of a narrative device deployed normally to enable them to lie to themselves about their position as viewing subjects.

The Blue Gardenia insists on this specular function of the offscreen in order to deconstruct it. One evening, Norah returns home in a daze, believing she has killed the Don Juan who had tried to take advantage of her drunk state the previous evening after inviting her up to his apartment.[8] She is, understandably, still dazed the next morning, and her behavior leads her friend, who shares the apartment with her, to interrogate her. Norah walks offscreen to get dressed, and there follows a shot of her friend looking offscreen right as she questions her. The latter shot, and hence the insistent look, is maintained without the film having recourse to a reverse shot, although Norah answers her friend. It is customary in such cases to cut from one speaking source to the other, and the film's refusal to do so cannot be put down simply to the fact that Norah is dressing: the upper part of her body could be shown, or she could be "shielded" by the door of her wardrobe, or simply revealed by the reverse shot to be more or less clothed. Instead, "all" we get is a long-held shot of someone else looking—and looking. The least one can say is that this frustrates the spectatorial desire to see by looking.

Such frustration—*unpleasure* would be too strong a word, although unease is certainly present—points out to the spectator the artificial nature of what is happening. Either we put the lack of reverse shot down to the prudery of the Hays Code, in which case a moral convention is ridiculed by an unusual use of framing and cutting. Or else we start from the enunciation as determining everything we see—and do not see—and are forced to see that nothing is natural, but everything is based on a choice at any and every moment. It is also pertinent to underline that such a long take plays against the psychic significance cutting takes on in classical cinema, where "continuity is built on fragmentation rather than the long take—on a segmentation for recomposition that can bind the spectator in the strong articulation of the unity it seeks to create" (Heath 1976a, 90).

An interesting comparison can be made between the sequence of *The Blue Gardenia* just analyzed and a shot, also held for a long time, in one of the earliest films of Josef von Sternberg, *The Docks of New York* (1928). The hero and a young woman he has just met go for a drink in a waterfront bar. If the camera remains fixed on them without any reverse shot, it is for the excellent reason that the spectator can follow what is going on in the bar thanks to a huge mirror on the wall behind the couple, and that mirror enables us not only to see the other customers but to fix the bar as a spatial unity. Although the Imaginary is thus central to the shot, it should be pointed out that, were von Sternberg to hold the shot indefinitely without cutting, a similar effect to the Lang would be produced, for the insistence on the mirror and the reflection would become artificial instead of appearing as a passing device enabling us to follow two different actions at the same time without cutting. As Heath pointed out in the passage just quoted, a certain breaking up of unity is necessary for the retotalization of image and ego, an ongoing process that needs a minimum of *change* for the repetition not to be experienced as such.

A sequence in *Man Hunt* stands midway between the two examples just cited. Quive-Smith has handed Thorndike over to the Gestapo to make him admit he was acting under orders from the British government to kill Hitler. Thorndike continues to deny it and is tortured for an indefinite period. Then Quive-Smith questions him again. At the beginning of the sequence, Quive-Smith is visible in the frame in the background, whereas only Thorndike's shadow can be seen in the foreground. Quive-Smith, who never takes his eyes off Thorndike and is therefore constantly looking offscreen right, advances to the foreground until he is on the same level as Thorndike's shadow. The two men therefore share the frame, one as a presence, the other as an absence. However, the shadow is very much present and tends to represent the offscreen, which is present thanks to the work of disavowal. The tactic is strengthened when the shadow shows Thorndike's mouth moving as he replies to Quive-Smith's questions. It is undermined, however, when Quive-Smith bends forward from time to time to talk to Thorndike, who is seated on a chair. The action of bending forward toward the offscreen can only insist on its existence and force the spectator to realize that, shadow or no shadow, Thorndike is absent from the frame. The sequence thus hesitates between an insistence on the offscreen, as in *The Blue Gardenia,* and a disavowal of it, as in *The Docks of New York.*

An example of a different kind is to be found in *The Ministry of Fear.* The hero and heroine, Stephen Neale and Clara, are fleeing from Nazi spies and, exhausted because of being forced to move around constantly, manage to find a place where they can sleep. When Clara wakes up, she looks offscreen right, her face contorted with horror. Then she turns her head to the left: Neale is there and it is he who woke her up. The shot works because of the general atmosphere created: one of fear, paranoia, and conspiracy in which nobody and nothing is to be taken at face value.

To leave it at that would, however, be to reduce the shot to a fixed place within the text having more to do with the general story line than with the unconscious thrust of the look. Given that we see nothing for a moment—only fleeting, but it is enough—we quite simply find ourselves looking at her looking, which becomes the object of the shot.[9] That a particular object at a fixed point of the screen is not at stake means that the spectator's look is no more fixed than Carla's, and it is a case of "the marginal distortion which ensues when the observer's eye is not correctly in position in the centre of the perspective projection but pulls to the edge" (Heath 1976a, 76). I would suggest that "marginal" be read as a pun: belonging to the extremity of the frame; and being limited and temporary in its effects. Which does not mean that such effects are to be dismissed as trivial: quite the reverse.

Clara's look, then, is to be seen as an element in the text's ongoing work on the look, and the aspect of horror it engenders is bound up with an earlier sequence, the séance, the element of the film that, both in theme and realization, brings *The Ministry of Fear* very close to the contemporary horror films of Jacques Tourneur.[10] The extraordinary power of the sequence, perhaps the most extended statement in Lang on framing and the look, stems from the careful placing of the spectator prior to the start of the séance: we know exactly where we are (in the house of the medium, Mrs. Bellane) and have had the chance to study the layout of the room used. Such classicism is vital for certainty to give way to doubt, all the more striking since we know where each person is seated in relation to the others.

Shot 1: The lights dim, then a lamp lights up in the middle of the table. Sinister music is heard.

Shot 2: Medium shot of Mrs. Bellane, her face in the light. She is looking directly into the camera.

Shot 3: Medium shot of the lamp from shot 1.

Shot 4: Medium shot of Mrs. Bellane in the act of closing her eyes.

Shot 5: Medium shot of Willi looking offscreen left. Then he moves his head slightly, while still looking offscreen left and to one side of the camera.

Shot 6: Medium shot of Neale seated between Mr. Newby and Mrs. Penteel. Suddenly Neale looks offscreen right.

Shot 7: Medium shot of Cost looking fixedly offscreen right, as if in a trance.

Shot 8: Medium shot of Neale, anxious, still looking offscreen right. The lamp can be seen to his left, Mr. Newby to his right. Track left so that only Neale and the lamp are visible. Neale's head is now facing left. On it is superimposed the image of the pendulum he was staring at fixedly in the asylum in the film's opening sequence. He bows his head as if trying to rid himself of the image, then raises it again and opens his eyes.

Shot 9: General shot of the room, from above. Everyone is seated around the table. A whispering can be heard.

Shot 10: Medium shot of Neale looking in horror toward the camera, but not directly into it. Someone is whispering "Yes, yes." Neale looks quickly left and right, as if seeking the source of the voice. Same sinister music.

Shot 11: Medium shot of Mrs. Bellane; it is she who is talking, her eyes closed.

Shot 12: General shot of the room.

Shot 13: Medium shot of Mrs. Bellane whispering indistinctly.

Shot 14: Medium shot of Cost (same as shot 7).

Shot 15: Medium shot of Willi. Track left to follow his look, which is changing direction slowly. Dr. Forrester appears in the frame, looking fixedly before him, offscreen left, slightly to one side of the camera. His look shifts left as the tracking shot continues. A woman enters the frame; both she and Forrester look offscreen left. Track right to frame Willi looking offscreen left. Both he and Forrester are in frame, the latter still looking fixedly before him. Suddenly a voice cries, "Stephen!" Horrified, Willi looks ahead of him, offscreen left, as in shot 5.

Shot 16: Medium shot of Neale, alone in the middle of the frame, a look of horror on his face. A voice starts to talk of his wife's death. Neale rises abruptly and moves left. Mrs. Bellane is now in frame.

Track back; Neale is no longer visible. We can see Newby and Penteel. A gunshot. The lights come up. Neale is standing in the background; he does not have a gun.

Shot 17: Cost is lying on the ground, blood on his temple.

Shot 18: Medium shot of Mrs. Bellane, seated, and of Forrester, who examines Cost and then looks offscreen right.

Shot 19: Medium shot of Neale. Mrs. Penteel accuses him of murder.

The constant changes in point of view and the looks offscreen fragment the sequence, but our knowledge of the layout of the room enables us to reconstitute the unity that is momentarily lost. The sequence is thus in many ways quite classical. When Willi's look shifts in shot 5, we know that he is looking at Neale, which makes of shot 6 a "logical" extension. The same can be said of shots 6 and 7, 15 and 16, and 18 and 19. Despite the complexity of shot 15, the combination of tracking shots and the presence in frame of two or three characters at any given moment lends it homogeneity. Shots 9 and 12 intervene to remind the spectators of the general layout of the room and follow a shot that shows a character in isolation without moving on to someone else. Shots 8 and 11 threaten the unity of the scene by functioning in the same way as close-ups, cut off from all elements likely to enable us to situate them, which questions our mastery of the visual field and thus our vision (Bonitzer 1971a, 19). Shots 9 and 12 remove such a danger.

If that is the case, then where does the interest of the sequence as a whole lie? Let us take shot 10. Whom does Neale look at in horror: Mrs. Bellane? Forrester? There is no way of saying. If Mrs. Bellane is the source of the voice, then the link between shots 10 and 11 is far from obvious, given that Neale's look lacks direction.

In fact, the problem is less one of suturing space than of knowing *why* X is looking at Y. Let us take shot 15. Each look within the shot is followed by another character being framed, which creates spatial unity. Yet nothing precise happens: the process just stops, then starts up again. Hence the look has no object or purpose except the look itself. Our look in turn is determined by the looks offscreen and between characters and, hence, is without purpose. The unity of the room may be maintained, but our own place and our role in the action become problematic.

It is surely revealing that Lang uses only cuts throughout the sequence. Whereas fades tend to create links and reinforce the imaginary referent, cuts run the risk of a spatial and temporal break, even though some link is inevitable, given the desire for continuity and the capacity to create it where none exists. As we are in the presence of a spatial and temporal continuity for the duration of the sequence, I would argue that each cut signifies the return of the repressed that is the enunciation. The spatial coordinates are not in fact given in advance but are re-created anew with every shot. The shots do not therefore form a coherent and harmonious totality with reference to the room, despite the attempts of the text to make us think so, but they signify only in relation to one another. Each shot becomes the signifier of the absence that constitutes the viewing subjects through their desire to see and, by seeing, to know and understand. A further angle, as it were, can be obtained if we study those elements that invite us in a very special way to look at them and, at a certain angle, return our gaze, with all that such a device implies: portraits.

4. Portraits and Paintings

It is quite clear now that, in the Langian textual system, all manifestations of vision and representation are bound up with questions of relativity and truth. Things may never be what they seem, but this tends to be elided in a desperate striving to pass belief off as knowledge in an attempt to maintain the ego as the center of a fixed network of concepts whose ideological nature is patent. One particularly potent force in this structure of disavowal is the portrait: it puts the subject back as an individual at the center of things. The dimension of resemblance, the fact that the person exists or existed converge to sweep aside even the possibility of any doubt as to the objectivity of the portrait. The question of the truth will not even arise, inasmuch as there is no reason to assume that such a question even exists. Even if one admits the existence of "stylistic flourishes" on the artist's part, there can never be any hesitation as to the interpretation. Indeed, the very idea of interpreting a portrait—What is it saying? What does it mean?—will seem absurd. That one can say that the portrait *is* such and such a person puts an end to the matter. The only possible discussion will be how lifelike it is.

In this system, of course, the very notion of subject positions can have no place. Likewise, the status of the artist is repressed: he or she will be talented or not, and if the portrait does not correspond to what people "know" of the person portrayed—significantly referred to as the subject of the painting—then this will be put down to incompetence or ignorance on the part of the artist. What is interesting about the portraits on display in Lang is that they must be seen as part of the overall textual system and therefore function as texts themselves. Leaving aside the very special case of the portrait in *The Woman in the Window* (see chapter 5), let us take a look at the portraits in *Scarlet Street, The Big Heat,* and *While the City Sleeps.*[11]

The portrait of the mother of gangster Mike Lagana in *The Big Heat* seems to function, at most, as a symbol of the son's Oedipus complex, but I would suggest that it is a very complex rhetorical gesture indeed. At one point in the film, the hero, policeman Dave Bannion, has one of the gangsters eliminated by spreading the rumor that it was he who betrayed Lagana. The film cuts to a shot of the portrait and a voice-off is heard telling how the gangster was killed. Why show us the portrait? What does it have to do with the killing of a gangster?

The portrait represents a woman, and women play a central and ambiguous role in the film: they are the signifiers of a discourse on the nature of Truth itself. Either they lie and are believed; or else they tell the truth and nobody believes them. Take the case of the wife of Duncan, the corrupt policeman whose suicide opens the film and sets off the investigation. Although she tells the truth by assuring the authorities that he killed himself, she lies inasmuch as she hides the reason for his suicide. The *énoncé* is the strict truth; it is her subject position within the *énonciation* that is a lie. Diametrically opposed is the case of the woman who frequents the gangsters. She tells Bannion that Duncan did not kill himself, which is quite untrue, yet she is telling the truth inasmuch as she knows why Duncan committed suicide.

Having Lagana stand under the portrait that therefore dominates him is a clear reference to his Oedipal hang-ups, made explicit in the film's dialogue, which, in turn, places the mother figure in a long and honorable tradition of powerful, enigmatic, scheming, and/or dangerous women, especially in *film noir.*[12] Lang's films of the 1940s and 1950s are very much part of this tradition, and the misogyny of all the films involved is clear, albeit varied. What is paramount is the woman as locus of a very special danger, never rendered explicit because totally unconscious: the castration complex. The fear women elicit is transformed into its psychic opposite: fascination, hence their presence via portraits. Thus Lagana's mother "contaminates" the other women in the film, who can never be the source of absolute Truth: there is always something about them that cannot be trusted. It is not surprising therefore that the gangster's moll who tips off Bannion should be killed: this fits in nicely with the cliché of "the tart with the heart of gold" and enables the film to smooth over a gap caused by such a contradiction in the genre's discourse on women.

The portrait in *While the City Sleeps* is of Amos Kyne, owner of a vast empire comprising press, radio, and television. He despises his son Walter, a weakling, and admires Ed Mobley, who defends the same values as Amos. The film is clear as to what these values are: power, selfishness, and the manipulation of others. Everyone in the film shares them in one way or another. After the death of his father, Walter summons into his office the men responsible for the running of the group's paper, *The New York Sentinel:* Griffith, Loving, and Kritzer. Walter Kyne is on the left of the screen, the three other men on the right. Kyne and Kritzer are placed so that each is presented as the mirror image of the other, an aspect that is reflected in their clothes: they are dressed identically, except that Kyne wears a bow tie and Kritzer a necktie. From this point of view Kritzer is the living heritage of Amos Kyne, whose portrait dominates the proceedings, and who is dressed like Kritzer. Since Kritzer is busy having an affair with Walter Kyne's wife, the general atmosphere is one of deceit and false appearances. Unfortunately, it is one of the rare moments when the notion goes beyond the theme to inform the very nature of vision and representation. The investigation is seen in moral terms and is far from the sort of signifying activity we can see at work in, say, *You Only Live Once* and *Beyond a Reasonable Doubt.*

Scarlet Street is somewhat different, for it concerns itself more with paintings as such rather than simply portraits. Lacan has shown the role of paintings in maintaining order within the psyche. He starts from Freud's observation that, if something created by desire takes on commercial value, it is because its effect is beneficial—profitable—to society. Admirers of paintings find it a relief to learn that people can earn a living by exploiting their desire, and that relief is overdetermined by the fact that the desire of the said admirers likewise finds relief: they renounce their own desire, and this raises up the soul, a most useful way of preventing disruptive forces from breaking free (Lacan 1973, 102).

One such disruptive force is scopophilia, sublimated by the look as pure admiration and fascination. The situation assuages what Lacan calls "l'appétit de l'oeil" (105), which, if voracious, he attaches to the evil eye, which creates the danger of disorder in the psyche. As I have pointed out, the look as *objet petit a* is that which has become separated from the subject, the (f)act of looking thus reminding the subject of that imaginary plenitude of childhood and the real lack—castration—at the center of existence. Fascination—and particularly admiration—are displaced forms of this reactivated desire. Inasmuch as desire is the desire of the Other, the disruptive potential of the look is sublimated, the viewing subjects finding satisfaction where they could have found unpleasure, thanks to the social value attached to works of art. Nor must another crucial component of the look be forgotten: the fact that portraits, in Lang as elsewhere, *always look back at us,* thus constituting us as objects of the look. Such is the special function of fascination: to defuse that "retaliatory" look that can trigger unpleasure, and to put renunciation in its place. Such renunciation is part of the structure of disavowal: we misrecognize our true position as voyeurs before the filmic text and the portrait, which is its stand-in, and displace scopophilia onto the socially acceptable activity of admiration for a work of art, a fetishistic activity that "contains" the lack in every sense. It is structured around the look as the return of the castration complex and at the same time masks the fact by rendering our look innocuous, even admirable, something to be cultivated. *Scarlet Street*'s discourse on art tends to underpin this ideology, and Cross's admission that he has never been able to master perspective suggests that some transcendental Truth can indeed be obtained.[13]

The nature of such a truth and of the search it triggers is the subject of chapter 3.

Belief, Knowledge, Truth: The Case of the Unwary Investigator   **3**

The look that the investigator poses on the object, animate or inanimate, of the quest, determines the way the spectator can grasp the object. However, the road to the Truth can be a hazardous one, riddled with holes, detours, and dead ends. Such a situation can be in keeping with the function of narrative analyzed in chapter 1 or, more interestingly, with the overall problem of representation, to what extent the audience's look is determined less by its identification with the protagonist—private eye, crime journalist, individual acting on his own account—than by the enunciative strategies deployed. These can serve to withhold information from the spectator to create enigmas, so that the suspense is created in turn by a slow unfolding of a truth that tries to pass itself off as being outside the discourse of the film and hence to repress the enunciation. It can also serve to place the spectator in a variety of shifting positions that endeavor to show the relative nature of knowledge and the profoundly problematic nature of vision. As Stephen Heath has put it, "truth is to be grasped not simply in the enounced, but equally in the enunciation, in the distances, gaps, contradictions of the two" (Heath 1977b, 63). The distance that separates the Langian textual system from most other Hollywood films can, I think, be most usefully judged by looking at a typical and highly effective example of *film noir* as enigma and investigation leading to Truth: *Mildred Pierce* (Michael Curtiz, 1945).

Mildred Pierce is structured around an enigma: Who killed Monty Bergano (Zachary Scott)? We see him being shot in the very first image of the film. He falls and, with his dying breath, whispers, "Mildred . . . ." In this way the enigma is introduced: is Mildred the murderer? The audience is encouraged to think so but cannot draw any conclusion. We then see a car driving away: a woman is behind the wheel, but it is impossible to see her clearly. The image is indispensable: the film cannot continue otherwise. In the next shot the camera cranes down and follows a woman who has emerged from the darkness, walking slowly. We then see that it is Joan Crawford, hence, Mildred Pierce. She is about to jump into the ocean when a policeman stops her.

The articulation of these few opening images is sufficient to plant firmly in the spectator's mind that there is every chance Mildred Pierce did kill Bergano: her name whispered by the murdered man, the car driven away at night by a woman, a woman walking alone, dazed and desperate. The enigma is impeccably put into place—and with it the spectator. Narrative and referential contiguity overdetermine each other, and the entire film plays brilliantly on its own ambiguity. By locking Wally (Jack Carson) in the house where Bergano has been shot, Mildred gives us the impression of wanting to pin the murder on him, and for a good reason: he has hurt her badly in some way, as we learn immediately when, on seeing her wandering about near his restaurant, he says, "You're not mad at me for this afternoon?" Another enigma, cleared up at the end: he has gained control of her chain of restaurants (the story is told in the form of a flashback). This he has managed to do only thanks to the complicity of Bergano. When she learns of it, Mildred rushes to a drawer, takes out a gun, and leaves her home. Everything indicates that she is indeed the murderer.

And she claims to be to the police, but for a precise reason: knowing it is Veda, her daughter, who has shot Bergano and feeling guilty at her treatment of the girl, she decides to take the blame. So the flashback, as has been pointed out, is duplicitous: we cannot possibly know that Mildred is innocent because information is withheld from us (Cook 1978). It is up to the detective in charge of the case to listen to Mildred, then to introduce new material that questions her story, and finally to force her to tell the truth.

The whole question of the status and representation of the enigmas is thus radically different from the Langian system, where it is not a matter of withholding information—even if that does play a role, as in the very special case of *Beyond a Reasonable Doubt* (see section 2, below)—but of constructing entire films on false evidence presented as such to the spectator, on the unreliable nature of eyewitnesses, and on the ways in which the spectators can be led into the same sort of snare as the investigator so that they are constantly in a position of doubt and hesitancy about the value to give to the image itself and hence about their way of reading it.

Such an issue is never at stake in *Mildred Pierce,* and for a very special reason. The enigma around which the whole film is structured is not a question of guilt concerning a murder but guilt on a far more redoubtable score: incest and the quest for origins. The fact is made fairly explicit when Mildred discovers her daughter kissing Bergano, her second husband and hence, legally, Veda's father. The script has already disavowed the theme: Bergano has ordered Veda to call him Monty, never father. If the film's ending is certainly "a reminder of what women must give up for the sake of the patriarchal order" (Cook 1978, 81), the enigma as displaced incestuous desire must also be stressed, for the element explains why the film is in no way concerned with the same problematics of vision and investigation as the various Lang under discussion here. The doubt and hesitation we experience when viewing Lang's films lead to an oscillation between different, often conflicting, interpretations, to a radical lack of knowledge that becomes knowledge of a more symbolic sort: not of what something "is" but of what our position is when we (fail to) understand. The central role of the mass media cannot but emphasize the dimension of the look and representation in the overall context of an investigation.

1. Newsreels

Although newsreel footage plays a central role in only one film, *Fury,* the importance it takes on in the film and the way the footage is shown as resembling a fictional film while at the same time differing from it are fundamental for grasping the thrust of the entire Langian textual system (Douchet 1981).

Firstly, a brief reminder of the circumstances. A crowd, out of control, convinced that Joe Wilson is the head of a gang of kidnappers, is determined to lynch him. Wilson has been put under lock and key by the town's sheriff until his story can be checked.[1] Journalists and newsreel photographers rush to the town in order to witness the hoped for confrontation between the crowd and the forces of law and order. The crowd storms the jail and sets fire to it. Everyone assumes that Joe has perished in the flames, and the ringleaders are charged with murder. The spectators know that Joe has escaped.

Thanks to newsreel footage used by the prosecution, those on trial are condemned to death. What the newsreel does not show is Joe's escape, and we are not shown it either: it is Joe who, at the same time as he tells his brothers, tells us what happened. We are thus given knowledge of a particular kind inasmuch as we can appreciate why everyone has jumped to the wrong conclusion. The conclusion, while understandable, nevertheless owes its existence to a "commonsense" philosophy, which states that seeing is believing and believing is knowing.

Such a philosophy is hardly esoteric, and one would be well advised never to underestimate the quite extraordinary ability on the part of those who swear by it (usually unconsciously) to fail to recognize the signification of the evidence they furnish themselves. Disavowal is the order of the day. Thus Lotte Eisner refers to an accusation leveled at Lang at the time: the story is not *vraisemblable* because newsreels were not admitted as testimony at the time: she adds that courts do accept them now (Eisner 1976, 162). The historical reminder is there to show us Lang's intuitive genius, how much in advance of his times he was. So far, so good, except for one little detail: twenty-two people in the film are condemned to death on the strength of newsreel footage *for a crime that never took place.* If one were to share Eisner's enthusiasm and to accept the *doxa* that film equals Truth, then one can only reflect with a shudder on the "fate" of those tried today on the "testimony" of newsreels.

Given such faith in the nature of the image, it is hardly surprising that the only people who remain sceptical about the newsreel are the two defense lawyers. The first insists that the prosecution must prove Joe was actually in the prison at the moment it was set on fire, while the second, faced with Katherine's claim that she saw Joe behind bars as the prison was burning, suggests to her that she may have been hallucinating because of emotional shock. The last point reduces the problematic to the behavioristic dimension of an individual error and sidesteps all question of the image. The remarks of the first lawyer are more interesting, although they boil down to the same ideology. What he is saying is that, were an eyewitness to swear to having seen Joe, then one could say Joe was in the prison and therefore that the accused are indeed guilty. The importance of *Fury*'s use of the newsreel lies in the way it sweeps aside such a line of argument. For the spectators know perfectly well that Joe was in the prison after it was set on fire: not only do they see him

Fury   The trial of the "murderers" and the "evidence," as reproduced on celluloid.

at the same time as Katherine does, but the crowd spot him too and throw stones and rotten fruit in his direction to drive him away from the prison bars and into the flames. If none of these elements is mentioned in court, it is because everyone refuses to talk so as not to implicate anyone else. If one person talked, the prosecution would win its case at once, which the film insists on. Yet we know that Joe has escaped.

At one point Joe says to his brothers, "They won't see me: I'll be hiding." For the entire country, therefore, Joe being invisible equals Joe is dead, just as Joe being visible in the prison equals Joe was in the prison when it was burned down. Since everyone knows Joe was locked up in the prison, what counts is his presence or absence *during the fire*. Every diegetic discourse sets up an opposition between presence and absence, which are seen as absolute. So, if the newsreel had managed to capture Joe's image during the fire, the accused would not stand a chance, and

Fury   The ringleader confronted by his "victim" offscreen after the projection of the newsreel footage.

the defense tries to exploit the lack of precisely such an image to show he may not have been in the prison. What is granted the image in all cases is its objectivity, its ability to capture some preexisting essence and present it unadorned to the world. Let us see how *Fury* proceeds with this way of seeing things.

As soon as the story gets around that something is happening in the town, people start flocking there, which leads a bus driver to say: "These newsreel men are on their toes. They must have found out about this before it happened." This observation is a remarkably subtle and effective way of pointing out that the media do not communicate information to the public concerning preexisting events but fabricate these events by the fact and manner of reporting them. The film is quite explicit about it. A brief sequence shows us a newsreel cameraman excitedly filming the riots and the burning prison. "What a shot this is! We'll sweep the country with this stuff." Pause. "The film's gone— reload!"

Of course, a segment of reality will be missing during the reloading of the camera, but the absence will not be visible in the film shown all over the country. Editing will have taken charge of that, editing that will fill in the gaps to fabricate a film that will, as a documentary, pass itself off as a faithful and objective account of a riot in which a number of people were responsible for the burning to death of an innocent man. *Fury* exploits the situation by having Joe spend a day at a cinema "watching myself burn to death," as he puts it. The spectators in that cinema and every cinema like it cannot but believe their eyes, given the status accorded to the image, which "speaks" for itself, surely as loaded an expression as one can find. As has been pointed out, all trace of any subject of the enunciation is masked behind the subject in the sense of logic: something is said (or shown), and it matters little who is responsible and under what circumstances (Descombes 1977, 73).

For the prosecution, all that counts is "the testimony of your eyesight." The district attorney is here victim of the *doxa* that assumes that testimony is a simple question of telling what one has heard or seen, of relating what one therefore knows. Yet testimony, by its very passage through language and dependence on memory, cannot but be a subject position, with all that implies. A testimony, as Lacan has pointed out, is not just a question of communicating a message, which ideology evacuates completely the unconscious (Lacan 1981, 49).

Since nobody will tell the truth—not even the sheriff—the court is transformed into a cinema, the lights are dimmed, and the show begins. We now see for the first time what images exist of that night. There is no doubt as to the identity of the citizens throwing burning torches or preventing firemen from putting out the fire. We, the subjects of the enunciation, relive that night *in the same way as the people in the courtroom,* for the simple reason that the cinema screen brought into the court fills exactly the cinema screen we are watching, that of *Fury* itself. In this way *Fury* is explicitly assimilated to the newsreel—and vice versa. The *doxa* pertaining to the image can now be applied to *Fury.* Because we know the newsreel does not tell the truth and the reasons for this, *Fury* succeeds in undermining the very nature of the images it itself presents as making up its own textual system.

The film now goes one step farther when the district attorney freezes certain frames in order to show the identity of the guilty citizens. After the freeze, the image "starts up" again. What follows will now be endowed with an extra dimension of truth, the frozen frame having shown beyond a reasonable doubt who was present that night and who did what. The moving image is what characterizes the cinema, the still image being of the realm of photography. A newsreel seeks to persuade spectators that what they are seeing is actually going on before their eyes, whereas the purpose of a photograph is to capture the past. Both past and present are now there before the stunned gaze of all those present, the moving images and the frozen frames thus overdetermining each other to present an even more "faithful" image of reality. As Roland Barthes has put it, the photograph says "This is how it was," and the introducfion of the past tense into the middle of a filmic discourse composed of moving images *in the present* eliminates any dimension, temporal and subjective, other than that of truth (Barthes 1964, 47).

Past and present overdetermine each other in order to disavow the fact, to disappear, absence rendered all the more simple by the presence of both kinds of image in court. If disavowal is possible for the spectators in the courtroom as it is for the spectator during that experience which is called "going to see a film," then it is not so for us, subjects of the enunciation. Both moving and frozen images are put in question for having been contextualized in an enunciative strategy that contains them both. The desired homogeneity and neutrality break down, for both what we have seen and how we have seen it are revealed to be partial. The fixed ego goes up in smoke (like the prison).

Newsreel footage plays a role—in the fullest sense of the expression—in two other films, *You Only Live Once* and *The Woman in the Window.* In the former, Eddie Taylor, found guilty of bank robbery and murder, is escorted from the court and through a hostile crowd. Near the police car that is to take him away there is a camera mounted on a tripod. As Eddie appears, it pans to follow him. Cut. The newsreel camera is now pointed directly into the lens of the camera of the enunciation. Eddie shouts at the crowd, "You'll never send me to the chair for a job I didn't do!" Cut. We see Eddie behind bars, looking into the camera of the enunciation.

As in *Fury,* people all over the country will go to the cinema and see a newsreel about a trial and people accused and found guilty of murder, which only the spectators of the two films know they did not commit. Because Eddie has been condemned without the law having the slightest doubt about the case, his shout will be interpreted as a threat, especially since he kills a priest on escaping and will be shot down by a policeman at the end. For the subjects of the enounced, the images communicated to them by the newsreel camera will bear the stamp of Truth: the future will fold back over the past and lend it meaning, just as the ending of a film of fiction will fold back over the preceding scenes and, through the meaning communicated, allow the spectator to disavow doubt and the various enunciative strategies deployed. In this way it will be said of Eddie that he was a born criminal and got what was coming to him. The discourse on justice and the discourse on the neutrality of newsreel images overdetermine each other to produce an ideology that is far from innocent: "there's no smoke without fire." The only problem is: Who lit the fire in the first place? The discourses in question, like the matter of testimony, serve to mask the place and status of the subject of the enunciation.

As in *Fury*, the newsreel footage in *You Only Live Once* builds an invisible bridge between two different moments of time, leading the spectators to believe they are faced with an eternal and ahistorical present, free from doubt and contradiction. As in *Fury*, again, the spectators of the enunciation cannot adopt this stance, and the fictional status of the newsreel—they know it does not reveal the truth—contaminates the status of *You Only Live Once* inasmuch as the visible camera and the invisible one through which we see gaze at each other: the former is not without the latter and, by functioning momentarily like the latter, stresses that we are not without the camera of the enunciation either. If the camera of the enounced is visible, it will not be so during the projection of the newsreel in cinemas, any more than the camera of the enunciation is visible during the projection of *You Only Live Once*—or any other film. Eddie's accusing look in the direction of the crowd is there to show us that we too would have accepted the verdict—a form of lie—had we not known the true situation. Knowledge is not absolute but depends on another kind of knowledge. Again, subject positions are not fixed but are an effect of the signifier.

The newsreel in *The Woman in the Window* seems, at first sight, to underpin the ideology subverted in the previous two films. We see Wanley reading a paper in which it is announced that the body of the murder victim has been found. There follows a shot containing a title stating that it was a boy scout who discovered the body, a shot that is then revealed as part of a newsreel being projected in a cinema. The frame of the screen of the enunciation corresponds exactly to the frame of the enounced, and each lends credence to the other, for we know the information communicated is the strict truth. Moreover, the newspaper is there further to overdetermine the message. Things are not that simple, however, for it is all a dream, and its only connection with reality is on the level of desire. The newsreel is as true—or as false—as the film itself and presents its images in the same way: as limpid and naturalistic, a form of representation that, in turn, stems from Wanley's desire, which is that of the spectator.[2]

2. Photographs

If *Fury,* Lang's first American film, gives pride of place to newsreel footage, *Beyond a Reasonable Doubt,* his last American film, does the same for photographs. Both films are centered on a trial and capital punishment, and the legal aspect has tended to be seen as the only subject matter of the two films. Such a reading has not harmed the reputation of *Fury,* for the antilynching message is certainly there, which means that the film can continue to be paraded as a serious social document. Displacing the center of interest as I have just done above will not prevent the film from being admired exclusively on these social grounds. Thus *Fury's* reputation remains intact, albeit for the wrong reasons.

The situation is quite different in the case of *Beyond a Reasonable Doubt.* It is not difficult to see why. The story consists of manufacturing proof against an innocent man in order to show that the Law can be wrong, that capital punishment is therefore to be abolished. Then the man in question turns out to be guilty and is sent to the chair. Clearly, this is not to be taken seriously: since the film is against capital punishment, an innocent man should have been executed.[3] The presupposition is that the film denounces the death penalty because one of the main characters, a crusading journalist, is opposed to its existence and goes to the extent of manufacturing false evidence to prove his point. Once again, the only thing that matters is the theme, not the way it is represented. This is quite striking in a film in which so much attention is paid to how the evidence is built up, down to the smallest details. This rigor and the extreme naturalism are, of course, what upsets critics who feel cheated, just as they were with *The Woman in the Window,* which operates in a similar fashion (see chapter 5).

Despite its naturalism, *Beyond a Reasonable Doubt* is really being accused of not being realistic, because, as Tzvetan Todorov has pointed out, the *vraisemblable* is seen in terms of the referent and not of the laws governing it (Todorov 1971, 93). Vincent Descombes has pointed out

Beyond a Reasonable Doubt   The editor's pipe, planting evidence, and filmic "proof."

Beyond a Reasonable Doubt   Multiplying the criteria of "objectivity" for   63
witnesses.

that verisimilitude is granted to what people say (or show, or believe) because the contrary is improbable, which sums up the situation of the Lang admirably (Descombes 1977, 102).

Beyond a Reasonable Doubt is a far-reaching film because it is an assault on the discourse of verisimilitude by showing what it means to take things for granted—they go without saying or, as here, without "showing"—not only in the context of the newspaper editor's crusade but also, far more crucially, on the level of critical judgments on the film—indeed, on what film "is." The editor believes firmly, like everyone in *Fury,* in the objective truth and reality of the image and uses his newspaper to purvey his notions on the subject. The editor's world, like that of the spectator staring fixedly at the screen, is a world "conceived outside of process and practice, empirical scene of the confirmed and central master-spectator, serenely "present" in tranquil rectilinearity" (Heath 1976a, 78). His death in an automobile accident and the loss of all the documents that can prove the hero, Tom Garrett, innocent can only cause suspense and anguish in the spectators as well as the man concerned, because they know nothing of the true situation. Why should the spectators be kept in ignorance here and not in *Fury?* I would suggest that the reason is that *Fury* created a link between two kinds of image—newsreel film, fictional film—in order to emphasize the fictional and partial status of both. *Beyond a Reasonable Doubt* turns on the interaction of two kinds of images: the moving images of the film and the photographs. The latter play a far more important role than the frozen frames in *Fury.* Another logic is needed to accentuate the enunciative strategies at work.

The editor trusts eyewitness testimony and distrusts circumstantial evidence: the perfect witness is the photograph because it cannot lie. In the film, however, it is the photographs that "lie" and the evidence brought against Garrett by the district-attorney that reveals the "truth." The textual system does not limit itself to turning the *doxa* upside down, however, for an essential piece of evidence used against Garrett is shown to us to be purely circumstantial. The police have found in the murder car a box of matches identical to those used by Garrett. It bears the mark of a burn, the kind a smoker would make when using the box to press down in his pipe the tobacco he has just lit. Since the killer smoked a pipe—according to an eyewitness who had seen the murder victim with a man shortly before her death—this explains everything. But the film shows us, without undue insistence, the editor using a box of matches in precisely the same way. It is also without undue insistence that the film never shows us Garrett smoking, which leaves the spectator with some active work to do. Garrett simply says he has never smoked a pipe, which the district attorney doubts. He does not believe in coincidences, which allows the film to introduce a detail that goes to the heart of the question of vision, truth, and representation. Another eyewitness has given a detailed description of the supposed murderer's hat and coat. Garrett is arrested because he has been seen dressed in an identical fashion. At the very moment when he orders Garrett's arrest, the district attorney is wearing a hat and coat that match the description perfectly. *Beyond a Reasonable Doubt* not only asks us to use our eyes but also questions the nature of decontextualized material.[4]

Two sequences will suffice to show what is at stake in the film. In the first, Garrett and the editor go to buy a coat identical to the one the murderer is said by an eyewitness to have been wearing. Garrett is reflected in two mirrors. The editor takes a photograph of him, and Garrett suggests that he take a second, in which the editor himself will be present, also reflected in a mirror. Garrett has his back turned to the mirror in order that his face be clearly visible. Both men are reflected in the mirror behind Garrett, with the editor also reflected in another mirror to the right.

The second sequence shows the two men at the spot where the murder victim has been found. Garrett throws his lighter into the undergrowth so that the police will find it (the investigation has hardly begun). Before doing so, however, he kneels beside the road, holding the lighter in one hand and, in the other, a copy of the editor's newspaper. The latter takes a photograph of the scene, taking care to make the name of the paper and, especially, the date visible. He then notes both date and spot on the back of the photograph.

No need to overemphasize the role of the mirrors: they grant an extra dimension of truth—completely imaginary—to the photographs by having the editor present in one of them. As in the case of the frozen images in *Fury,* the photographs here say to us, "This is how it was," thus repressing any embarrassing questions about subject positions, especially since the editor shows that it was he who took the photographs. The sequence reinforces the *doxa* in order to unmask it later. This is, I would argue, the great merit of the scene. The editor's lack of awareness of the truth about Garrett is less important than his lack of awareness concerning his own place in the fiction. If a proposition within an enounced is false, then there is an error or even deceit, whereas, from the point of view of the enunciation, it is the speaking subject who misrecognizes its true status (Descombes 1977, 74).

For the editor, to point a camera at someone and to ensure the presence of one's own image within what is recorded is one and the same thing: only the image counts. The spectator reacts in a like fashion in the two sequences under discussion. Either the subject of the enunciation (the editor) is present in the photograph, or the time and place of the enunciation are, with the presence of the paper adding an extra dimension of truth. The editor has taken the photographs, what they show is strictly accurate, verisimilitude is satisfied—and it's all a lie. Thus the reason is made explicit: it is the enunciative strategy deployed that is responsible.[5]

The editor is anxious to seize Garrett in a frame to advance his cause, and "frame" him he does. Every time a photograph is taken, the textual system intervenes to frame all the necessary elements for us. At no point do we see Garrett from the editor's point of view when the latter is recording the situation on film. There is no shot where we see Garrett through the viewfinder of the editor's camera. We observe what is going on without participating, which is crucial for placing us in relation to the enounced. Thus we can become the subjects of the enounced without ever assimilating this status to our real position as subjects of the enunciation. We are witnesses of an enunciative strategy within the enounced, which reinforces our position on the level of the enunciation: we are shown—in the fullest sense of the word—what it means to take a picture inasmuch as it is the entire film that is involved with the lie being unfolded.

What the camera of the enunciation shows as the editor takes his photographs of Garrett is the offscreen of each photograph. It is precisely this overall context that is hidden to anyone looking at the pictures afterward. The person who takes the photograph does not see the offscreen either, but he knows not only that it is there but also what it contains. Such knowledge is denied any subject viewing the pictures elsewhere, just as it is denied the spectator watching any film. As I have shown, the editor misrecognizes his position as subject of the enunciation because he takes the image-as-object for the truth it is meant to communicate. Hence a representation (a choice of framing) passes itself off as a presentation of a given event). If the spectators' imaginary inscribes them into the enounced, they will find themselves part of the offscreen, which will return them at once to their real position: able to note that an image is more than just what is seized by the lens and shown on a rectangular piece of paper. We are able to see how we have been led astray over Garrett, just as the editor has (and, faced with the "evidence," the district attorney). What is represented masks the very space enabling it to exist, which in turn bestows on the viewing subjects the feeling that they are not implied in that space, in at enunciative activity, but can function as a simple passer-by: neutral to the bitter end (Bergala 1976, 42).

And the end is bitter indeed, for Garrett, for the spectator—and for Lang, who, having put a final nail in the coffin of the neutrality of vision, sealed his own death warrant as far as Hollywood was concerned. Believing in the image-as-Truth can be as dangerous as unmasking it, as Garrett's "fate" reveals. It almost proves fatal too for Professor Jasper in *Cloak and Dagger*. He goes to Europe as a spy for the United States government in an attempt to find out what has become of certain famous scientists in a position to help the Nazis build the atom bomb. On his arrival in Switzerland, Jasper is photographed by a man whose clothes code him at once as a "typical" Swiss. As he is being photographed, Jasper hides his face. A most unwise gesture: since he is meant to be a traveling salesman, why try to hide his identity? Jasper's face is unknown, so there is no need to hide it. If he does, then it can only be because he has something to hide. The neutrality of the image breaks down at once. Jasper, knowing who he is and why he is in Switzerland, is coded unconsciously to do everything in his power to keep it a secret. He believes that a photograph goes beyond appearances to reveal some hidden truth, whereas it is his gesture that reveals, if not the truth, then that there is more to Jasper than meets the eye (literally). The gesture is the return of the repressed: Jasper as subject of the enunciation, the effect of the signifier, which is better appreciated by the photographer, a Nazi in disguise. By being taken for what he is not, he succeeds in leading Jasper to take the image for what it is not and to reveal that he is not what he seems to be. The discourse of the Other structures the entire sequence, both for the characters and for the spectators.

One of the most ironic uses of photographs in all Lang is to be found in that most bitter of films, *The Blue Gardenia*. The entire film is built around an unquestioning and sexist belief in stereotypes of women, which code a cynical and unscrupulous journalist in his attempts to sell copy. No trick is too base, no lie too gross, to draw the supposed murderess out of hiding: punishing a killer is far less important than journalistic sensationalism. Lang keeps his venom for the end, where the heroine, now officially recognized as innocent (another victim of a "frame"), emerges from the halls of justice in time to be photographed. One can imagine the caption "This woman is innocent," whereas the same photographers and journalists would have been happy earlier to publish her photograph with the caption "This woman is guilty" (compare *You Only Live Once,* section 3, below).

3. The Press and Television

The way police and journalists collaborate in *The Blue Gardenia* is taken up in *While the City Sleeps.* The key difference is that the person sought by the authorities is the murderer, although the behavior of the journalists is identical to that in *The Blue Gardenia:* the only thing that matters is one's career, with no holds barred. The problem is that the film remains on the level of the general theme and does not show any more interest in the problems of representation than do the characters. That Ed Mobley is seen having make-up applied before appearing on television and that the most dangerous woman character uses make-up and wears dark glasses can hardly be taken as serious criticism and certainly gets us nowhere. It is a great pity that Lang was unable to exploit the articulation of press and television, especially when one remembers what he did with the question of vision in *Fury* and *You Only Live Once* and what he was to do with it in his next film, *Beyond a Reasonable Doubt.*

Fury skillfully uses the press as a device to advance the story, while at the same time showing that such a device is never there just to communicate a preexisting event. The following two headlines are represented on the screen in two shots linked by a fade:

> Kidnappers caught; confess!
> G-men nab whole gang!
>
> Innocent man lynched;
> Burned alive by mob!

The first headline is as true as the second is false, but by presenting them in the same way and linked by a fade, the film suggests that they are identical and that one is not without the other. The second headline is revealed as false almost immediately when Joe suddenly turns up at his brothers', which gives the spectators no chance to forget the virtual coexistence of the two headlines—and it is just this "virtual" that is exploited by the textual system as resulting from an enunciative device. The first headline at once becomes problematic: it is not going to be dismissed as false, but its status—and especially the status of the people who composed it—can no longer be taken for granted. We have again the equating of discursive contiguity and referential contiguity in order to place the spectators in such a way that they can see the falsity of such equations.

This becomes clearer for the audience later in the film when we know the truth about Joe's escape. Following the showing in court of the newsreel, we are presented with three headlines:

> Identity of 22 proved
>
> Movies identify defendants
> in Wilson lynching trial
>
> 22 face death!
> Judge Hopkins clears courtroom

Lang does not use a fade here but passes from one headline to the next by a sort of "wipe," so that we have the impression of turning the pages of a newspaper. Using a specific cinematic code to represent what is specific to the press is a particularly cunning device on the film's part. Moreover, as the papers are quite simply reproducing what everyone assumes to be the truth thanks to the newsreel, the specificity of film and the specificity of journalism overdetermine each other. The spectators know the newsreel does not reveal the truth, which means that the press has fallen victim to the same snare and that the film reveals a discursive strategy as responsible for the snare.[6] Since the textual system has highlighted the unreliable status of the newsreel, then film, newsreel, and press are all enmeshed in a basic snare, a situation that is reinforced by the use of the term *movies* to designate the newsreel.

Fury never questions the truthfulness of what one reads in the papers without inscribing the theme into an overall context of representation, a tactic repeated in Lang's very next film, *You Only Live Once*. Lang cuts from a shot of Eddie Taylor being arrested for robbery and murder to a picture of a smiling Eddie, with the caption "Taylor freed." A track to the left reveals a picture of a serious-looking Eddie, with the caption

"Taylor jury deadlocked." Track back to reveal a picture of a sinister-looking Eddie, with the caption "Taylor guilty! Chair awaits killer." The final track is accompanied by a reframing of the scene: a journalist is inspecting the three front pages reproduced.

A further backtrack reveals, on the left and behind a desk, the editor, as well as the journalist responsible for the three front pages, now on the right of the screen. The latter asks, "Do you think the jury'll bring in a verdict before our deadline?" The editor replies, "It already is our deadline." The phone rings; the editor answers, listens, then turns and points. Track forward to a close-up of the third front page: Eddie has been found guilty.

Once again the information contained in these few shots moves the film forward rapidly and succinctly, according to the laws of narrative, a mastery of which was indispensable for anyone wanting to work in Hollywood. We are also treated to a very special vision of the press: the search for the truth is of less importance than a deadline, and that determining factor introduces an element of uncertainty that worries the journalist responsible for the three front pages. The articulation of the shots of Eddie and the accompanying captions presents a variant of the nature of the image. The verbal aspect of each front page is really redundant: how Eddie looks is sufficient to communicate the verdict. The caption is there in each case not to explain the photograph or even to communicate a message (although these factors do have a role to play), but to "prove" that what the photograph shows corresponds exactly to what it is being called upon to "say." The caption naturalizes the picture, rendering it transparent: it cannot possibly mean anything else, and its signification (its signified of connotation) becomes its meaning (its signified of denotation). Thus the need to intervene on the part of the press, not only in the fabrication of front pages that create events before they have happened but also in the "judicious" choice of photographs, is evacuated in favor of a message, as are the subject positions involved.

Taylor is innocent; it is normal that he should smile. Taylor is smiling; he can only be innocent. For the ideology of neutrality, these two statements are identical. Picture and caption refer back to each other and, as the man they represent exists in the real world, a supplement of truth is duly bestowed on both of them. Along with this "truth" goes the question of the nature of our knowledge. It is not until the third front page is presented to our gaze that we realize what is happening. Prior to that we have been placed by the film's *mise en scéne*—framing, cutting, camera movements—in such a way that we realize retrospectively just to what extent we have been victims of the journalists' own little *mise en scéne,* which hence functions as a metaphor for the work of the film. The meaning of the sequence—how we see—is therefore to be found in the enunciative strategies and not in some vague remark on the press.

The way the press in *You Only Live Once* represents people via stereotypes that pass themselves off as truth is central to *The Blue Gardenia,* but this time on the level of language first and foremost. A journalist writes of the murderess that she was dressed in black. A friend of the heroine's—who was wearing a black dress and assumes she is the suspect—is sceptical: "That kind of girl never wears black." The codes she is subject-ed to are quite clear: such a woman must be blond and beautiful, as "they all are." The next step is simple: since a waiter claims to have seen a blond with the future murder victim, a newspaper writes of "the blond murderess." The situation is made more complex for the spectator because the heroine is blond and was in the victim's company that evening. Were it not for certain information we dispose of, we realize that we could fall for the same line (like the lines written in the press). A neat—and negative—link is drawn between press and television when a colleague of the journalist says he has been watching too many TV serials, which makes explicit the theme of social coding inscribed into the very representational devices exploited by the film.

It is the partial nature of all these devices that the Langian textual system insists on, and nowhere is it so central to a film as in *Beyond a Reasonable Doubt.* Just as a jury is meant to represent society in general, so a paper is there to communicate facts: subjectivity can exist only in certain well-defined circumstances, such as a campaign to abolish capital punishment. "Bias," however, is believed to function only on the level of the enounced, the content of one's argument. However, as I have already pointed out, the film goes to great lengths to show how the evidence is manufactured.

It is essential that the various textual manifestations of the newspaper in the film should not function in the same way in order that we be able to situate each instance in a precise context. Thus the first headline we see gives us an objective and accurate piece of information: "Peters executed." As from the second use of a newspaper, however, the situation changes: the photograph of Garrett and Dolly (a friend of the murdered dancer) is there to lead the readers to believe their friendship is more than that. One reader who certainly reacts in this way is Garrett's fiancée, who refuses to believe his story that he is doing research for his book: the information communicated by the picture enjoys an even greater weight than those taken by the editor because it has appeared in a newspaper.[7] When Garrett questions another friend of the murder victim and mentions the color of her hair, the woman suspects him immediately, and she is not satisfied until Garrett says he read it in the press. Now it is just this special status of the press that brings about his downfall. At one point he uses the victim's former first name, a slip of the tongue his fiancée is quick to pick up. Garrett replies that he read it in a paper, but she knows that the name has never been mentioned and exposes him as the murderer.

Every time a character uses the argument "I read it in the papers," it is accepted as gospel. The spectator is no exception here. The film's most striking use of the ploy is to be found in the articulation of two remarks and two specific codes, a cut and a reframing. The district attorney finds a letter written by the editor and says, "Garrett has been telling the truth." The next shot treats us to Garrett's fatal slip of the tongue. His fiancée leaves the room, and we see an anguished Garrett, alone. Cut. Close-up of a headline: "Garrett is Innocent." The paper is being read by a friend of the fiancée, who now enters the room. The articulation of these shots maintains the referential illusion, but to the detriment of the ideology of representation it sustains. Not only is the district attorney wrong (having been right all along), but so is the headline. At the same time the editor's scheme is revealed for what it is and the entire film with it.

No Hollywood film has gone so far in undercutting the spectators' certainty about their position, and this is inextricably linked to a whole network of concepts of representation. A shot of the editor claiming that a paper is there to tell the facts—an extraordinary example of disavowal on the part of a man who is busy proving the opposite—is followed by a shot of the district attorney. The spatial coordinates are identical, which suggests that justice, like the mass media, is just another *mise en scène* that refuses to recognize its true status.

This blindness is shared by Garrett. I would suggest he is in the same position as the minister in Poe's "Purloined Letter" (Lacan 1978, 225–40). Just as the queen thought herself safe because of the king's obtuseness and just as the minister thinks himself safe because of the police's identical obtuseness, so Garrett thinks himself safe because of the obtuseness of the editor and the police. The former will furnish the "evidence" the latter need—and cannot find—enabling Garrett to exploit a literal-minded equation of sign and referent. But Garrett makes the mistake of assuming he is all-knowing simply because he is far more intelligent. He is unaware that, like everyone else, he is an effect of the signifier and that the Truth—the unconscious—can insist when one is least expecting it. It is ironic that Garrett should be revealed as a liar and a murderer at the very moment when the district attorney says he has been telling the truth, for it shows less that the police are stupid, than that Garrett has, precisely, *told the truth* to his fiancée and the spectators, in his slip of the tongue in which the subject (re)emerges through language. And it is through a person's name that he betrays himself by telling the truth, a name that is, literally, a different arrangement of letters from those constituting the name used up to this point in the film. As Lacan says, a letter is something that always reaches its destination (Lacan 1978, 240) and, in the case of *Beyond a Reasonable Doubt,* is it the letters of the alphabet that insist—and send Garrett to the electric chair.[8]

The concern here is with a particular manifestation of the articulation of Truth and the vraisemblable. For the purposes of the discussion, the film may be divided into two parts: part 1 goes up to the point at which Garrett makes his slip of the tongue by using the real name of the murdered woman; part 2 goes from the uttering of the name to the end. Part 1 presents us with a situation allowing us to formulate the following propositions:

1. The district attorney believes Garrett is guilty.

2. The spectators "know" he is innocent.

Both positions belong to the *vraisemblable.* Part 2 presents us with a situation allowing us to formulate the following propositions:

1. The district attorney believes Garrett is innocent.

2. The spectators know Garrett is guilty.

The district attorney's position still belongs to the realm of the *vraisemblable,* whereas ours is now one of knowledge based on the emergence of Truth, of a genuine subject position dictated by the signifier.

What leads us to this Truth? Quite simply that the elements of the enunciation employed by the editor so as to appear plausible— *vraisemblable*—while telling a lie, in fact turn out to tell the Truth. The purpose of the *film noir,* like the detective story, is to maintain a gap between Truth and verisimilitude. As Todorov points out—he is referring, precisely, to *Beyond a Reasonable Doubt*—when the two merge, then you have the end of the story and the death of the character (Todorov 1971, 98). Garrett has tried to be God, exerting an absolute control over life and death, an untenable position stemming from narcissism and the Imaginary. The Truth being *l'instance de la lettre* and a slip of the tongue an element of the enunciation, Garrett becomes a *mise en abyme* of the spectators' miscognition of their real place in and towards the textual system and, in the last instance, a destruction of that miscognition through the signifier, which places the subject of the enunciation. Thus, once again, "truth is to be grasped not simply in the enounced but equally in the enunciation, in the distances, gaps, contradictions of the two" (Heath 1977b, 63). We shall see Gruber in *Hangmen Also Die* filling the same function as Garrett and suffering the same "fate," death.

4. The Meaning of Truth

The Langian textual system is concerned first and foremost with the spec(tac)ular nature of the image and how we see it. As I have demonstrated, this theme is often inscribed into the diegesis via the search of an investigator who believes that knowledge is a question of clear vision but who fails to understand that such vision is a matter not just of seeing things as they are but of grasping one's place in a discourse as subject of desire, of the unconscious. One character who does understand and who pays the penalty in a way that is highly instructive for the spectator's place in the Langian textual system is Inspector Gruber in *Hangmen Also Die*.

Gruber's task is to find the assassin of Heydrich, whose identity is known both to the spectators and to Mascha Novotny: Dr. Svoboda. Svoboda has become a symbol for the Czech Resistance, which must ensure Miss Novotny's silence and complicity or else lose Svoboda to Gruber and the Nazis. To do so, the Resistance puts on for everyone's benefit a little show.

Svoboda goes to see Miss Novotny to persuade her not to denounce him, but he suspects, rightly, that the Nazis have installed a microphone in the apartment in order to be able to "spy" on its occupants. As soon as she lays eyes on Svoboda, she says, "You killed . . . ," then continues, "any feelings I ever had for you." Svoboda has managed to convince her of the urgency of the situation, for she was about to add "Heydrich." That the camera is present in the apartment on Svoboda's arrival but shifts to Gestapo headquarters as Miss Novotny speaks is crucial, for Gruber is listening in. We are therefore *with* Gruber, while at the same time understanding how Svoboda turns the situation to his own advantage. We are also at an advantage in relation to Gruber: we have a visual aid that enables us to appreciate the ruse, an enunciative device destined to lead certain subjects astray as to the significance of the verbal discourse they overhear. If the Gestapo concludes it is a simple love affair, Gruber is sceptical. He feels something is wrong and our knowledge that he is right to be suspicious puts us in a very special relation to him.

Everything shows that Svoboda is innocent: he has an alibi, a colleague who will say that he was in the operating room at the time of the assassination. We, however, know that he was replaced by another colleague, and in two shots Lang shows us the limits of an eyewitness. During a meeting of the Resistance, we see a man resembling Svoboda: it is the surgeon who took his place. At the end of the film, Gruber—who, as we shall see presently, has succeeded in finding out the truth—goes looking for Svoboda at the hospital. He runs into two masked surgeons and addresses his remarks to one of them, calling him Svoboda. The man takes off his surgeon's mask: it is the colleague. Now before this unmasking—a neat theatrical touch in a resolutely "theatrical" film—the spectator too is unaware who is who behind the masks.

How then does Gruber unmask the plot to hoodwink him? Svoboda realizes that Gruber does not believe their story, so he puts on another act for him: Gruber catches Svoboda and Miss Novotny "in the act," as it were, pretending to be making love. All the pertinent traits are summoned up to convince the inspector: she is half-naked, he has lipstick on his face. Present with Gruber is Miss Novotny's fiancé, who falls for the *mise en scène* and spends the night with Gruber in the company of prostitutes in order to forget his misery. The next morning the fiancé draws Gruber's attention to the presence of lipstick on his face. Gruber looks in the mirror—and understands everything.

> The passage through the mirror, through reflection, usually intensifying the impression of mirrored semblance, here functions as a reversal of appearances: one has to reach the real by way of the image: the denaturalisation of the visible, its designation as such, its self-representation and its reflex conceptualisation, means that the snares can be avoided, the simulacra rejected. . . . On the other hand, this business of the reflected look is precisely what captures our own look and inscribes it in the mirror, superimposing it

in the reflection on Gruber's look. The "placing in the abyss" also places us in the abyss by including our view . . . in the circulation of represented views. A pattern is established of which we, in our position as spectators, form part. Gruber sees himself seen—He sees himself—He sees himself see himself—We see him seen—We see him—We see him see himself—We see ourselves see him. And, one might venture to say, he sees us see him. (Comolli and Géré 1981, 141).

If Gruber grasps perfectly what is at stake, he forgets the lesson when faced with the two masked surgeons, as does the spectator. Such a slip is essential for our status as spectators capable of overlooking the obvious, all the more so because Gruber is our representative within the diegesis. "His investigation tells us nothing we do not already know. But by accompanying him, by following this sort of initiatory journey in his wake, we learn, as he does, the meaning of this truth that is finally unveiled and the price that is to be paid for it: death, his death. And our death a little bit, too, since Gruber has for a time been our most direct representative in the fiction. Like us, Gruber is a reader of fiction" (Comolli and Géré 1981, 135).

Let us now go back over these scenes in the light of the remarkable analyses of Comolli and Géré. A dual tension is at work at the heart of the film. We hesitate between admiration for Gruber, a highly intelligent man with whom we identify as someone who wants to find out the truth, and support for the Resistance, our ideological hero. At the same time we want the secret to be unveiled in order to reduce an intolerable suspense stemming from the nature of the intrigue and from our split identification. The sexual nature of this tension is well known: orgasm leads to peace, that is, death. Our libidinal investment in Gruber allows the continued functioning of the metonymy of desire: a resolution of doubt, hesitation, and conflict within the signifying chain, displaced onto Gruber, who, by becoming the locus of the death instinct, enables us to breathe easily again.

The lipstick sequence overdetermines our unconscious identification with Gruber in two ways: by his looking at himself in the mirror (he is us) and by the look of the fiancé watching him (we displace our identification onto the young man as spectator). This enables us to disavow our real status by believing ourselves outside the whole set-up: the sequence is an extraordinary *mise en abyme* of the structure of disavowal. Inasmuch as it is Gruber who dies, I would suggest that he fulfills, within this structure of disavowal, the same role as the death's head in the now famous Holbein painting *The Ambassadors,* all the more so because the film insists on his bald head, which he is always stroking when he thinks and which brings him closer to the smooth skull, the "néant" of death (Lacan 1973, 86).

Comolli and Géré have underlined (1981, 144) the significance of the murder of Gruber by Svoboda and his colleague: the shot–reverse shot structure of the sequence puts us alternately in the place of the two men and in the place of Gruber. We watch them advance on him from two different viewpoints condensing our own dual status as spectators. Writing on the shot–reverse shot Raymond Bellour has pointed out, "The effects of this cinematic code par excellence evoke the structure of the cinematic apparatus, and thereby of the primitive apparatus it imitates, namely the mirror wherein the subject structures himself through a mode of narcissistic identification of which aggressivity is an indelible component" (Bellour 1979, 118).

The aggressiveness that Gruber shows throughout his investigation and the aggressiveness of which he is a victim at the end are but two textual manifestations—in a reversed form—of our own aggressiveness as spectators within the structure outlined by Bellour. I have shown that scopophilia is an aggressive desire to see and that the links between vision and knowledge mean that the desire to know is also invested with an aggressive component. Such aggressiveness is now overdetermined by another form of aggressiveness: that which stems from our unpleasure at being brought face to face with our true status as spectators, an aggressiveness displaced by the structure of disavowal that inscribes it into the text as the death of the villain Gruber, our alter ego. The enunciation is eclipsed by the enounced. It is most fitting that the last shot of the sequence where he is killed should be of his bowler hat rolling onto the floor, for the hat is the Langian textual system's privileged signifier of the unspoken psychic content—death—of the link between desire and the look.[9]

The immense merit of the sequences discussed is to have insisted on the gap between belief and knowledge instead of simply reproducing narcissistic gratification, whatever the disavowal that intervenes. The split nature of the spectator's ego is also made clear in the sequence with the microphones planted in the Novotny apartment. What are they, these voices that the Gestapo hears and that lead them astray, that are taken as revealing the truth because those listening never dream of questioning the nature of the source? Surely they are voices-off, the same voices that normally bestow on the spectator a privileged but imaginary position as holder of truth and knowledge. If we do dispose of real knowledge this time, it is because of a variety of subject positions given us by the articulation of the scenes with the microphones, the lipstick, and the two masked surgeons.

It is necessary, however, that we remain ignorant of the full implications of this and can grasp it through the structure of disavowal, by proxy as it were, thanks to the death of Gruber, whose death is just one of many in Lang's films, where "the truth is what kills, what condemns to death" (Comolli and Géré 1981, 132). Nevertheless, the spectator strives to know, but the knowledge is imaginary because it is based on a refusal to recognize the signifier. Truth and Knowledge are seen in terms of knowing who and what one is dealing with, and not to know is to introduce doubt, which returns within the textual system through the dimension of identity.

4 Identity and Identification: Seeing Is Believing

When quoting Stephen Heath in the opening lines of chapter 2, I left to one side his articulation of the look and "the basic apparatus of identification exploited in narrative film" (Heath 1977a, 11), the camera. Christian Metz has also shown that the spectator identifies firstly with the camera and secondly with the characters (Metz 1977b), and Lacan has insisted on the need to see the ego as "a sum of identifications" (Lacan 1978). The two previous chapters have attempted to show how this ego position is constantly compromised and rendered untenable for the spectator in the light of the Langian textual system's construction of such problematic aspects as the offscreen, unreliable means of representation, not to mention unreliable agents of these means and ambiguous occupants of these absent spaces. The massive insistence on vision and the investigator condenses both kinds of audience identification, thus rendering problematic both the enunciative strategies and the diegetic world put into position by them. To this dimension of identification must be added that of the very identity of the films' characters, who, as I shall show, are never quite what they seem or claim to be, who always fail to live up to that fixed, alienating "sum of identifications" we expect, both from the cinema (on the basis, let it not be forgotten, of the star system) and from life in general.

Summing up the overall implications of the Langian textual system—and anticipating to a certain extent what is to follow—one could say that the spectators' desire to see leads them, through identification with a variety of characters, to investigate a problematic situation in order to understand and, hence, to fix themselves through knowledge. The situation, as Freud has shown, goes back to the early years of childhood.

> At about the same time as the sexual life of children reaches its first peak, between the ages of three and five, they also begin to show signs of the activity which may be ascribed to the drive for knowledge or research. This drive cannot be counted among the elementary instinctual components, nor can it be classed as exclusively belonging to sexuality. Its activity corresponds on the one hand to a sublimated manner of obtaining mastery, while on the other hand it makes use of the energy of scopophilia. Its relations to sexual life, however, are of particular importance, since we have learnt from psychoanalysis that the drive for knowledge in children is attracted unexpectedly early and intensively to sexual problems and is in fact possibly aroused by them (Freud, SE 7:194).

In other words, a desire to know stems from a desire to see, with all that such drives can signify for a subject wishing to constitute itself as a unified ego, sure of its origins and identity.[1]

In a study written in 1973 and delivered in the course of his 1974 seminar, Christian Metz analyzed, with that didactic striving for precision that makes his research invaluable, the importance of our perception of our environment and our need to be able to name what we see so as to avoid any hesitation (Metz 1977a).[2] He points out that what is vague in outline will tend to be given a clear, fixed form that can at once be identified by a word the meaning of which is, for the subject, eternal and nonproblematic. A frequent manifestation can be seen in the way guides to France's innumerable prehistoric caves invite visitors to "see" anything from cauliflowers to castles (with the Virgin Mary high on the list) in the variety of stalagtites and stalagmites offered to their gaze. It is not necessary for a drawing or a photograph or a filmic image to reproduce a given object or person in great detail for us to be able to recognize—and hence name—the thing or person presented: a few carefully chosen lines can be quite sufficient, as the art of the caricaturist amply testifies (Metz 1977b, 346, 356). A capacity to represent via a network of absences is part and parcel of perception as a cultural code and puts into place that quest for unity, homogeneity and identity that is constantly being stressed in these pages.

In a like fashion, we do not need to see the source of a noise to be able to identify the noise (Metz 1977b, 371). However, should that noise be menacing in some way or apparently in a relation of radical hetero-geneity vis-à-vis the diegetic world, anxiety can easily set in, and the need to identify the source takes precedence over other factors. This is clear in thrillers and horror films, as the magistral opening sequence of Lang's *Last Will of Dr. Mabuse* shows: what is making that regular, throbbing noise that we hear as we watch the character on the screen attempt to escape without being seen? I would suggest that the tenden-cy to need to attach a name to every object and to identify a source—which one usually does without the slightest effort, hence the fact that it seems unimportant—probably functions more insistently in the case of characters in a film than in the case of objects, sound, and so on, for obvious psychological reasons arising from narcissistic strategies of identification. It can, I think, help explain the particular problematic surrounding the character of Inspector Prentice in *The Ministry of Fear* (see section 2 below), a problematic that is intimately caught up in the work of genre and the status of the "anti-Nazi" films that are central to this chapter. I shall begin by discussing the first of them, *Man Hunt.*

1. Identity and Characters

Man Hunt is structured around a number of trajectories, both physical and metaphorical: the trajectory of Thorndike's bullet, which may have been destined for Hitler; the trajectory of the arrow with which he kills the Nazi Quive-Smith; Thorndike's own trajectory as character, at the end of the film doing finally what he denied he wanted to do at the outset. The last element is at the center of the thrust—or trajectory—of the unconscious of the text.

Thorndike has been arrested by the Germans and accused of at-tempting to assassinate Hitler under instructions from the British gov-ernment. Thorndike is an enthusiastic hunter and claims he had only one thought in mind when pointing his rifle at Hitler: to see if the weapon's telescopic sights were as effective as claimed. It is hardly surprising that the Gestapo is sceptical, and the story line turns on Thorndike's refusal, under torture, to sign a confession that would enable Nazi Germany to declare war on Britain.

A number of formal elements show that Thorndike is Quive-Smith's double, although, on the explicit level of the script, their moral values are opposed. Quive-Smith sees in Thorndike a kindred spirit: both of them are interested in hunting. For Thorndike, however, his adver-sary—or counterpart—understands nothing about hunting, which is a

sport, not a question of life and death.³ But a shot—reverse shot introduces a new dimension. Quive-Smith ushers Thorndike into his office:
the former is seen looking offscreen right, the latter offscreen left. The
mirror-image effect is clear and adds a little ideological spice to the
sequence analyzed above (chapter 2, section 3) where Quive-Smith
(onscreen) is interrogating Thorndike (offscreen). It enables the unconscious of the spectator, coded by that of the text, to represent this
sequence with the roles reversed, not flattering for the British "fair
play" that Thorndike claims to symbolize in his hunting. This element
returns in *Hangmen Also Die* (see below).

At the end of the film, Thorndike, who is being pursued across
England by the Nazis, unearths a hideout, a cave whose entrance he
blocks up with a flat, round stone that he keeps in place with the aid of a
stout branch. However, Quive-Smith tracks him down and traps him by
setting up an identical branch on the outside. The dialogue is as explicit
as one could ask for. "I admired your stone door so much that I imitated
it," says Quive-Smith, which takes up an earlier remark by Thorndike
that he would become invisible so as to avoid capture and, by so doing,
"imitate" the Gestapo (which acts "under cover"). The shots of Quive-
Smith on the outside and Thorndike on the inside repeat the shots in the
former's office and, in another way, the interrogation sequence, in which
Thorndike was present through his shadow. Outside, Quive-Smith is
standing; inside, Thorndike is sitting, exactly as before. That Thorndike
is always visible this time can only serve to underline his resemblance to
the other.

There is nothing coincidental about this, as other elements will show.
Furthermore, Quive-Smith urges Thorndike to sign the confession so as
to avoid "an unpleasant conclusion" for them both. On the conscious
level of the dialogue, the remark means that Quive-Smith does not want
Thorndike to die of starvation, but on the unconscious level other
factors are at work. It is the Nazi who suffers an "unpleasant conslu-
sion" when Thorndike kills him with his makeshift arrow, but the
conclusion is also unpleasant for Thorndike, who is now forced to
admit that hunting is a matter of life and death, not a sport for gen-
tlemen. As a result he draws the only possible conclusion: return to
Germany to hunt Hitler.

The theme of the double, which I shall analyze in detail in the
context of *The Woman in the Window,* makes its entrance here, and by
no means in an isolated fashion. When Thorndike escapes, he is pursued to England by one of Quive-Smith's henchmen, who uses Thorn-

dike's passport to enter the country. The Nazi therefore becomes literally Thorndike's double and pursues him all over London, hunting him in much the same fashion as Thorndike hunted Hitler, the only difference being in the motive. During one stage of the hunt, the Nazi is joined by a colleague: there are now two of them, a sort of doubling.[4] Thorndike hides in the doorway of a building (see *Hangmen Also Die,* below, for a repetition) as the two Nazis approach, one from the left, the other from the right. The two men therefore occupy the positions occupied in earlier sequences by Quive-Smith and Thorndike. As the men converge on him, Thorndike can be seen as the mirror image of each, the condensation of all the characters involved, the crossroads at which the various paths of the unconscious of the text converge.

On the wall at one point can be seen an advertisement for Black and White Scotch. During the interrogation in which he was tortured, Thorndike was wearing black, whereas Quive-Smith sported a white jacket (as if dressed for a reception, unless it can be seen as an ironic way of giving Thorndike a "sporting" chance).[5] According to the *doxa* it is an example of classic binary oppositions, which does not apply at all to *Man Hunt,* where appearances are misleading. Advocates of a certain sort of "realism"—read: surface naturalism—will protest that I am reading too much into an advertisement. Not a bit of it. The advertisement does not just happen to be there: someone (I do not know who; that is quite irrelevant) chose to put it there and Lang chose to film it. The reasons for the choice are evident everywhere in the film. It is a question of a text, each of whose elements signifies in relation to all the others, be they present or absent. In such a context, Thorndike's absence from the screen except as a shadow can be seen as the text's unconscious commentary on its own signifying activity. The presence of "Black and White" on the wall is a perfect example of a signifier whose unconscious effects inform the entire film, via other signifiers (the clothes mentioned above).

Quive-Smith returns constantly to the subject of the hunt to unmask Thorndike's hypocrisy and force him to admit the truth. Though he does end up admitting it, he claims he acted alone, not under instructions. The detail is important because it eliminates the "propaganda" aspect of the film in favor of an analysis of Thorndike's psychic trajectory. As Quive-Smith says to him: "I've anticipated the pleasure of meeting you for years. I should have recognized you on sight, a man whose brother was a guest in this house." The evocation of the relationship with Thorndike's brother, who clearly resembles him, also shows that

Quive-Smith expected Thorndike to be like his brother in other ways: to share his values, which, it is suggested, are Quive-Smith's.[6] The Nazi adds a remarkable observation: "You've been lying to yourself. You refuse to face your secret self. From the moment you crossed the frontier, you became an unconscious assassin." The frontier, of course, is the other scene, the unconscious, and when Thorndike, sporting a rifle again, returns to Germany to carry out his "destiny," he is only doing what he wanted to do all along.

Lacan has said that "our acts come and find us out" (Lacan 1978, 240), and an interesting comparison can be made here between Thorndike and Oedipus, whose every act is dictated by the oracle—which equals his unconscious as the locus of the discourse of the Other—and who, by setting out in life in ignorance of the fact, is other than what his biographical self realizes (245). Everything is there to hide the truth from him. As such, Thorndike becomes a metaphor for the spectator, whose going to the cinema does not mean what it is meant to mean socially.

The project of the film is to lead Thorndike to admit what he persists in denying; after all, we do see him put a real bullet in his rifle, after firing a blank, and giving a salute—a parting gesture?—to his "prey." The enunciation shows this is the case down to the smallest detail. At one point, Thorndike scrambles down a slope to escape his pursuers, a slope that recalls the shot where he is dumped over a cliff by the Nazis after being tortured so that it will be thought that he killed himself. The articulation of the two shots within the textual system—the one representing (literally) the other—shows that Thorndike will be pursued (like the hero of *M*) until he confesses openly.

It is not surprising in a film based on hunting that a rifle figures as a signifier for Thorndike's trajectory—and that of the film. A rifle appears behind the credits and is present in the first and last shots. The weapon has its double: the brooch Thorndike gives Jerry, the young prostitute who hides him in London and is killed by Quive-Smith and his henchmen. The dialogue during its purchase is eloquent. The jeweler suggests that Jerry pierce Thorndike's heart with it, and a laughing Thorndike refers to it as "a dangerous weapon." And it is just this brooch—in the form of a miniature arrow—that Thorndike uses to kill Quive-Smith by tying it to a stick. Killing Quive-Smith with the arrow is a realization of the metonymy of desire: the arrow for the absent rifle that was to have killed Hitler.

Thorndike offers the brooch to Jerry on the grounds that "every good soldier needs a crest for his cap." The fact that he does not evoke love is not innocent, for the observation is a condensation. The use of the expression *dangerous weapon* means that the textual system is putting into place its own conclusion and showing the inevitable nature of what will happen. Moreover, the jeweler is an elderly German, which worries Thorndike, not because of some simple hostility, but because he unconsciously sees himself face to face with his double, Quive-Smith, an experience that provokes anguish at the thought of the (inevitable) coming encounter, in which he will kill him. For killing one's double is tantamount to killing something in oneself, which Thorndike has done in London when he killed his Nazi double who was hunting him down.[7] That the brooch functions as a condensatory signifier is apparent from the arrow painted on the plane that transports Thorndike back to Germany at the end.[8] Just as the rifle figured behind the credits, so does the brooch figure behind a montage of images of war. The brooch having stood in for the rifle as an arrow, the rifle now returns when the brooch-as-arrow is represented as the crest-as-arrow on the plane, a striking condensation of metaphor and metonymy. In the shot where Thorndike jumps, both rifle and crest-as-brooch are present, a doubling and a condensation that sum up the entire project of the film: Thorndike's dual nature and the enunciative strategies deployed by the film to show it.

The reader will have noticed that I earlier put the word *destiny* within quotation marks. The first reason is simple: the word is used in the dialogue by an offscreen narrator who informs us that Thorndike is returning to Germany to "accomplish his destiny." The fetish word is present, but it has nothing to do with its official meaning. If the "destiny" is Thorndike's, then it becomes apparent through the text's enunciative devices, starting with the use of the rifle behind the credits. Let us rather see it as the destiny of the enunciation itself, whose trajectory has included the constitution of the double to serve as metaphor for the real nature of the spectator's subject position and to highlight the question of how we grasp character through procedures of identification. Lang's next film, *Hangmen Also Die,* has much in common on all scores.

Hangmen Also Die presents the struggle of the Czech people against the Nazi invader. If there can be no doubt as to the need for that struggle, doubt does creep in as to the methods used by the Resistance, especially in the elimination of a double agent. This doubt takes the form of a textual hesitation as to drawing a line between seemingly opposing forces.

From the moment Svoboda appears, we know that something has happened: he is running and looks anxious. Suddenly he hides in the entrance of a building to avoid a group of German soldiers obviously looking for someone. The spatial coordinates are crucial for what follows.

Svoboda hides behind the right half of a double door, the left half of which is open; he is thus in darkness, and we can see the movements of the soldiers through the other half. As they move down the street, the camera tracks slowly so as to maintain constant the spatial relation between the two halves of the door and the characters associated with each of them. The opposition open/closed and the opposition light/dark return repeatedly throughout the film.

Svoboda is forced to seek shelter at the Novotnys', for the hideout prepared for him by the Resistance is no longer accessible. He rings and Miss Novotny, thinking it is her fiancé, opens at once. The right half of the door is closed, and the young woman is framed in the open left half of the doorway, looking offscreen right. Although he is absent from the screen at the moment the door is opened, Svoboda occupies, in the context of an imaginary shot–reverse shot overdetermined by memory, the same position as the one he occupied when hiding behind the door from the German soldiers. Moreover, Miss Novotny occupies the same space as that filled by the soldiers in the earlier shot. Svoboda's "place" within the textual system is thus reinforced, while Mascha Novotny is assimilated to Germans.

The Gestapo does not trust her and places her under close surveillance. When she leaves her apartment at one point, we can see a detective standing in front of a door on the other side of the street. As she walks out into the street, the left half of the door of the apartment block is open, the right half closed and in darkness. The shot is an exact repetition of the one that showed Sbovoda hiding, and, once again, Miss Novotny occupies the same position as the German soldiers. The detective occupies the same position as Svoboda, with one difference: he is not hidden in the darkness. The difference is less important than the similarities set up, especially since Miss Novotny is the center of the scene. Moreover, it must not be forgotten that both she and Svoboda are playing a game of hide-and-seek with the Gestapo, which means that they can never be what they seem, willingly or not. Finally, the detective must be in a position where he can observe all comings and goings, and his being visible to suspects (the enounced) is less important than his being visible to the spectator (the enunciation). There is nothing *invraisemblable* about this, for he does nothing to draw attention to himself and Miss Novotny suspects nothing.

At the end of the film—the lipstick sequence analyzed in chapter 3, section 4—Gruber knocks out the fiancé, ties him up, and leaves to confront Svoboda. The fiancé is discovered by Mascha Novotny's younger brother, and the two of them set off in pursuit of Gruber. At one point they are forced to hide from patrolling troops behind the closed right half of a double door, the soldiers being framed within the open left half, a repetition of the earlier shot of Svoboda hiding.

That the fiancé and the brother should be assimilated to Svoboda is normal: the latter has assassinated Heydrich, the former wants to confound Gruber. There is therefore a classical opposition Resistance/Gestapo. But that Svoboda at one point should be assimilated spatially to a Nazi detective and Miss Novotny to German troops is less obvious. I would suggest that, although she comes within an inch of denouncing Svoboda because of the danger involved for her family,[9] the real reason for these comparisons lies elsewhere.

If the Resistance is opposed to the Gestapo, one would expect the opposition to be clear-cut on all levels. On the contrary: it becomes more and more ambiguous as the film progresses. The Gestapo has recourse to threats, violence, executions, and subterfuges to confound the Czech people, but on the last score the Resistance is more cunning.

The business with the microphones and the lipstick shows the ruses employed. At one point the Germans get collaborators to read speeches inviting the population to denounce the assassin. The speeches are passed off as the personal opinions of the speakers but in fact have been written by the Gestapo. They are broadcast over the radio, and the Czech people hears voices, just as the Gestapo did when listening in to the conversation between Svoboda and Mascha Novotny. The Resistance succeeds finally in confounding the enemy by fabricating, with the aid of testimony—including that of eyewitnesses—false evidence intended to destroy the alibi of the double agent Czaka and "prove" it was he who killed Heydrich. The Gestapo officers fall for the ideology of the *vraisemblable:* they consider that, because it is improbable that so many people should lie, then Czaka must be guilty, and they kill him. Despite having recourse to all kinds of deceit, the Gestapo cannot believe that others can do so, and thus it falls into its own snare: one is what one says, and what one says is and can only be the truth as from the moment one is not believed to be lying. The Gestapo underestimates the intelligence of its enemies and cannot conceive of them functioning

in the same way as itself.[10] From this point of view they can be compared to Garrett in *Beyond a Reasonable Doubt* and, via Inspector
Gruber, pay the ultimate penalty, death (see chapter 3, sections 2, 4).

The final sections of the film involving the framing of Czaka are
rather disquieting, and we need to ask ourselves why. Certainly Czaka is
not innocent: he has been responsible for the deaths of many members
of the Resistance. On the other hand, he is not guilty of the crime he is
accused of, and having someone executed for a crime he did not commit
is difficult to shrug off; *Fury* is built around this question. The disquiet
surely also stems from the textual system's persistently comparing the
Resistance to the Gestapo. The comparison is followed through to its
logical conclusion. A shot toward the end shows us Debic, the head of
the Resistance, who has been killed. It is as though he is lying in state, his
head to the right of the screen. After the murder of Heydrich we see *him*
lying in state, his head to the left of the screen. Each man becomes the
mirror image of the other.

I referred in chapter 1 to the function of stained-glass windows at the
opening of the film and the scene in which Czaka is snot down. The
image returns again in the shot where the fiancé and the brother hide
from the soldiers behind the door. The upper part of the door resembles
an opaque stained-glass window, which sets up yet another comparison.
Moreover, as Svoboda has his double as an alibi, it is not surprising that
this doubling process should occur elsewhere: the signifier follows its
own logic, that of the unconscious. It is not a case of saying "the
Resistance equals the Gestapo," but of insisting that any text built
around a system of games, lies, deceit, and subterfuge in the domain of
vision and representation cannot be expected to produce anything
clear-cut, hardly the term one would spontaneously apply to the
Langian textual system.

Further investigation is required, especially in the light of an observation by Comolli and Géré concerning the need for solidarity against
Nazism, and the tactics involved. "Since Nazism had taken particular
care over moulding its own presentation, it had to be taken over and
repostulated in a counter-presentation which would brand the Nazi
mise en scène as just that, a *mise en scène:* manipulation of appearance,
bogus show, machination" (Comolli and Géré 1981, 128). As I have
shown—and everything in the study of Comolli and Géré points in the
same direction—the Resistance behaves in a like fashion. The fact that,
in death, Heydrich and Debic are mirror images of each other not only
reinforces this but can be seen as a condensation of the split status of the

spectator analyzed in chapter 3, section 4. As I have indicated, the whole Langian system works massively against any simple and simplistic "black and white" opposition, and it is this system that, given the function of the signifier, cannot but take precedence over such a vague signified as "international solidarity." There are, however, two other factors at work that overdetermine this state of affairs and serve further to destroy the "message" one expects.

One of these is genre and intertextuality. Inspector Gruber is much closer to the "positive hero" than he is to, say, the Gestapo man who tortures the unfortunate Mrs. Dvorak; he is surely the Hollywood equivalent of Inspector Lohmann, who appears in *M* and *The Last Will of Dr. Mabuse*. I have mentioned in the opening chapter in my remarks on genre the intimate relationship between *Hangmen Also Die* and the gangster film, on the level of both dialogue and representation. Surely it is a perfect example of one discourse—the gangster film—taking over another discourse—the anti-Nazi film—via tactics of repetition and memory destined to satisfy audience demands for the same? Let us not forget how the Resistance *takes over* Czaka's discourse and how the Gestapo *takes over* the discourse of the collaborators for their own ends. It is impossible to approach Gruber outside an interaction of Hollywood as system and Lang's cinema as system, hence my remarks on the need to rethink *auteur* theory by placing it—and oneself as critic or spectator—*elsewhere*.[11]

The second factor is, precisely, the presence of this "elsewhere": the return of the repressed from the other scene. With brilliant insight, Comolli and Géré have pointed out how, at the beginning of the film, Svoboda removes his worker's cap and puts on a bourgeois homburg. One disguise for another, certainly, but much more crucially a displacement of the accent from the popular Resistance to Resistance by an elite (Comolli and Géré 131). That the cab driver commits suicide means that the proletariat is essentially eliminated, leaving the middle-class intellectuals to do the thinking. The cab driver is literally made to become part of "another scene," is literally "dis-placed": he jumps through a window and falls to his death, or, if one likes: becomes part of an offscreen that is kept firmly "in its place," that is, offscreen. Now there is nothing imaginary about the existence of the proletariat, but only bourgeois values can be represented onscreen and, when one remembers History (which has the unfortunate tendency to return when least expected), then one remembers that large sections of the Western ruling class were only too happy to make a pact with Nazism against the proletariat. It seems to me that *Hangmen Also Die* is both saying this *and* disavowing it: saying it via its enunciative strategies, which make clear links between the Nazis and the bourgeois-led Resistance; disavowing it by eliminating the proletariat in favor of the bourgeoisie and trying to overcome this disavowal with calls of "No surrender!" The highly unconvincing nature of the ending—simple propaganda—stems from an endless series of ideological and discursive contradictions.

These contradictions lead spectators to question the significance of what they see, a significance that depends on the means of representation used. Hesitation is set up through the assimilation of elements ideologically supposed to be in total opposition. Another form of hesitation occurs when there is doubt about the very identity of the characters. Such doubt can occur within the enounced where one character is deceived about others *(Rancho Notorious, The Blue Gardenia);* and within the enunciation where the spectator is deceived *(Cloak and Dagger, The Ministry of Fear).*

2. Aspects of False Identity

Rancho Notorious tells the story of Vern Haskell's search for the men who raped and murdered his wife, stealing from her the jewels he had given her. His quest becomes obsessive to the point of his being unable to distinguish between guilt and innocence: everyone is guilty. His obsession leads him to read the signs on the basis of an absence: ignorant of the context, he imposes on everyone and everything an identity in keeping with his fantasies. The spectator is caught up in his pathological system.

Significantly, what Haskell is looking for, knowing that his wife scratched one of her aggressors, is a face. A sequence shows with exemplary clarity what is involved for both the hero and the spectator. At one point, Haskell says he is looking for a face, a remark that is is followed by a series of close-ups of faces, all of them unknown to us. Any man, literally, could be the one he is hunting down. Because we have seen none of these faces, we are able to grasp the extent to which the search is based on chance and appearances. Nor do we know if the faces are those of men he has seen or not, or even if they were present at the same time and in the same place. The close-ups are cut off from all diegetic coordinates, from everything except the obsession of the main character, thus becoming a metaphor for his subject position based on ignorance and, by extension, ours.

There is no offscreen enabling us to constitute an imaginary space, and even when there is one, the film can lead us astray. At one point the bandits think someone is pointing a rifle at them. There is indeed a rifle, but nobody is holding it: it has been tied in position in order to fool the bandits—and the spectators. The offscreen is absolute: someone must be there to suture space as a unity. On the level of the enounced, there must be someone outside the window; on the level of the enunciation, there must be someone beyond the screen, and "beyond" becomes an imaginary offscreen on the level of the enounced.

Either certain elements are not shown, so as to stress the relativity of vision; or else the elements *are* shown, so as to highlight the relativity of representation. Haskell reacts at once when he spots the scar on the face of Wilson, an outlaw with a reputation as a ladies' man. He stares at his face constantly throughout a meal at the outlaws' hideout, where he has been accepted as being on the run. The sequence takes up that of the montage of faces, except that Haskell now has one face to concentrate on. The theme is repeated later when Haskell notices that Altar Keane, the woman leader of the outlaws, is wearing one of his wife's jewels, given to her by her outlaw lover, Frenchy Fairmount. Haskell stares at the jewel, and the stare is followed by a close-up of the jewel. Then his look shifts offscreen. Cut to Frenchy smiling. We do not see whom he is smiling at, and this aspect of the shot could be a pure fantasy on Haskell's part. His look now shifts elsewhere: to Wilson, who is also smiling, which would tend to reinforce the idea that it is Haskell who is representing them this way, for we do not see whom Wilson is smiling at either. So both Fairmount and Wilson are potential rapists and murderers in Haskell's eyes (literally). There follows a montage sequence of all the outlaws present, as with the faces. Then a final close-up of Haskell. The meaning is clear: they could all be guilty, or innocent. For Haskell, that is what is at stake: all or nothing. His attitude leads him to cause the deaths of all those present. Once again the search for absolute knowledge can terminate only in death.

Haskell looks but sees nothing, which is summed up by the remark "He looks right through a man." It is the real murderer who makes the remark, an irony the spectator can appreciate: Haskell suspects an innocent man, whereas the guilty man he looks at without seeing is present. On top of that, the famous scar leads him astray: it is less a question of mistaking X for Y than of basing an identification on an incoherent way of seeing that stems from a belief in absolutes cut off from context. When she catches Haskell staring at her, Altar Keane says, "You're always using your eyes," which prompts him to reply, "That way you see things you never expected to see." Again, the irony is obvious to the spectator because Haskell never sees the truth, but the remark should also be taken literally as far as the place of the spectator is concerned.

A flashback shows us an episode in the life of Altar Keane at a time when she was a singer in a saloon. She is fired without being paid and decides to get her money by other means. One of the games that the saloon uses to amuse its customers and part them from their money is a big wheel that turns and, on stopping, designates a number. But it does not stop of its own accord: the employee responsible presses down on a disguised floorboard to arrest its course, thus enabling him to choose the winner—or prevent anyone from winning. Altar Keane knows the trick, but the man operating the wheel is unaware she has been fired: when she gambles, he stops the wheel so that she wins. Only the privileged look of the camera allows the spectators to occupy a position of knowledge that separates them radically from the spectators of the enounced. It is right after this episode that Fairmount makes the observation, "The greatest skill consists in not showing." He is talking of his prowess with a six-gun, but he has intervened to protect Altar when the employee realizes the game she has been playing. Now Fairmount also cheats so that she will win again, so his remark becomes a metaphor for what the film is busily showing by revealing how it can be hidden: the function of the enunciation and our position as spectators with regard to it. Hiding elements from the characters accentuates the relativity of vision, while hiding elements from both characters and spectators assimilates the latter to the former for enough time to make them aware of how they have been duped. All identification in such contexts must be partial for a shift in position toward a different kind of knowledge to be possible within the spectator.

The question is approached with force in *The Blue Gardenia,* in which the dimension of ambiguous appearances is manifest from the outset. The Don Juan who is to be killed is seen on the phone to a woman he wants to avoid. He informs her he is busy, which he is: making a sketch of the heroine, whom he has seen and lusts after. The sketch now becomes, in the very next shot, the heroine "in the flesh."

What is seemingly a classical example of narrative suture is in fact something quite different, for the dress the heroine is wearing in the sketch is also the dress she is wearing when we see her, which stresses that both shots are images and products of the activity of the textual system.

The dubious nature of appearances and stereotypes is manifest everywhere. Both police and press are convinced they have only to find a woman wearing a particular dress to discover the murderess. And the heroine was, indeed, wearing such a dress the night of the murder, when she accompanied the future victim to the restaurant. Just before the sequence in question, however, we are treated to a brief scene that undermines any simplistic ideology of cause and effect. Harry Prebble, the Don Juan, makes a phone call from the restaurant where he is awaiting his guest. As he talks, a young woman wearing a dress identical to the one the heroine will be wearing later that evening comes in and sits down. The point is simply and effectively made. Moreover, when Prebble calls the heroine's apartment, it is her friend he wants to talk to, and the heroine pretends she *is* the friend, which leads to her being invited out in her friend's place, an expression that is hardly innocent, given that people are taken for other people and often resemble one another closely. This is the case of the heroine and her friend, who has already pretended to be a third woman. And the heroine looks like the actual murderess, the only difference being in their ages. In such a context, the presence of the young woman in the background is an invitation to the spectators to use their eyes, which we usually fail to do, given that only the foreground is of importance.

Such an abusive assimilation of A to B returns in a sequence that takes place in the post office where the heroine works as a switchboard operator. It was a favorite haunt of Prebble's, and the police investigation starts here. Various women are being interrogated, and their employer asks at one point, "Who's next?" A policeman points to a name on a list we are not shown. Cut to a general shot of the operators: we recognize only the heroine and therefore assume it is her turn. Not a bit of it: the police want to talk to the woman sitting beside her. The presence of the heroine provides spectators with a fixed center, enabling them to position themselves in relation to the diegetic world and the narrative. Such has been the situation in classical cinema since World War I through the star system, which means that several generations of filmgoers and an entire economic set-up are behind the way we

read this shot by homing in on the heroine, not to mention the func-
tion(ing) of the ego, that indispensable adjunct to capitalism's ideology
of the individual.

In *The Blue Gardenia* identity is problematic not only on the level of
the enounced—the police and the press are always wrong—but also on
the level of the enunciation. Although we know at any given moment
who the heroine is, the way she is assimilated to other women through
face, hair, and clothes shows us how easy it is to make a mistake. For it is
always a question of images and representation. Within the diegetic
world certain women are expected to behave in a certain way and dress
in a certain way, which is never natural but based on systems of representation that the film's textual system exploits to emphasize for the
spectators that they are faced with images too. The sketch is revelatory
here, and not only in the way discussed above. For nobody except the
spectators knows that Prebble had shown any interest in the heroine.
There was therefore no way she could figure on a list of suspects, but
our tendency to consume images passively and to forget or treat as
insignificant what is not insisted on means that this essential information is not retained. We assume she is suspected because she becomes
the center of the shot, so the codes function nevertheless.

Whenever a film has recourse to an explanation that has functioned
as an "insignificant" detail, critics start caterwauling. "The final explanation, based completely on chance, blames the deed on a character
who had hardly even existed in the film beforehand" (Jensen 1969,
182). Jensen is forced to say "hardly," which reveals the truth: the
character *has* figured in the film, but not centrally. Once again the old
problem arises: everything is insignificant unless stressed, whereas we
know that the presence of *any* element, however obscure, means something. Freud has taught us at least that, as I shall show in detail in
chapter 5. The conclusion to be drawn, then, from Jensen's remark is
that everyone and everything must be neatly pigeonholed and given a
precise identity. The violence of many attacks on Lang shows that
doubt, hesitation, and ambiguity are not to be tolerated in the hallowed
realm of vision and representation. If the camera cannot be trusted,
where does that leave us? Where indeed! *Cloak and Dagger* and *The
Ministry of Fear* will provide some answers.

In the first sequence of *Cloak and Dagger,* where we are informed of
the activities of the Resistance in Europe and Nazi retaliation, characters function as part of a sign system devoid of psychology and individual identity. A French railroad worker goes into a bar and knocks on

a door. The barman gives a sign—so to speak—and the man enters. Immediately two men in the bar stand up; clearly they are Nazis following the worker (the credits have already informed us we are watching a spy film). We now see the worker knocking twice on another door (since he knocked once the first time, we realize that this is a sign too). In the room he enters is a colleague busy extracting a radio from under a pile of logs: one thing hides another, is a sign of something else. Suddenly the Nazis burst in and gun down the two men. Cut to the headquarters of the U.S. Secret Service, where we see a map of Europe covered with pins. Two of them are removed, sign of the death of the two Resistance workers.

The codes at work in this sequence are easy to decode and function to inform the spectator of the way to decode the rest of the film, in which nobody is what he or she seems. This was already obvious in the analysis I offered (see chapter 3, section 2) of Jasper being photographed, where the accent was on clothes and role playing. It is repeated on several occasions. A man sits down in the box at the opera where Jasper is already installed, but he is there to give him information. Given the circumstances, however, the man must not be taken for what he is, so he has been careful to put on evening wear so as to pass unnoticed. Later, Jasper is approached by a man who has taken him for an American because of his clothes. The man talks of "our cause," but a woman Jasper meets soon after warns him of "our Gestapo friend." She is immediately revealed to Jasper as a Nazi agent by the man at the opera, and we can see how her bluff succeeded: by having an American accent, she lent the aura of truth to what she said, which means that she was able to hide her real subject position.

Jasper turns the tables on her by inviting her out and offering her flowers, which he does to compromise her in the eyes of the Nazis. He achieves this by forging her signature, the ultimate sign in our society of a fixed individual identity. Then he shows her a letter that he claims has been written to him by a pro-Nazi and that accuses her of receiving American funds. The audience understands at once that this is a further ruse, for it has come to recognize that, in this film, everything that is normally taken for granted must hide something else. The woman is less astute and reveals her real feelings.

Given the nature of disavowal, nobody can fail to fall for such tactics at one time or another, and the film shows that both we and Jasper are no exceptions. Jasper is sent to Italy by submarine, and, when it surfaces, somebody signals from the beach. The person's identity is hidden: all we can see is a vague outline wearing trousers and a hat. We are just as astonished as Jasper when the person takes off the hat and is revealed as a young woman. It has less to do with the clothes—an element, although socially coded, that is naturalized as being part of the enounced only—than with the conventions of the genre that form an enunciative strategy. That women can be spies, granted—as long as they occupy the place of the Nazi agent already unmasked. These conventions are played on in a far more complex manner in *The Ministry of Fear.*

The doubt and hesitancy that function so strongly stem from our far more intense identification with Stephen Neale than with Jasper and from the possibility that Neale is unbalanced. The opening sequence serves that narrative function. It is not until near the end that we learn that Neale is perfectly sane and why he was incarcerated in an asylum: for helping his incurably ill wife to commit suicide. Nothing, however, is allowed to interfere with the impeccable creation of doubt, suspicion, fear, and paranoia that reign supreme until the very end and are at their most intense in the scenes involving Inspector Prentice.

That Neale is robbed by a blind man (who is not blind) of a cake he won at a garden party (a cake meant for someone else) and that he is framed for a murder that turned out to be a fake (the "victim" being none other than the man who should have won the cake) show that he is being hunted. Everyone and everything become suspect in his eyes— and ours. Before the séance, Neale had hired the services of a private detective. After the "murder," Neale rushes off to find him, only to discover that the man's office has been ransacked. His own room having suffered the same fate, we, like Neale, tend to see a link. When Neale arrives at the building in which the detective's office is located, we see a man appear opposite, then disappear. At one point, Neale looks out of the office window: the man is there, obviously spying. The disappearance of the private detective can only help to persuade us, with Neale, that this mysterious man is responsible in some way, an interpretation supported by the codes of the genre.

The question then is: Which genre? The thriller or the anti-Nazi film? I have already pointed out the extent to which the two are interdependent in Lang, and the presence of the mysterious man outside the building recalls the Gestapo agent posted opposite the Novotnys' apartment building in *Hangmen Also Die.* There is also the dimension of the general story line, which gives the impression of watching a modern Sherlock Holmes tale rather than a film on Nazism.

Neale comes to suspect a certain Dr. Forrester of being at the head of a spy ring and of taking advantage of his position (a delightfully poly-semic word) at the Home Office to hand secret documents over to the enemy. In order to get access to Forrester's apartment, Neale persuades a librarian to allow him to deliver a package containing books ordered by Forrester. The package turns out to be a bomb—which makes the librarian a spy too—and Neale recovers consciousness after the explo-sion to find himself in a strange room with, sitting near the bed with his back to him, the mysterious bowler-hatted man. Neale accuses the man of being a Nazi, and he replies that Neale should never have been let out of the asylum. He introduces himself: Inspector Prentice. They are at Scotland Yard.

It is Prentice's general appearance, as much as the narrative codes, that encourages us to take him for another Nazi: after all, the film is full of them. His bowler hat and dark suit make him an ideal partner in crime for Forrester and the man at the garden party, who are dressed in an identical fashion, just like their predecessors in *Man Hunt*—and *The Ministry of Fear* is also a manhunt. The man who should have won the cake works at a tailor's, which nicely puts the spectator's unconscious on the sartorial track.[12] It is this, I would suggest, that is at the origin of a misreading of the film by Lotte Eisner.

At the end of the film, Neale and Clara, a young Austrian refugee whose brother has been revealed to be a Nazi too, are pursued by the spies and take refuge on the roof of a building. Neale and the Nazis exchange gunfire, and it is clear that the latter are gaining the upper hand. Suddenly they turn around and start shooting in the opposite direction, down the stairs leading onto the roof. More gunfire, and the spies are hit. A light comes on, and a man with a revolver emerges onto the roof, slowly, to the accompaniment of sinister music. Eisner de-scribes the scene as follows: "The police arrive just as Dr. Forrester emerges menacingly" (Eisner 1976, 246). But it is Inspector Prentice who "emerges menacingly."

Let us now see the sequence in its context. Neale has gone to the apartment of Carla and her brother Willi, who now reveals himself to be a Nazi spy using his humanitarian organization as a front. Neale and he fight, and Carla shoots her brother down as he tries to escape. But the couple cannot leave the building because the spies are on the staircase, hence their flight up to the roof. Forrester arrives, wearing a homburg and a long grey coat. His henchman Mr. Newby—whom we have already seen at the séance—is wearing a black suit and a homburg. They are accompanied by two gunmen whom we have not seen until now.

The camera is placed beside Neale and Clara on the roof so that we see things from their point of view. Neale shoots Newby, whom we recognize from his clothes, and Forrester turns off the lights on the staircase. After various exchanges of gunfire, the lights suddenly come back on again, and we see Forrester standing near the top of the stairs by the open door leading onto the roof. More shots, and Forrester collapses: we recognize him because of his height. Nobody is in sight for the moment, then sinister music is heard and a man slowly emerges. The bowler hat and the dark suit tell us that it is Inspector Prentice.

That vision is curtailed and clothes in particular enable us to identify characters certainly make the sequence anything but clear-cut. But other factors intervene. One of the gunmen is shot down just before Forrester, so, were it the latter who emerged "menacingly," then it must have been he who shot the gunman, which makes no sense. From a diegetical point of view, to see Forrester emerge onto the roof is quite illogical. From the point of view of the enunciation, however, the meaning is clear. That the camera should stay with Neale and Clara is a question not just of heightening the suspense but also of preventing us from witnessing the arrival of the police at the building and their climbing the stairs to rescue the hero and heroine. We are kept in a position of uncertainty as to what is going on beyond our vision.

We have always seen Prentice in the same way: as someone menacing and unknown. In theory, once we learn that he is a policeman, the threat should be dissipated, which goes on the assumption that we can forget everything that has gone before. The unconscious forgets nothing, however; it does not forget the links forged by the text's enunciative strategies between Prentice and the Nazis, which means that Prentice can function henceforth only as a signifier devoid of any precise identity as an individual. That he can be put in the place of another character—and not just any character, but a Nazi—after the revelation of his "true" identity shows the extent to which he is part of an enunciative strategy that is ongoing and therefore carries with it all those elements, past and absent, that it had earlier placed within the fiction. When Prentice-as-individual emerges onto the roof, Prentice-as-signifier brings with him all the unconscious memories connected with the look.

In Eisner's case this continued after the film was over. Since she knew Lang's films well and was in the midst of writing a book on them, I would suggest that the unconscious memories in her case are massively overdetermined by the well-dressed Nazis in *Man Hunt* and, in particular, by the bowler-hatted Gruber of *Hangmen Also Die,* whose bowler hat plays such a prominent role in the film that it comes to stand in metonymically for him when he is killed. Prentice-as-signifier can be seen as a textual manifestation of the metonymy of desire on the spectator's (Eisner's) part: bringing back at a crucial point an element existing elsewhere in the text (*The Ministry of Fear* and the Langian text in general) in an attempt to form a whole that makes sense, an attempt that points up the ego's miscognition of its real status and its failure to recognize itself as an effect of the signifier.

Analyses of three individual films, *The Woman in the Window, House by the River,* and *Secret Beyond the Door,* will allow the drawing together of the strands of the previous chapters in order to see how the spectator fits into this signifying intertextual chain.

The Woman   5
in the Window:
Home Sweet Home

Richard Wanley is a psychology professor at an American University. Following a lecture entitled "Psychological Aspects of Homicide," he sees his wife and two young children off at the station. He spends the evening at his club with two intimate friends, a doctor and the district attorney. The three men talk about growing old and desiring women much younger than themselves. Left alone, Wanley orders a drink and asks the waiter to wake him at 10:30 P.M., which he does. Outside the club, Wanley stops to admire the portrait of a young woman whose beauty had been responsible for the discussion on growing old. Suddenly the subject of the portrait appears and invites Wanley up to her apartment for a drink. After some hesitation he accepts, and they broach a bottle of champagne while chatting. Their discussion is interrupted by the arrival of the woman's lover, who, insanely jealous, slaps her, then turns on the protesting Wanley, who kills him in the ensuing struggle. Together they get rid of the body, but there has been a witness, the victim's bodyguard, who starts to blackmail them. They try to kill him too, but he is too smart to fall for their amateurish tricks. Cornered, Wanley commits suicide in his apartment at the very moment when the police shoot down the bodyguard, convinced he is the murderer. As Wanley dies, he is suddenly shaken by a hand. It is the waiter come to inform him of the time. It has all been a dream.

    "It was only a dream!" That is how the film presents its own ending, and, of course, it has been taken at its face value. Lang was accused of choosing a conformist ending (Méraud 1956, 16), an opinion that Jensen echoes. "This ending is a cheat used to rescue the director, who had painted himself in a corner. Killing off the hero was a far from common practice in the Forties. . . . Neither could the movie code let an actual killer go free and live happily ever after, so the only solution was for the film to pretend that nothing at all had happened" (Jensen 1969, 156). Jensen then adds that "the killing was completely in self-defence, and Wanley was only guilty of being present at all" (157). Precisely. A dream is a realization of desire, which explains why Wanley went to the apartment of the woman in the portrait in the first place. This aspect of the film is now seen as perfectly acceptable by critics, but Parker Tyler seems to have been the only person to have understood until recently. "In making the professor's crime occur *in his dream* its psychological reality, its mental precipitation . . . is established. . . . Since the murder takes place as the direct consequence of an indiscreet sex adventure, the dreamer is dominated by both fear and desire" (Tyler 1947, 167–68). Far from confusing the issue, the revelation that it was a dream lends the film its coherence and explains its power. Let us look at this more closely.

In the course of Wanley's lecture, the name of Freud appears on the blackboard. An important change in the point of view intervenes as Wanley talks of varying degrees of guilt: a forward tracking shot reframes him in relation to the blackboard, thus making Freud's name visible. If critics of a naturalistic bent were a little more sensitive to such modifications—usually shrugged off as "insignificant"—they might just have noticed that something was happening. They might even have taken the trouble to read what was on the board under the very name of Freud:

Divisional Constitutions of Mental Life

1. unconscious, preconscious, conscious

2. id, ego, superego

Such critics demand, through the ideological presuppositions of their discourse—"this film lacks realism"—an accumulation of details so that they can say the film reflects reality. This means, of course, that if a sequence in a film is set on a farm, it must show cows grazing in a field, since anyone who walks about a farm cannot help but see cows grazing in a field. It is a question yet again of the age-old confusion between

The Woman in the Window   Wanley returns to see the woman in the window after
disposing of the corpse.

discourse and referent, between the articulation of contiguous elements
by a given choice of angles, framing, cutting, and so forth and the
chance contiguity of such elements in real life. It is in no way surprising
therefore that critics should fail to notice such a change as intervenes
here: overlooking the obvious is part and parcel of the human psyche
and, in such a case, to notice the camera movement would be to recognize explicitly that what is happening is crucial to the filmic discourse
and hence to our apprehension of it.

Wanley makes a distinction between two kinds of murder: murder in
self-defence and "murder for profit." As he pronounces these last
words, the image fades, and we find him at the station saying goodbye
for the weekend to his wife and children. The wife is presented as both
fussy and well-meaning, treating her husband like a child who will have

The Woman in the Window   The second woman asks Wanley for a light as he admires the portrait after waking from his dream.

the greatest difficulty in surviving without her. The word *profit* must be taken as a signifier and interpreted rather as "taking advantage of a situation to put one's plans (that is, desires) into operation." My interpretation is perfectly justified by the film itself without looking elsewhere: Wanley gets what he wants by going to the woman's apartment, and money plays no role for him. Moreover, we can say that Wanley's distinction is false in another crucial fashion: he is certainly forced to defend himself against the lover, but his presence there stems from motives that cannot be admitted except in the context of a dream.

Killing the lover belongs to the dimension of the id, whereas the appearance of the bodyguard provides a warning: certain social codes are not to be transgressed, and punishment awaits anyone who transgresses them (the dimension of the superego). That the lover and the bodyguard work in the club, as we see at the end of the film, confirms Freud's theories in two ways: the dream incorporates elements from the previous day; and the discussion between Wanley and his two friends shows at work an oscillation between the id and the superego that is worked out in the dream. The club thus becomes the locus of hesitation: convention or adventure, the interior (the club, the home) and the exterior (the street and the woman's apartment, which functions psychically as an exterior).

Before entering his club, Wanley admires the portrait, which obviously fascinates him, as it does his friends. The district attorney calls her their "dream girl," which shows that the dimension of the dream is not just thought up in desperation at the last moment to save the situation. In the eyes of his friends, Wanley is enjoying his "first night as a bachelor," hardly an innocent statement. They express amazement that he is not in some night club, and he admits that he would not mind bringing a dancer to perform in the club, which elicits cries of feigned disapprobation. Wanley now admits that encroaching old age makes him regret that he cannot behave in such a fashion, to which the district attorney replies: "We've no business playing with any adventure we can avoid. In the D.A.'s office we see what happens to middle-aged men who try to act like colts."

Wanley's drinking more than usual could cause the spectator to attribute to liquour his spirit of adventure, but a remark by the district attorney stresses the dimension of desire: "Trouble starts from little things, from some forgotten, natural tendency." The terminology is imprecise, but it does at least introduce the concept of repression: alcohol may reduce the ego's defenses, but it cannot be the cause of what follows. When Wanley asks him friends mockingly, "Is it safe to leave me alone in this rebellious state of mind?" his conscious tone reveals what he cannot say: he wants to show he is still a man by having an affair with the woman in the portrait. That Wanley and his wife are past middle-age and are ignored by their two young children indicates a late marriage where the sexual dimension has ceased to play a role, however fond of each other they may be.

On arriving at the young woman's apartment, Wanley admires a statue representing a naked woman without a head, which shows that his desire is not simply for the woman in the portrait but for Woman as something forbidden. The lack of a head inscribes into the text the problem of vision and the dimension of castration via the *corps morcelé*. Here is the junction of the unconscious of Wanley, the unconscious of the text, and the unconscious of the spectator within an element of the diegesis functioning as a condensatory signifier. The lack of head means that the statue, unlike the portrait, cannot return the professor's gaze, so his scopophilia remains in a state of noncontradiction and exists as pure fascination. The dimension of fascination is insisted on massively to begin with, since the woman in the portrait and the portrait itself are approached fetishistically by Wanley and the spectator. Being looked at poses no problem because the dimension of castration is displaced and disavowed. It is only later that anxiety creeps in inexorably as the professor feels trapped, unable to escape a desire that controls him. The anxiety is, of course, the manifestation of the original repressed, castration, and the real significance of the look, repressed in favor of fascination, will also hasten the return of the repressed.

The statue functions as a signifier that triggers new signifying systems. Let us examine the sequence where the bodyguard visits the woman in Wanley's absence to blackmail her. A shot frames them as follows: the woman and the bodyguard are standing near the mantel bearing the statue. The woman is standing to the right of the statue, the bodyguard to her right. They are in front of a large mirror and framed in such a way that only the upper parts of their bodies are reflected. The next shot reframes them as follows: the woman and the statue, plus the bodyguard seen only as a reflection in the mirror. He is beside the statue, and the woman is no longer placed between the two. Through spatial contiguity, a literal displacement, the bodyguard is thus assimilated to Wanley, whom we have already seen in the same position in relation to the woman and the statue. The bodyguard thus becomes Wanley's "mirror," his *double.*

The textual system has now introduced the theme of the double via its enunciative strategies. Not only are there reflections in a mirror and the prolongation of the problematic introduced by the portrait and the look, but in addition, different characters are assimilated to one another, underlining that the concept of the unified ego is a snare, which is now starting to close on Wanley (and, hence, on us). The bodyguard now plays his second textual role: as he takes his leave of the woman, he raises ironically the hat that the *mise en scéne* has so insisted on throughout the scene. I think the moment has come to look in detail at that ultimate sartorial signifier, the hat.

The hat in question is a straw hat, and the way the bodyguard wears it—rakishly, on the back of his head—is obviously meant, by the film's conscious discourse, to create a "natural" link between character and dress. So far, so good, especially since the murdered lover wears an identical hat and is portrayed in a similarly negative fashion. So far, so good—but that is as far as it goes, for the district attorney also wears a straw hat, as does a man who crosses the path of Wanley and the woman in a corridor where they have met to plan the murder of the bodyguard. And when Wanley goes to pick up his hat from the cloakroom of his club, a whole line of such hats is on display. The appearance of the same actor in the double role of the cloakroom attendant and the murdered lover indicates, as I have shown, that the unconscious incorporates elements from the previous day's events for use in dreams. But it does not explain the district attorney's hat, for he is quite a different character from the lover and the bodyguard. He is, however, a similar character to Wanley, which is precisely the point. He too could have had a similar dream, given the conversation in the club. His warnings exist as much for himself as for Wanley: as guardian of the Law (both legal and patriarchal), he cannot afford such extramarital activities.[1] The resemblance between Wanley and the district attorney is a way of condensing the various interpretations, of showing that the processes of the unconscious are common to all of us—including in particular *us,* the spectators—in the light of the enunciative strategies used to implicate us in a diegetic world that turns out to be the manifestation of desire.

Referring to the "pictographic script" of the dream work and its "characters," Freud points out that "if we attempted to read these characters according to their pictorial value instead of their symbolic relations, we should clearly be led into error" (SE 4:277). Samuel Weber (1982, 28) has chosen to translate the original German *Zeichenbeziehung* as "*semiotic* relations" (*Zeichen,* "signs"), which means, clearly, that a hat in the textual system is in no way a simple hat but an element whose meaning depends on its articulation with all the other elements, present and absent. In other words, a *signifier.*

The straw hats in *The Woman in the Window* function as signifiers in the fullest Lacanian sense: they structure the spectator's unconscious whose reading of the text is an effect of their place in it, a place that determines the spectator's. This is the same process that I have already examined, especially in *You Only Live Once* (chapter 2, section 1) and *The Ministry of Fear* (chapter 4, section 2). What is at stake here, I would suggest, is the functioning of the entire Langian textual system. Johnny, the vicious pimp of *Scarlet Street,* wears an identical straw hat. Tom Conley has drawn attention to this detail, but in order to suggest that a straw hat in New York in 1945 is an anachronism ("old hat"?) and that such a garment "resurrects a time of the silent film and the early days of the Depression" (Conley 1983, 1099). Perhaps, but the major reference of both films is *Hollywood as an intertextual space*. The hat is therefore part of a cinematic convention, and it is interesting to note that the Jack Carson character in *Mildred Pierce* (also made in 1945) sports one too—and there is nothing old-fashioned about him. One could certainly put the hats in this film and *Scarlet Street* under the heading "flamboyant corruption, Hollywood style," but that says little about the hats in the various Lang under discussion. One must look elsewhere.

Both the bodyguard and the pimp are played by Dan Duryea, who had already worked for Lang: he is the bowler-hatted Nazi tailor Mr. Cost in *The Ministry of Fear*. It must also be remembered that the main roles in *The Woman in the Window* and *Scarlet Street* are played by Edward G. Robinson and Joan Bennett (who also played a hapless prostitute in *Man Hunt* and would play an "enigmatic" female in *Secret Beyond the Door*). Nor must one forget that such intertextuality goes far beyond Lang's films to embrace the kind of role that character actors such as Duryea were associated with and the very special ideological status of the *femme fatale* that I discussed above (chapter 2, section 4) in the context of portraits (and, after all, Joan Bennett is a portrait "come to life" in *The Woman of the Window* and a woman turned into a portrait in *Scarlet Street*). I would suggest that we must see hats as a metaphor for the entire cinematic machine, the Imaginary Signifier analyzed by Christian Metz, and its dialectical relationship to spectatorial desire: the constant reappearance of hats is a *mise en abyme* of going to the cinema as a form of *repetition compulsion*.

Before drawing any conclusions, let us examine other textual manifestations of the functioning of the unconscious. I am thinking especially of the condensatory role played by the incident in which Wanley is forced to use scissors to open a bottle of champagne. It is just these scissors that are used to kill the enraged lover. As he struggles with him, Wanley indicates to the woman that he needs her help (the lover is stronger than he and is slowly strangling him). She obliges with the scissors, and Wanley stabs the man to death. A weapon was necessary, but not just any weapon. The logic of the text demanded that the weapon be already present. Thus the bottle of champagne that Wanley could not open was indispensable, not for the *énoncé* but for the *énonciation*. The diegesis flows backward: a weapon being necessary and the scissors fitting the bill, they had to be handy so as not to call attention to the narrative strategies being deployed. This in turn is simplified by the fact that nothing could be more "natural" in the circumstances than a bottle of champagne. The scissors have therefore a double function: introducing the concept of the double while at the same time masking the fact that it is the narrative logic, or enunciation, that imposes the double, not the story line, or enounced.[2] Thus the spectators are enabled fo forget the true status of Wanley as subject of desire within the diegesis and, through the strategies of identification, to repress their own identical status as subject of the enunciation positioned by desire. The text now seems to be totally transparent, which, as I shall show presently, is crucial for another logic that is at work.

In the case of the scissors, the dual role is hidden because the demands of the diegesis hide the narrative strategy deployed. Elsewhere, however, this is not the case, as we have seen in the way the bodyguard "doubles" Wanley. The bathroom mirror in the woman's apartment, for example, is flanked by twin fluorescent lights, in Wanley's home by twin lamps. There is nothing more normal than this sort of decor, but such "normality" is of a very special kind, and decor in a real bathroom has nothing to do with decor in a text. I have referred to the scissors: Wanley cuts himself with them, just as he will cut himself later on a barbed-wire fence when disposing of the body. Again, perfectly natural, but the first time was not necessary diegetically, only as part of the unconscious logic of the text that imposes doubles everywhere.[3] I have also referred to the champagne bottle: it is in fact a second bottle that is responsible for Wanley cutting his hand. Again, this second bottle is really unnecessary: Wanley is already somewhat drunk and, anyway, they have little chance to broach it, for the lover suddenly makes his entrance. However, there are two bottles of champagne, and they figure prominently in a scene where Wanley kneels to examine the body. The woman is standing reflected in a mirror, while a small mirror near the floor allows for Wanley to be reflected too. The second mirror is, in fact, in such an unusual position—you would have to kneel or bend *double* to see yourself in it—that it clearly is there solely to enable the text to double Wanley by his reflection.

I have summed up Wanley's predicament as a snare that closes on him to the point that his desire controls him completely. He is in no way master of his words and actions, which is made clear by a whole series of parapraxes that serve to indicate just to what extent the unconscious takes precedence over the conscious. Thus he refers to the disappearance of the lover as a murder though the district attorney has made no such supposition and heads for the scene of the crime without being told. When this is revealed to Wanley, he is shocked, less, I would suggest, because he is afraid of being discovered than because he is suddenly brought face to face with his unconscious as something that controls him.[4] The feeling of being trapped goes back to *M,* and Colin McArthur has quoted the murderer's words: "I am always forced to move along streets, and someone is always behind me. It is I, I am myself behind me, and yet I cannot escape" (McArthur 1972, 71).

It is no coincidence that there is a remarkable representation of this in *The Woman in the Window* where there is, through framing and context (it is night) the repetition of automobiles drawing up outside the woman's apartment. It is a perfect example of the way the Langian textual system exploits genre (the role of the combination of night, streets, automobiles, and suspense) within a vaster and more complex problematic, that of the double. Each man—the lover, Wanley—is to a certain extent "behind" the person who preceded him inasmuch as he comes along later, a sense in which the hero of *M* is taken literally. This also concretizes in the very body of the text the idea at one and the same time of a repetition compulsion and a split personality, each man resembling the other (it is dark, they are both burly and wearing hats—and I have already stressed the link between Wanley and the bodyguard on the one hand, the lover and the bodyguard on the other) and showing that the imaginary identifications that make up the ego of each of us (we "recognize" the scenes in question) place us in a position of radical heterogeneity. Just what is at stake will, I think, be clear from Freud's study "The Uncanny" (SE 17).

The original German title of the work is "Das Unheimliche," and Freud gives a detailed semantic analysis of the linguistic paradigm "*heimlich/unheimlich.* The former term means not only "intimate, pleasant, cosy" (such as feeling at home within one's four walls), but also "concealed, kept from sight, . . . withheld from others" (Freud, SE 17:222, 223). The latter semantic field also corresponds exactly to one of the meanings of *unheimlich,* so *heimlich* comes to have the same value as *unheimlich,* which leads Freud to note that "*heimlich* is a word the meaning of which develops in the direction of ambivalence" (226). Referring to the research of Schelling, he makes the following point: "Everything is *unheimlich* that ought to have remained secret and hidden but has come to light" (225).

Freud then analyzes in detail certain aspects of the work of E. T. A. Hoffmann, in particular "the phenomenon of the 'double.'" "The subject identifies himself with someone else, so that he is in doubt as to which his self is, or substitutes the extraneous self for his own. In other words, there is a doubling, dividing and interchanging of the self. And finally there is the constant recurrence of the same thing—the repetition of the same features or character-traits or vicissitudes, of the same crimes" (234). Although it would be premature to draw any hard and fast conclusions, one cannot fail to notice the way in which these remarks apply to those aspects of the textual system already elucidated: clearly Freud had viewed *The Woman in the Window.* Freud's conclusions on repetition coincide perfectly with what we have seen concerning the snare that precipitates Wanley into a situation beyond his control. "It is only this factor of involuntary repetition which surrounds what would otherwise be innocent enough with an uncanny atmosphere, and forces upon us the idea of something fateful and inescapable when otherwise we should have spoken only of 'chance' " (237). As there is nothing "innocent" about Wanley's presence in the woman's apartment, we can conclude that it is not the story line of the film but the text as a system of enunciative strategies that is responsible for the oppressive and anxiety-ridden atmosphere *The Woman in the Window* creates. "Fate" has now nothing to do with the "message" of the film but is a question of the way the narrative and representational devices "place" the spectator.

It is, however, in his comments on the various functions of the double that Freud provides the key.[5]

> The theme of the "double" has been very thoroughly treated by Otto Rank (1914). He has gone into the connections which the "double" has with reflections in mirrors, with shadows, with guardian spirits, with the belief in the soul and with the fear of death; but he also lets in a flood of light on the surprising evolution of the idea. For the "double" was originally an insurance against the destruction of the ego, an "energetic denial of the power of death," as Rank says; and probably the "immortal" soul was the first "double" of the body. This invention of doubling as a preservation against extinction has its counterpart in the language of dreams, which is fond of representing castration by a doubling or multiplication of a genital symbol. The same desire led the Ancient Egyptians to develop the art of making images of the dead in lasting materials. Such ideas, however, have sprung from the soil of unbounded self-love, from the primary narcissism which dominates the mind of the child and of primitive man. But when this stage has been surmounted, the "double" reverses its aspect. From having been an assurance of immortality, it becomes the uncanny harbinger of death (234–35).

A bulwark against death and castration on the one hand, the "harbinger of death" on the other. Given the narcissistic component of spectatorial scopophilia, it is surely no exaggeration to say that the two meanings of the double are simultaneously present in the film, which reveals therefore the structure of disavowal—the simultaneous presence of mutually exclusive opposites, of belief and knowledge—and shows itself as an elaborate *mise en abyme* of what it means to go to the cinema, which recalls remarks already made concerning the repetition compulsion. The simultaneous presence of opposites gets to the heart of the matter—the representation of the events narrated—and it is here that various reactions to the film are particularly helpful.

Courtade uses the word *inquiétude* ("disquiet") to describe the feeling the film generates (Courtade 1963, 69), and Henri Agel says the film is a "nightmare that exudes a mysterious climate of anguish."[6] The precise nature of this mystery has been elucidated by Moullet, who claims it stems from "the natural, anodine and realistic nature of the details shown. . . . It is the absence of all disquieting elements that creates anxiety for the spectator, as the nature of the action should normally be disquieting" (Moullet 1963, 63–64). It is not the situation, then, but the way it is represented that creates the feeling of something uncanny. Moullet's brilliant insight repays close study.

The Woman in the Window has disappointed, indeed infuriated, critics, precisely because it adheres so closely to the *doxa* of naturalism: everything in the film, down to the smallest detail in the decor, strikes the spectator as normal, realistic, corresponding perfectly to "life." Then, suddenly, all these "insignificant" elements are revealed as a dream, as the product of unconscious desires, which imply ours, the spectators', drawn as we have been into the mesh of the snare by the tissue of the text. Talking of hallucinations, Freud has written: "Let us be clear that the hallucinatory wishful psychosis—in dreams or elsewhere—achieves two by no means identical results. It not only brings hidden or repressed wishes into consciousness; it also represents them, with the subject's entire belief, as fulfilled" (SE 14:230).

By leading us to believe that what we are witnessing is to be taken at its face value, *The Woman in the Window* at one end and the same time shows that its discourse has enabled us to fullfil our desire to live out Wanley's fantasies and that such desire is the real reason behind any person's going to see a film. As Freud has pointed out, "an uncanny effect is often and easily produced when the distinction between imagination and reality is effaced, as when something that we have hitherto regarded as imaginary appears before us in reality" (SE 17:244). This is most obviously the case when the portrait "comes to life" for Wanley, but it also sums up critical reactions and the status of the spectator. On one level the film is taken for reality and is suddenly revealed as imaginary. On another, far more fundamental level, it is seen as mere imagination (just another film), then turns out to be reality inasmuch as the real nature of desire becomes apparent through the revelation that it is a dream. The realistic devices show that they are just that, devices, and destroy abruptly and brutally the desired narcissistic identification. The revelation constitutes a return of the repressed, hence the negative reaction. What is so particular about "unconscious (repressed) processes" is "their entire disregard of reality-testing; they equate reality of thought with external actuality, and wishes with their fulfilment" (Freud, SE 12:225). The critic, like the spectator, has been hoodwinked.

It is the entire function of the imaginary signifier that is being revealed, but this unpalatable fact cannot be swallowed. Instead, the critical discourse displaces the problem in the best tradition: it is not the discursive devices that have caused disquiet, but the mere content ("it was only a dream"). At work here is the highly ideological way "common sense" represents dreams to itself: as weird, unreal, surrealistic, never to be taken seriously. Since such a position is a means of denying the unconscious as the discourse of the Other, some remarks are in order.

Following the research of the psychologist René Zazzo, Christian Metz has pointed out that, if the manifest content of a dream were filmed as such, the result would be a completely unintelligible film (Metz 1977b, 149). Such a project is, of course, impossible. Condensation and displacement occur without any concern for reality inasmuch as they are part of the primary processes based on the pleasure principle. Whatever role the unconscious may play in a director's decision to frame X and not Y, to use a fade rather than a cut, or, to return to a recurrent theme in this book, to choose one kind of hat rather than another, the fact remains that these decisions are manifest through *language,* whose grammar and syntax belong to the secondary processes and hence obey the reality principle (Metz 1977b, 151). It explains the unsatisfactory nature of the dream in Hitchcock's *Spellbound* (1945): Dali's self-conscious approach means that the absurd stems from a logic belonging to the intellect and is not absurd at all, just "bizarre."

It is therefore perfectly logical that there should be only one realm where the dream is tolerated: the *fantastique.* However disquieting or unsettling the film may be, as long as the whole venture can be safely pigeonholed as belonging to the supernatural, everyone is happy. A perfect example is the British film *Dead of Night,* (1945), in which everything is explicitly supernatural. That one of the stories narrated by the film—whose purpose is to show that there are things psychoanalysis cannot explain—is a humorous ghost story enables critics to place the entire film in that category. What is striking is that the story in question is the only one that is not *unheimlich,* for the simple reason that the others, via secondary revision, are realizations of the unconscious: the episodes "The Haunted Mirror" and "The Ventriloquist's Dummy" give the impression of having been written and directed by Lacan to illustrate his theories of the mirror-stage and the discourse of the Other.

One thing is as plain as a pikestaff: there is nothing remotely *fantastique* about *The Woman in the Window.* Indeed, it is, along with *Beyond a Reasonable Doubt* (another Lang film that has infuriated the critics), the film that corresponds least to the *doxa* of the *film noir:* no oppressive lighting (how different from *The Ministry of Fear* and *Scarlet Street*), a simple tale simply told. As Samuel Weber has stressed, "the language of the dream is one in which identity and non-contradiction are strategic, calculated and misleading after-effects of differential relations, transformations, and displacements" (Weber 1982, 67). What shocks and surprises is not that it is a dream but that the unconscious is revealing itself in such a way what the viewing subject ceases to be an ego in full control and is forced to recognize its true status, a recognition that explains why strategies of disavowal and the metonymy of desire are called upon to deny the fact.

One returns to that quality of the film that insists so massively: being controlled by forces one does not understand. It is a key element in *Dead of Night* too, where doubling and repetition are the basic enunciative strategy along with the feeling, made explicit in the dialogue, of "I've been here before." Freud has pointed out "that every affect belonging to an emotional impulse, whatever its kind, is transformed, if it is repressed, into anxiety" (SE 17:241), suggesting that, given the frightening nature of the uncanny, "the frightening element can be shown to be something repressed which *recurs*" (241). He adds, "We can understand why linguistic usage has extended *das Heimliche* ("homely") into its opposite, *das Unheimliche* (p. 226); for this uncanny is in reality nothing new or alien, but something which is familiar and old-established in the mind and which has become alienated from it only through the process of repression (241).

What this familiar yet uncanny element is must be seen, as I have suggested, in the light of "I've been here before": the "mother's genitals or her body" (SE 17:245). Freud sees the prefix *un-* as "the token of repression" (245) and we can see a clear link between the double and repetition on the one hand, castration and scopophilia on the other. It is precisely what is at stake in *The Woman in the Window,* and Freud's remarks on works of art are precious. He stresses that whenever the uncanny "proceeds from repressed complexes," then it is "more resistant and remains as powerful in fiction as in real experience. . . . But where it is given an arbitrary and artificial setting in fiction, it is apt to lose that character" (251). The extreme realism of *The Woman in the Window*—attested to by critics—eliminates the latter possibility, except on the mode of displacement: the ending is described as "arbitrary." What has returned is not only the repressed of the castration complex, but the enunciation, *discours* as opposed to *histoire.* The latter strives to pass off the narrated as existing without a narrator, as in a dream or a fantasy (Metz 1977b, 114), which only goes to show that it is not a dream at all: it is only a film.

Just to what extent the textual system invites one to take literally a remark such as "it's only a film" (rather than to use the observation on the mode of disavowal) can be seen (literally again) in the sequence where Wanley leaves the club (the dream has now started, but we do not know it yet) and stands and admires the portrait, which gazes out at us, therefore at the camera of the enunciation. Suddenly the reflection of a woman, the woman in the portrait, appears on the window behind which the portrait is being exhibited. Wanley cannot believe his eyes. The camera pans left to reveal the woman in question standing on the sidewalk smiling at the professor.

Several things are happening here. One can say that the relation between Wanley and the portrait is a *mise en abyme* of the status of the spectator watching the film, especially as the gaze of the portrait is fixed on us, the spectators. In other words, if Wanley equals the spectator, then the portrait must look not at him but *offscreen*. If Wanley is a metaphor for the spectator, the latter occupies his place in the diegesis: the portrait does not look at him but looks offscreen. On the other hand, that the portrait should be looking at the spectator but not at Wanley means that, at *this precise moment,* the spectator is *not* Wanley.

Although we are led to identify with Wanley throughout the film in general, we are separate from him inasmuch as we are looking at him looking at the portrait. The point of view hence upsets our imaginary status as subjects of the enounced identifying with Wanley and puts us back in our real positions as subjects of the enunciation. However, if we occupy our imaginary position as Wanley, then the portrait looks not at us but offscreen, in the direction from which the woman herself emerges. That the portrait should be looking at us both reinforces our scopophilic status as subjects of the enunciation and inscribes us into Wanley's offscreen. The portrait's look symbolizes our double status as spectators: placed both outside and within the diegesis thanks to our look.

That the woman appears first as a reflection—having formerly appeared as a portrait—means that the film is insisting on its real status as image, which shifts the attention from the referent to the signifier. Moreover, the woman's emerging from the offscreen, as if from nowhere, fits in with the Freudian concept of the unconscious as "the other scene" and also other aspects of the diegesis, such as the sudden appearance of the lover and, later, of the bodyguard. The image corresponds to spectatorial desire.

In this way the film allows the spectators' imaginary to function, while at the same time maintaining the bar between enunciation and enounced through the role played by the portrait's look. When the woman emerges from the offscreen, she is emerging from the imaginary of the spectator, who identifies with Wanley as subject of the enounced. At the same time, she emerges from the offscreen of the space created by the look of the portrait *and* the look of the spectator, which makes of her the manifestation of the spectator's real position in relation to the textual system. Lang has recourse here not to a shot–reverse shot, which would have reinforced the imaginary, but to a pan, which reveals progressively the offscreen, which is the metonymic space of the onscreen, its prolongation (Bonitzer 1971b, 18).

What is revealed is thus the spectator's phantasm, there to mask what is unbearable about the cinema, what questions the very status and structure of the spectator as subject of the signifier (Oudart 1970, 47). It is surely pertinent to reflect for a moment here on the portrait, which so fascinates Wanley, and which is not without reminding us of the most famous portrait in the classic Hollywood cinema, that of the heroine of Preminger's *Laura* (1944, the same year as *The Woman in the Window*). Readers will recall the extraordinary scene in which Dana Andrews, who believes Laura to be dead (as do we), and who has fallen asleep under her portrait, wakes up suddenly to find himself confronted with the real Laura, there before him in the flesh. The Laura of the portrait, wearing a black dress, dominates the scene, whereas the real Laura stands there in a white raincoat. The juxtaposition within the same frame, from which all extraneous elements have been eliminated, is a remarkable comment on the entire cinematic machine.

To begin with, it is a metaphor for the purely technical nature of the filmic process: the film in the camera produces a negative, which is processed to give the positive image we see on the screen (or in publicity stills). Thus, prior to processing, the negative frame shows faces as dark and dark-colored clothes as light. More than that, however, is happening. The portrait of Laura functions, for the characters of the film, as a means of fixing her image forever, outside time and confined to the space of a living room wall. As such, it becomes an idealized representation of Laura, Laura as she was at the moment of posing, Laura as she wanted to appear, but especially Laura as others, particularly men, wanted to see her. From the spectators' point of view, the portrait functions rather as a signifier of desire: Laura condensing in her portrait the cinematic image of Woman that we have all become used to seeing in films and have come to look upon as the only way to represent women. This fetishistic mentality enables us to maintain the myth of women in film as pure objects of fascination and scopophilia: they are there to be admired—a hypocritical way of saying "stared at."

Laura's portrait and our relation to it as spectators are a perfect illustration of Stephen Heath's observation that "mental processes exist to begin with in an unconscious phase, only from which do they pass over into the conscious phase, 'just as a photographic picture begins as a negative and only becomes a picture after being turned into a positive' " (Heath 1976b, 252). The quotation from Freud that Heath includes shows to what extent the unconscious and the conscious are condensed in the shot from *Laura* under discussion here. The irruption of Laura the woman into the privileged space of Laura the portrait is not just a question of a return from the dead but rather of a return of the repressed.[7] A real Laura is there for the Dana Andrews character to contend with, not an image of her fixed for eternity. It will no longer be possible for him to fantasize about her in the same way—who was this enigmatic woman?—because she will be there to present another image of herself.

Such is not the case, I feel, for the spectators, who find themselves confronted with yet another *image* of Laura, one that coincides perfectly with that of the hapless heroine who does not understand what is going on. It is reinforced by what follows: the need to unravel the enigmas, for Laura is the center of these enigmas, the signifier of desire. Nothing can be explained without her, and the final revelation about the guilt of Waldo Lydecker only goes to stress this enigmatic status of hers, a status that is explicitly linked to death: "I remember the weekend Laura died," says Lydecker's voice-off at the beginning of the film, a voice cut off at the end by his own death.

For the spectator Lydecker's death constitutes the classical ending and maintains the unity of the self-satisfied ego. From the point of view of the unconscious, it represents the end of the Oedipal quest, the solving of the riddle, the realization of the oracle of sexual difference. Applying an observation of Lacan's, one can say that the spectator passes "from myth to existence," just as Oedipus does (Lacan 1978, 268). Hardly surprising then that this unconscious project of the text displaces the issue onto an individual problem: Lydecker is a repressed homosexual, which makes it easier to defuse the unbearable link between death and castration inscribed into the film through the interplay of the look, the portrait, and the woman.[8]

These values and unconscious processes are at work in *The Woman in the Window.* Let us take the title: it is not a woman who is in the window, but a *portrait* of her. Not exactly the same thing, except ideologically: the fetishization of Woman as absolute, the condensation of all the lost objects thus retrieved in the Imaginary. One must not forget that the real woman appears firstly as a reflection in the window, as another *image,* which enables both Wanley and the spectator to overdetermine desire by multiplying images, which in turn makes the explanation even more significant for the unconscious nature of the image—and even more disappointing for the narcissistic component of the ego. The role of the double is more insistent and systematic in *The Woman in the Window* than in *Laura.*[9]

That the themes of the double and repetition, linked as they are to the look and hence to castration, are central to the textual system of *The Woman in the Window* is nowhere more obvious than in the final sequence. Overcome by the realization that it was a dream—overcome in the double sense of "relieved" (equals disavowal) and "shattered" (equals an authentic subject position)—Wanley staggers from the club, only to go and take another look at the portrait. As in the first instance, the woman in the portrait gazes back, not at Wanley but at us, the viewing subjects, who are thus looked at as if we were a painting (Lacan

1973, 98). It is as if she were admiring us in turn, as if we desired to be
gazed at, which indicates that scopophilia is a variation of basic narcissism, the latter defusing the dangers inherent in the former (castration; a subject position defined by the unconscious). The way the in-
terlocking gazes inscribe us into the diegetic space means, as I have
shown, that we can fantasize a situation where we are Wanley, meeting
and having an affair with a beautiful woman. The ending is, of course,
where the film goes too far. Its comic aspect is not to be taken at its face
value because the entire sequence, once again, is set in motion by the
look of Wanley. This time, however, the look, by doubling that of the
first occasion, emphasizes repetition, which in turn is overdetermined
by the second woman's fixing of Wanley with her look: she may be
"vulgar" as compared to the first woman, but her very presence makes
her function as a version of the double, as the locus of the lack we have
been trying to elude and on which the film's discourse insists.

Wanley's gasp of horror is, then, the full recognition by the ego of its
true subject-ivity.[10] The spectacle is too much for him, and he rushes
away, seeking refuge from the "other scene" that is making its presence
felt. He disappears offscreen left, while the young woman saunters
offscreen right, leaving an empty screen as the image fades. The spectator faced with the empty screen is thus faced with the Truth: a fade-
out can become a fade-in; an empty screen can suddenly accommodate
someone who walks in from offscreen, summoned by the spectator's
look, which cannot tolerate the void, yet can fill it only through the
Imaginary by the reactivation of desire. The fade-out becomes a way of
keeping desire going: one film finishes, another will take its place (in
this case, *Scarlet Street*). But the empty screen is also a reminder of the
need to look, and it looks back, at the spectator. This is all the more
striking in a film that has applied the orthodoxy "Seeing is believing" in
order to deconstruct its ideology. Stephen Heath has pointed out the
importance of the window as a theme in Renaissance and post-Renais-
sance painting (Heath 1976a, 81), and one can see it at work in a very
special way in *The Woman in the Window*. The spectator's look is
channeled, inscribed into a frame in order to fix it, but the effect is not
to defuse the dangerous implications of the look as the locus of desire
but rather to accentuate it, especially in the context of the role of the
young woman and the momentarily empty screen. Normally "the frame
is the reconstitution of the scene of the signifier, of the symbolic, into
that of the signified, the passage through the image from other scene to

seen" (Heath 1976c, 260). I would suggest that rather the reverse is the case here: that there is, albeit fleetingly, a passage from "seen" to "other scene." This constitutes the radical nature of *The Woman in the Window,* whose themes and devices return, in a more displaced form, in *House by the River.*

House by the River: **6**
Pinups and Hang-ups

Stephen Byrne, a novelist, takes advantage of the absence of his wife, Marjorie, to try to seduce their maid, Emily. The young woman rejects his advances, which leads him to attempt to take her by force. When she screams for help, he tries to stifle her cries, only to finish up by strangling her. Horrified, he lies about the circumstances of her death in order to get his older brother, John, to help him hide all trace of the crime. Reluctantly John agrees, and the brothers put the body in a sack, which they dump into the river during the night. But the sack is washed up by the tide, and Stephen rows up and down the river by night in a desperate and unsuccessful attempt to recover the object. Finally it is the police who succeed in doing so, but they cannot pin the crime on the brothers because only circumstantial evidence links them to the death. John, however, is increasingly worried over the behavior of Stephen, who becomes more and more violent and deranged as the days go by. When John reveals he intends to confess, Stephen goes berserk and attacks him. Thinking his brother is safely dead, he then attacks Marjorie, who he thinks is John's lover. John, who was only injured, returns in time to save Marjorie. The insane Stephen, thinking he sees Emily in the folds of a billowing curtain, falls downstairs and is killed.

At the beginning of *House by the River*, Stephen Byrne is writing in the gazebo at the bottom of his garden. His neighbor Mrs. Ambrose calls out to him, and he puts aside his work to go and talk to her. At that moment, Emily appears carrying a small parcel. Stephen tells her to place it in the gazebo, adding that, if she takes a bath, she must use the bathroom upstairs belonging to his wife, the one downstairs being out of order. Emily smiles and moves off. Her swaying hips clearly attract Stephen, something that does not escape the notice of Mrs. Ambrose, who also leaves the scene. Stephen goes back to writing in his gazebo.

If this summary introduces us to two important elements of the film—creativity and sexual desire—it tells us absolutely nothing about the way these are presented (like any summary, it is summary). Let us therefore go back to the beginning. The scene opens with a point of view, that of the camera, which shows us in the background the houses of Stephen and Mrs. Ambrose. A slow track forward enables us to see the two characters. Mrs. Ambrose is gardening. She straightens up to adjust her hat, then stops suddenly and looks offscreen left. Cut. The spectator can make out the body of an animal floating on the river. If we are obviously seeing the scene thanks to the camera, the look of Mrs. Ambrose, followed by the cut and a change of viewpoint, leads us to assume we are seeing what she is seeing, hence to adopt her point of view. The process of inscribing the spectator into the diegesis is beginning.

The look and the point of view are therefore central to the textual activity being elaborated. When we see Stephen for the first time, it is through a window of the gazebo in which he is framed. The shot is a metaphor for our position as spectators whose look is determined by the frame of the cinema screen, the word *frame* being anything but innocent, as I shall explain. A few shots later we view Emily in an identical fashion when she places the package in the gazebo. Since both Stephen and Emily look offscreen from the vantage point of the gazebo, the repetition within the diegesis takes up the repetition of our look as subjects of the enunciation, thus reinforcing our increasing identification with what is happening in the film, inasmuch as it is determined by looks. Stephen's looking offscreen left when Mrs. Ambrose speaks to him activates the offscreen as a real space in which the spectator locates the absent Mrs. Ambrose. It is made all the more easy because the spectator has already occupied the same diegetic space as her by disavowing the role of the camera.

Exactly the same process is at work when Emily looks offscreen: the absent Stephen immediately becomes present, and his occupying the same diegetic space as Mrs. Ambrose reinforces our inscription into the film as subjects of the *énoncé*. We are both spectators who are looking

House by the River   Stephen: writing, looking, and the offscreen.

(subjects of the *énonciation*) and spectators whose looking finds an exact parallel within the activity of the characters of the text. This double status is part of the Imaginary, for we cannot function on both planes simultaneously. The spectators will repress their real status in favor of an imaginary inscription into the diegesis through the system of identifications analyzed. The repression at work here will enable us to understand the meaning of Stephen's look at other points of the film and, by extension, our function as spectators.

The packet Emily brings contains the manuscript of one of Stephen's novels. It is not the first time, as he points out bitterly, that a manuscript has been rejected by a publisher and returned to him. Mrs. Ambrose advises him to give the public what it wants, lurid stories. There follows a shot where we see the two of them looking offscreen right. The next shot, manifestly intended to be from their point of view—and therefore

House by the River   The sack that contained Emily's body: Stephen faced with the
return of the repressed.

ours, given the logic of the film's enunciation—shows Emily moving
away, her hips swaying. A remarkable number of elements are present in
these two shots: the creative process, repetition (the manuscript that
keeps returning), sexual desire, the look. The meaning of their interaction, now that the spectator has been placed in the imaginary position
described above, finds its first extensive elaboration in the following
sequence.

A light goes on upstairs in Stephen's house. Cut to Stephen smiling
lasciviously. We know at once, given what has gone before, that Emily is
taking a bath in Marjorie's bathroom. But this shot of Stephen does
more than just inform us of what is happening. The shot of the house
has not been preceded by a shot of Stephen looking, as was necessary in
the opening shots of the film. The spectators having been led to the

position where they believe they are seeing from the point of view of the characters, the identification process is now sufficiently advanced for such positioning shots to have become superfluous. We "are" now Stephen, and desire can be given full rein.

Stephen settles down in the gazebo and starts to read over what he has written. He picks up a pen, crosses out a sentence, and begins to write. As he picks up the pen there is a change in the point of view: we no longer see him; we are in his place. The identification is all the stronger because we see Stephen's hands writing, just as we would see our own if we were sitting in the gazebo. A further change in the point of view shows us Stephen again. He stops writing, pushes his chair back, and stares fixedly in front of him. The codes, both social and cinematographic, are perfectly clear: Stephen is thinking. The next shots are as follows:

Shot 1: Cut to a shot of the window lit up.

Shot 2: Cut to Stephen thinking.

Shot 3: Cut to a close-up of the window.

Shot 4: Fade-in to a close-up of a bath filled with water. Someone's right arm enters the shot from the left of the screen and removes the plug.

Shot 5: Cut to a close-up of a small wall mirror all steamed up. A hand wipes it off until Emily's face appears reflected in the glass.

Shot 6: Cut to Stephen in the gazebo. He rises and leaves.

That shots 1 and 3 each follow a shot of Stephen thinking allows us to conclude that the entire sequence is the realization of his desire to know what happens as Emily takes her bath. Given the identification process now functioning, it is our own desire we see reflected on the screen. Inasmuch as Emily is present in the sequence as a reflection in the mirror, the shot is a metaphor for the cinematic machine: we are in the presence of an absence (the actress playing Emily is not present), but this does not prevent us from wanting to see or seeing her. Henceforth the spectators are part of the textual system that will dictate their interpretation and way of seeing the film, just as the events following the death of Emily will dictate to Stephen the novel he will write based on her death. By the way it creates and sets in motion desire, the Imaginary, and voyeurism, the bathroom sequence is a condensation of the dual activity of writing a novel or seeing a film. If I add that the steam on the mirror can also be called *condensation,* this is then more than just a play on words.

If Emily as an immediately recognizable character appears in the sequence only as a face reflected in a mirror, that is not, however, the only part of her anatomy to figure: shot 4 also shows us her arm. But the position of the right arm is not the same as that of Stephen when he picks up the pen; if we are Stephen, we are certainly not Emily. Our identification with the former's desire is reinforced by the fade linking shots 3 and 4 and hence two stages in the realization of this desire, whose object gradually takes form: Emily's face appears in the mirror bit by bit as she wipes the steam away. The young woman's face is now the locus of her own look. The fact that she is looking at or admiring herself enables spectators to displace onto her their desire to see her, making her the mere object of their desire.

It is a perfect example of that "reversal into its opposite" that Freud pinpointed as one of the "vicissitudes" of a drive (SE 14:126).[1] He goes on to describe as one of the stages of scopophilia and exhibitionism the "introduction of a new subject to whom one displays oneself in order to be looked at by him" (129). The new subject is Emily, but it is she who displays herself in order to hide, on the one hand, that she is simply "on display" for Stephen and the spectators and, on the other hand, that her displaying herself is, on the spectators' part, a psychic reversal of their former narcissism, present in the film via Stephen. The spectator "surprising" Emily wiping off the condensation so as to admire herself in the mirror is a case of the other (Emily) surprising the viewing subject as a hidden look that is revealed in its true status (Lacan 1973, 166).

The spectator's voyeurism, which comes into being through Stephen's look and the whole process of the camera's point of view, becomes Emily's exhibitionism. Paul Willemen has pointed out that Freud considered that the first object of scopophilia is the voyeur himself as a child (Willemen 1976).[2] The voyeur is therefore looking for someone like himself, the woman being a displacement and scopophilia the displaced locus of repressed homosexuality. The desire to see the naked female body is then the desire to disavow the absence that one nevertheless knows exists. Homosexual libido and the castration complex, both surmounted in the subject's psychic evolution, can therefore both return to threaten the correct ideological functioning of the text unless the appropriate displacement strategies are at work. All the more reason, as we shall see in due course, for the spectators' interest to be displaced onto John. In the bathroom sequence the castration complex is present metonymically through Emily's face and her arm, both features of the *corps morcelé* and a condensation of all the factors determining the spectators' reception of the text: looking, desiring, disavowing, creative activity.

The bathroom sequence is triggered by Emily bringing the packet containing Stephen's rejected manuscript, which, as he puts it in a highly significant phrase, "keeps on coming back like the tide." Return and repetition, themes central not only to the plot of the film but to the meaning of Stephen's desire and that of the spectator. The Freudian *fort/da* (SE 18) should be seen not as the simple mastering of the mother's absence (after all, experience shows the child she has not gone forever) but rather as the absence that is central to the human psyche—castration—a failure to come to terms with which compromises the entrance into the Symbolic and the mastery of language, itself based on absence. That writing and a constantly returned manuscript are at the center of the sequence shows how uncertain is Stephen's mastery of the signifier. It is not surprising therefore that, having disposed of Emily by dumping her body in a sack into the river, Stephen is treated to the sight of it returning with the tide, a repetition of the scene with the animal. Nor is it surprising that, whenever he pursues the sack by boat, the object is never at the place where he saw it: his pursuit symbolizes his desire for presence where there can only be absence.

It is clear then that libido, in one form or another, is central to the film. It is worth noting here that Stephen and Marjorie have no children, that they do not sleep together, and that his advances are brutal, in the nature of a kind of rape, which has led his wife to reject him. His "creativity" has been displaced onto writing, with uncertain results. He has acquired a certain notoriety, especially with women, because of his writing, but its superficiality is underlined in the film. It would seem to indicate Stephen's inability to overcome his desire for his mother as a child and the castration complex. The importance of this dimension can be seen in the sequence in which Stephen and John dispose of the body of Emily. A fish jumps, and what little light there is from the moon is concentrated on its scales, which shine brightly, causing Stephen to give an anguished look in its direction. It is not the fish as some phallic symbol that matters here, but the darkness, the darkness of the primal scene where the child discovers its parents making love. Most of the film takes place in surroundings where shadows prevail. The darkness means that Stephen keeps on reliving an early experience, but one that he can disavow, precisely because of the lack of light, which keeps his desire going through repetition. Hence he extinguishes a candle in order to be able to spy on Emily. Seeing without being seen gives the illusion of control, of being able to choose what one sees, whereas Stephen's situation is really a metaphor for that of the spectator: looking in order to disavow what one has originally seen, returning repeatedly to the cinema to keep the disavowal functioning.

If John helps Stephen in the disposal of Emily's body, it is not simply because it needs two people. John must be involved with Stephen in order to facilitate the audience's future displacement onto him as center of attention. Superficially, John seems to have even more personal problems than his brother. For a start, he limps, the classic image of castration. He lives only for figures—he is an accountant—and has few human contacts.[3] A closer look at John will show how he functions in relation to the spectator.

John is the elder brother and spends his time coming to Stephen's rescue whenever the latter finds himself in some predicament. John is forever repeating the same gesture, an apparently minor but, in fact, important detail in a film in which repetition is central. At the same time he plays the role of a father looking after a wayward son, hence Stephen's jealousy: he believes John and Marjorie are lovers, which keeps alive the Oedipal factor. Stephen is living out in real life the imaginary role of a child, which explains his need to have desire satisfied at once, in a typically narcissistic and aggressive fashion. It is interesting to note that, in order to persuade John to help him, Stephen says that Marjorie is pregnant. Stephen plays the paternal role in a lie that John soon exposes, whereas John plays the paternal role in the Imaginary of the text, one of its discursive strategies. This role is destined to reinforce the spectators' desire to identify with him at Stephen's expense.

Inasmuch as John represents constancy, stability, and reason in the face of his brother's irrationality, one can say they represent respectively the ego and the id. More decisive for the functioning of the film is the relationship of John and Stephen to each other: the former is the latter's superego, his moral conscience, the severe father figure who protects but also represents the Law, castrating the son who desires access to the mother. John does not seem to have a sexual life, having sacrificed everything in order that Stephen succeed as a writer. It is Marjorie who comes out with this piece of information in an intimate scene with John where she reveals her love for him and he in turn declares his affections. Such a situation can only precipitate a further stage in the process of displacement and audience identification, especially as Stephen is behaving in an ever more odious and pathological manner.

The courtroom sequence shows perfectly how a textual system is built up in order to impose its logic. John is accused of the murder of Emily because his name has been found on the sack used to dispose of her body. Because John claims the sack was stolen, the police have no proof.[4] However, the neighbors all believe John to be guilty, which isolates him more and more from the community, thus enabling him to come into ever closer contact with Marjorie, a further ruse in the logic of the text. During the trial, John and Stephen are seated side by side on the front bench. Mrs. Ambrose is protesting against the whole pro-cedure (including therefore John's being accused), saying that she will not accept such insinuations against a man who would not harm a fly (we must not forget that, for the authorities, suspicion also hangs over Stephen). Although she makes a dramatic gesture offscreen left, in the direction of both John *and* Stephen, the camera does not follow suit to frame John (or Stephen). Why? Because, at this precise moment the unconscious of the text cannot choose between the two brothers be-cause of the ongoing displacement. For a displacement of another kind is taking place. Mrs. Ambrose's observation is not just due to chance. During her conversation with Stephen at the beginning of the film, he picks up a sheet of paper and notices an insect crawling over it. He shakes the sheet carefully over the lawn. The insect is a beetle, but it functions as a fly inasmuch as Stephen, literally, *would not harm a fly.*

The courtroom sequence is exemplary because it shows the conflict between the two projects of the text, each with its own logic. In one system there is Stephen: everything pertaining to him is retained, even such a "superfluous" and "insignificant" detail as the beetle. This ele-ment, like a foreign body (the animal, Emily) returns at the very mo-ment when the logic of the other system is taking over, the system in which the spectators are being led to identify with John, who is becom-ing more and more the center of attention, so that they can disavow their former identification with Stephen, whom they resemble far more in their real role as spectators. The text *hesitates,* which means that the camera cannot cut to John. To cut to John would mean that a choice had been made, a choice fatal for the original project of the text, which is to maintain an identification with Stephen as the signifier of spectatorial desire, of the very social function that is called "going to the cinema." By not cutting at so crucial a point, the text refuses to *show,* hence to *see,* thus at one and the same time highlighting and disavowing the related concepts of scopophilia and castration. The text panics before the return of the repressed, linked as it is to repetition (Mrs. Ambrose's observation repeats, within the logic of one system, what has already gone before). The theme of repetition is far from being an abstract one; on the contrary it informs the text at every level, verbally and visually, as I shall now demonstrate.

On two occasions Mrs. Ambrose tells us that she hates the river at the very moment when an object—the animal, then the sack—is washed up by the tide. Here, then, both repetition and the return are linked, the two concepts being remarkably condensed in an expression—itself repeated—that describes the situation and its endless movement: *back and forth*. She also uses the word *filthy* to designate the animal, and it becomes a privileged signifier. Stephen speaks of "the filthy moon," which suddenly lights up the darkness as he and John are disposing of Emily. John's housekeeper refers to Emily as "trash," and Mrs. Ambrose assumes the sack contains "rubbish." *Trash* condenses the literal and metaphorical levels of the signifier by evoking the absent signifier *filthy,* now endowed with a sexual connotation. When Stephen accuses Marjorie of being in love with John, she says he has a "filthy mind." This in turn continues the process of displacement onto John, who now represents normal sexuality as opposed to the evident abnormality of Stephen. The primary identification with the camera is becoming a thing of the past.

The film's credit titles are accompanied by shots of the river at night, its banks covered with waving reeds and trees. These images are presented to us via slow lateral and forward tracking shots. The same images and tracking shots intervene in the sequences where Stephen desperately rows up and down— "back and forth"—at night in search of the elusive sack. We even occupy his physical position in the boat and do the rowing. These images of repetition facilitate our identification with Stephen, which must be kept up until the displacement onto John can take over, the logic of one project of the text entering into conflict with the other, as I have already noted. It also allows a certain constancy to exist, in keeping with the pleasure principle: jumping from one character to another would jeopardize such constancy. At the same time the gradual and subtle displacement introduces into the repetition and the return an element of *change* indispensable for the correct functioning of the reality principle.

That Stephen is the locus of repetition both verbal and visual calls for closer analysis, given our primary identification with him and the ongoing process of displacement of identification onto John. Thus Stephen's use of the expression *filthy moon* in the scene with the flashing scales of the jumping fish is hardly coincidental but rather the return of an image that can find expression only through language. It is what Stephen has "seen" that is filthy. We know from Freud that "anxiety is not newly created in repression: it is reproduced as an affective state in accordance with an already existing mnemic image" (SE 20:93). Whether Stephen actually witnessed the sexual act between his parents or has fantasized it is irrelevent, as "the Wolfman" shows (see chapter 1). Nor is there any need to overemphasize the link between the sexual and the excremental forged by the signifier *filthy,* a regression to the anal stage and a manifestation of the repressed homosexual component of Stephen's scopophilia.

What does need to be insisted on, however, is the activity Stephen is so obsessively involved in at the moment of this observation: rowing up and down the river looking for the sack, an activity that is a condensation of the repetition compulsion and the desire to refind the lost object. Stephen's rowing is a question of acting out. "The patient does not remember anything of what he has forgotten and repressed, but acts it out. He reproduces it not as a memory but as an *action;* he *repeats* it, without, of course, knowing that he is repeating it" (Freud, SE 12:150). Likewise Stephen's horror before the leaping fish indicates that a repressed memory has returned, but a "memory" of a very special kind. "Something is 'remembered' which could never have been 'forgotten' because it was never at any time noticed—was never conscious" (149).

Referring to Freud's observations, Lacan has stressed that repetition must be seen in relation to something that has always been lacking (Lacan 1973, 131), which can be interpreted as the phallus as the signifier of castration. One must also keep in mind the function of the sack: however much Stephen pursues it, however close he gets, he never puts his hands on it because it is never where he expects to find it but always elsewhere. What is important, then, is what drives Stephen to pursue the sack, inasmuch as no object can satisfy a drive (Lacan 1973, 153). "The object of a drive is the thing in regard to which or through which the drive is able to achieve its aim. It is what is most variable about a drive and is not originally connected with it, but becomes assigned to it only in consequence of being particularly fitted to make satisfaction possible" (Freud, SE 20:122).

Stephen's desire is one of disavowing the lack as a means of overcoming castration, massively present in the film through the motif of the look, which means that, by extension, the sack must be designated as an *objet petit a.* The lack of satisfaction involved—quite explicit in Stephen's case—renders the process of repetition dangerous for the overall project of the film, which is to enable the spectators to indulge scopophilia and its attendant pleasures, not its attendant unpleasure. Hence the need of the textual system to find ways of centering attention on John at Stephen's expense.

If repetition brings constancy and aids identification, it also allows the text to pursue its strategy of shifting identification from Stephen to John. A frequent image in *House by the River* is that of a character framed in some way: Stephen and Emily in the gazebo set the tone here. When the brothers dispose of Emily in the river, the boat is framed between two trees. During a reception, John is framed by a window and, on two occasions, by a French window. He is therefore assimilated to Stephen in the gazebo, a link reinforced, then displaced, by John's being framed in this way when we learn that he and Marjorie are in love. The assimilation of John to Stephen in order to shift the audience's attention to the former is most striking in a further detail at work in the shots of John just mentioned: each time he is all but engulfed in a curtain. This image prepares us for the end of the film, when Stephen is caught up in and strangled by a curtain. The text displaces onto John what is connected with Stephen, thus revealing again that hesitation and oscillation pertaining to the problem of identification. John is literally in the place Stephen will occupy at the end of the film, which means that Stephen's role has been taken over by John.[5]

The last textual manifestation of the framing process—the public at the trial, framed within the courtroom by the door—contains an element repeated several times throughout the film: the wall to the right of the door is lit by sunlight. What is of interest here is the interplay of light and dark and the position of the light concerned: Emily in the bathroom, a lamp on the wall; Stephen in front of a mirror in the hall, a candle on a table; John at the reception, a lamp on the wall.

On each occasion there is a source of light situated to the right of the character in frame, a light that must be seen in the context of its (absent) opposite: darkness. I have pointed out that Stephen has to be in darkness in order to observe or spy on Emily and that darkness is a metaphor for the situation of the spectator in a darkened cinema. In both cases the darkness is not total: just as there must be at least a faint source of light for Stephen to be able to make out Emily, so there is also some light in any cinema. It is the nature and source of the light that matter here. The spectator, who sees a lighted screen, forgets that this light comes from the projector, a constant presence and a reminder of something outside the diegesis that is disavowed in favor of immediate identification with the story and its characters. The same spectator is also ignorant of the real source of light in *House by the River:* for the purposes of the *énoncé* it is, say, the moon; for the purposes of the *énonciation,* a studio light. The moon's suddenly coming out and lighting up the river and its jumping fish wakes Stephen from one "frame" of mind and plunges him into another that causes anguish, just as the lights that come up suddenly during the projection because of some technical fault abruptly change the spectators' relation to the diegesis, causing unpleasure (called frustration or disappointment).

A condensation of these factors is at work in two scenes that intervene, respectively, after Emily's bath and the disposal of her body. The spectators are therefore aware of Stephen's desire and of its consequences. In the first scene the bathroom door opens with a creak and Emily emerges. All we see of her (shades of *The Old Dark House* or any of the horror films of the 1930s and 1940s that put such emphasis on lighting) is a shadow on the wall of the landing, the light emanating from the bathroom being projected—so to speak—onto the wall to the right of the (door-)frame. She starts to come downstairs very slowly, and all we see of her is the lower part of her body: she is wearing a robe that reveals her legs up to the top of her thighs. We have a variant of what we have seen in the bathroom: there it was Emily's face that set in motion scopophilia and the concomitant disavowal of the lack; here it is her legs, revealed, but not too much. Cut to an overhead shot of Stephen looking up and offscreen right, smiling lasciviously (another repetition). Though he can make out the young woman, she has no idea he is there until he makes a movement that frightens her. It is at this point that he makes advances that end with her accidental death by strangulation.

The second scene is in every way identical, except that, when Stephen looks, he gasps in horror, "Emily!" The woman, of course, is Marjorie.

I say "of course," but the situation is by no means so obvious. It could be argued that Stephen has retreated into his fantasies to the point of being psychotic, which is all very well except that it keeps the discussion on the level of the *énoncé* and represses the status of the spectator. Much more pertinent is the dimension of disavowal, in which the subject places belief before knowledge (the two, of course, are always present together), especially in the context of the castration complex, which functions massively here, given the question of scopophilia. Just as the spectators come to believe momentarily in something they know does not exist, so Stephen believes he sees a dead woman. Our seeing part(s) of a body and a dress means that we are dealing with a network of signifiers and not two women as *individuals*. Both by the way they are framed in individual shots and by remarks they make to Stephen, Emily and Marjorie are assimilated to each other to the point of representing, not themselves, but a certain image of Woman that is the product of Stephen's desire—and our own, whether it be in the context of *House by the River* or that of "going to the cinema."

The object of desire is constantly pursued, never attained: Stephen's pursuit of the sack is eloquent proof of that. It is highly appropriate therefore that Stephen and the object of his gaze should not figure together in the same shot: it is the offscreen, and hence an absence, that triggers desire, the object of which can only be possessed in the Imaginary (the sack as *objet petit a*). Appropriate too that, at the moment when Emily seems to return and an earlier scene is apparently repeated, Stephen's look and cry of horror—triggered by something unmentionable offscreen—should be so powerful an instance of the Uncanny, one of the component factors of which is precisely the feeling of déjà vu, the unsettling experience of having been here before, which I analyzed in detail in the previous chapter. The definition of the Uncanny as "something that should have remained hidden but has come to light" is "uncannily" in keeping with the leitmotif of darkness and obscurity in *House by the River.*

By identifying with Stephen the spectators have been able to give free rein to their scopophilia, a shameful social activity that the cinema could nevertheless not exist without.[6] Stephen is therefore the locus of a contradiction, all the more so because the pleasure looking brings can suddenly turn into unpleasure in the case of the return of the repressed (the fish, Marjorie on the stairs). Stephen is neurotic and, for Freud, unpleasure for a neurotic is a pleasure that cannot make itself felt except as its psychic opposite. Hence it is dangerous for the correct functioning of the cinematic machine that the identification with Stephen should prevail. If Stephen's look is indeed a metaphor for our own look as spectators, the displacement from our place as subjects of the enunciation onto Stephen as subject of the enounced—essential for one aspect of this functioning of the machine—must in its turn give way to the more necessary displacement onto John, crucial for the final triumph of another logic of the same machine. John's textual function is to allow the spectators to assuage their desire to see without running the danger of unpleasure; then to replace this desire, with all its dangers and ambiguities, by another desire, a far safer one: the desire to see John and Marjorie happily united, the desire for the narrative to run its "normal" course toward that "happy end," which does not fail to materialize.

Morality triumphs in a way that enables the spectators to "forget" their illicit—but nevertheless enforced—identification with Stephen. Now completely insane, Stephen attacks his brother and tips his body into the river, yet another example of repetition. But John, of course, is not dead and soon returns to save Marjorie from her demented husband. John is guilty of a momentary weakness, which he overcomes by showing that, limp or not, he is a man after all.[7] To identify with John is thus to identify with that masculine order whose reward is the woman. Society's values are intact and we can all breathe again.[8]

It is not, however, so easy to dispense with Stephen. The spectators enjoy an imaginary control over the diegesis, all the more so because they have "created" it by identifying most fully with Stephen when he is writing or acting out his desire unrestrained (Emily in the bathroom). We are also in Stephen's place when he holds in his hands the manuscript of the novel he has written, inspired by Emily's death. The very last shot of the film shows us this novel, which has ended with Stephen's death. Stephen has set the fiction in motion by telling John that Emily died falling downstairs. The form Stephen's death takes has been prepared for in another sequence where Marjorie occupies his position at the bottom of the stairs, while Stephen occupies that of Emily or Marjorie on the stairs. Stephen on the stairs equals Stephen who will die in a way that condenses fact and fiction: on the one hand he is strangled by the billowing curtain, just as he strangled Emily; on the other hand, he falls downstairs, which is how he claimed Emily met her death. Thus Stephen's fictional account of the death of Emily, which has kept going the fiction engendered by the bathroom sequence, merges into fact and thus disavows the textual elements destined to stress the fictional nature of the text and, by extension, the very nature of the cinematic machine.

As we have "been" Stephen, we have written the novel and hence the film. Hence we control our destinies as spectators, which is precisely the function of the superego, the role John plays in relation to Stephen (and, briefly, to us, who have identified with Stephen). Such control is, however, typical of a narcissistic overevaluation of one's intellectual capacities that is part and parcel of Stephen's problems (Freud, SE 17:240). The original logic of the text therefore returns at the very moment when our identification with John allows us to disavow it. We disavow what *was* in favor is what *is,* just as we disavow what we experienced during the film in favor of what we want to believe as we walk out into the street ("After all, it was only a film"). The intimate link between the desire to see (a film), castration, and death cannot normally be inscribed into the classical cinema, except in a displaced form (Stephen's death).[9] We must be allowed safely to ignore the lessons of what we have seen or lived through—at least until the next time we see (a film).

Secret beyond the Door: **7**
Romance in a
Low Key

All the aspects of the Langian textual system analyzed up to now return, insistently, to the global strategy of emphasizing the enunciation and what that implies for the spectator. *Secret beyond the Door* takes up these concerns and adds another: the voice-off. This was discussed briefly along with the role of the microphones in *Hangmen Also Die* (see chapter 3, section 4), but its role assumes other dimensions in *Secret beyond the Door:* not only is it the voice of the main character that is involved, but she is not what she seems. One could sum up the general thrust of the film by saying that its conscious project is subverted by its unconscious project. The film presents itself as a case of a devoted wife trying to cure the psychological problems of her husband and succeeding, whereas the other project—and the only one that stands up to scrutiny—consists in showing that she is as neurotic as he is.

Celia and Mark meet in Mexico, fall in love, and get married. During their honeymoon in that country, Mark talks of his secret passion: reconstituting rooms where acts of violence or crimes of passion have taken place. Celia has always considered him "inhibited" and now calls him "mad," which elicits from him the reply, "Yes, probably I am." Such a response introduces the favorite illusion, which consists in saying that, if someone recognizes a fact considered to be the truth, then it is indeed the truth and there is a coincidence between belief and knowledge, as if the fact of recognizing one's illness is necessarily to be taken at face value, as if it is the same thing as recognizing the reasons for being ill in the first place. The ego reinforces itself by a recognition that is, in fact, a radical miscognition, as the textual system will show in Celia's case. By accepting such an ideology, the spectator will also accept Celia as all-knowing "guide" through the "labyrinth" of Mark's psyche and hence identify with someone whose discourse and behavior introduce a fundamental heterogeneity into an apparently nonproblematic situation.[1]

The real situation is, however, somewhat more complicated. In one of the earliest scenes of the film, a female friend of Celia's and her own brother accuse her of having broken off her engagement to another man, to which she replies, "I never dreamed of marrying him." Since the preceding scenes have shown us that she has just married Mark—the scene in question is told in flashback and shows us Celia before her meeting with Mark—a certain frivolity is implied on her part. More important is Celia's incestuous relationship with her brother Rick, referred to by her as "mother, father, and check-signer." She even goes so far as to wonder if she will ever find a man of his worth. His being in charge of money matters condenses the ambiguity of the film that I shall try to explain at the end of this chapter: it could indicate irresponsibility on Celia's part, but it also indicates the way women are forced to rely on men in the domain of the Law, both legal and patriarchal. It is the lack of responsibility that is stressed here: Rick's sudden death forces Celia to look after her own interests—but she is helped by a lawyer who is in love with her. Significantly, much later, when things seem to be going from bad to worse, she says, "If only Rick were alive, I could go home to Rick."

Let us return now to the sequences in Mexico. Celia is present at a fight between two men over the favors of a woman. Celia feels "strangely held" by the fight and says of the woman involved, "I felt how proud she must be." What is striking here is not only that Celia is fascinated when confronted with this violence, but also that she chooses to recount the scene as part of her memories of Mexico, which means that it is her desire that is talking. To begin with, however, this element is masked because Celia is presented as the film's narrator and therefore enjoys the status of someone who knows because she is recalling something. According to Freud, "there is no guarantee of the correctness of memory; and yet we yield to the compulsion to attach belief to its data more often than is objectively justified" (SE 5:515). The observation is particularly pertinent for spectator attitudes. It is worthwhile remembering that Celia and the film encourage us to attach belief to the meaning of

Secret beyond the Door   The first night of the honeymoon and the locking of the
door.

dreams and that Celia claimed she never "dreamed" of marrying a
former suitor.

It is at this sexual combat that Celia spots Mark for the first time,
and, commenting on what attracted her to him immediately, she tells us,
"He saw behind my make-up what nobody else had ever seen, what
even I didn't know was there." The remark is followed by a cut, as if to
mask the introduction of an unknown element that might compromise
Celia's status as someone who will be able to understand and cure Mark,
but the repressed returns at once when Mark says to Celia, "You're not
a bit like you, I mean; you aren't what you seem to be." But his next
observation allows a less disquieting reading: Celia is a sort of Sleeping
Beauty woken out of a trance by Prince Charming. The image is taken
up by a friend of Celia's: "When you finally snapped out of your trance,

Secret beyond the Door   Celia stealing the key to Room 7.

you looked as if you'd seen Death himself." She is referring to the emotional impact Mark has had on Celia, which allows one project of the text to slip in the theme: Mark will prove dangerous to Celia because he is now linked to Death.

The project is undermined, however, by the way the film represents the sequence where Celia watches the two men fight: violence is involved, she is attracted by it, yet she will use Mark's passion to show him that his interest in violence is affecting him mentally. Moreover, Celia admits that she was really looking for such a man as Mark when she evokes her dream of daffodils, which, according to the logic of the conscious project of the film, represent danger in a dream. To discuss Mark and the dream together suggests that she is looking for danger, which she finds: a knife thrown during the fight nearly kills her. The film tries to mask these contradictions by having Celia recount a number of events in flashback, as a voice-off. It is precisely through this tactic of homogenizing disparate elements that the conscious project starts to come unstuck.

Secret beyond the Door opens with a woman's voice-off talking about dreams and daffodils. Then follows the marriage, intercut with other scenes in Mexico prior to the marriage. All is told in flashback, to the accompaniment of Celia's voice-off. As from the scene of the honeymoon, the flashbacks cease, but not the voice-off. The voice-off, recognizable at once as Celia's, presents and comments on the flashback sequences, which, by the very nature of things, belong to the past. I say "presents" deliberately, because the past is thus literally re-present-ed and exists, because of the images, on the same level as the present. The past being shown through memories enjoying the status of Truth—the *doxa*'s way of fetishizing the "I remember"—the present is also invested with the same aura and, vitally, the position of Celia, subject of the enunciation within the enounced. The imaginary situation whereby the two exist on the same level, to the detriment of the former, is now firmly in place, despite the implicit doubts concerning Celia, henceforth an unproblematic narrator.[2]

A voice-off is not, of course, "off" at all: it pervades everything, but since the spectators cannot see the person talking, they are forced to accept what it is saying, which means that a subject position is inscribed into the enounced and hence naturalized. As in scientific discourse, what is said goes without saying and the speaker becomes a simple purveyor of knowledge and truth (Descombes 1977, 141).

Celia as voice-off is not talking to anyone, but the particular situation implied means that we take it as if she were addressing her observations to us, which inscribes us into the diegetic world and disavows our status as subjects of the enunciation, which in turn removes the little contradiction of Celia's desire, her unconscious. Celia's words can thus be safely assimilated not to *discours* but to *histoire,* along the lines of the distinction elaborated by Emile Benveniste (1966b, 239). The comparison can only be partial, for historians never say "I," in order to pass their discourse and subject position off as anonymous objectivity. However, despite the presence of Celia's narrating "I," I would suggest that the voice-off accords a "historical" dimension to her sort of interior monologue, which is, precisely, *not* a monologue, because it sets up an imaginary situation in which we are her interlocutors. We can have access to the past only through her. However, Celia being part of this past, she is obliged to furnish us with information on herself in order to make the past complete, and it is here that the conscious project of the film fails to maintain order and unity. For we do not see and grasp everything through Celia. What she says is part of a discourse and is in no way to be passed off as a simple story.

The person who says "I" refers to himself every time that he so speaks, which means that he reproduces himself anew with every "I," that the "I" can never be the same twice, that meaning is produced within the discourse. The subject being the effect of the words used, it is what is said, how, and in what circumstances that allows us to grasp the position of the speaking subject. One is supposed to say what one means, but what one means and what one wants are very different, neither necessarily producing what the speaking subject intended to say or believed he was saying. What, then, do Celia's remarks on various topics reveal to us of her real subject position?

On the first night of their honeymoon, Celia is alone in the bedroom, brushing her hair (one must remember that the exchange about Mark being "mad" has just taken place). Suddenly, for no apparent reason, she smiles and goes to lock the door. Soon after, someone tries the handle insistently, then gives up. Celia continues smiling, but when the person goes away, she jumps up with an "Oh Mark!" and opens the door. There is nobody there, so she goes downstairs, where she finds Mark. He has just received a telegram and must go to New York. He denies having come upstairs.

The sequence is important for the story because it sets off Mark's neuroses: the ideology of cause and effect must be strictly adhered to, *vraisemblance oblige*. More interesting from our point of view is what follows. The maid assures Celia that there has been no telegram, and Celia tells her she must be mistaken. Celia's reply is purely for class reasons, for she reacts differently when alone: "Of course there was no telegram. The pain started. Why had he gone? Why had he lied? He said he hadn't come up, but I knew it was Mark, I knew it all the time."

Granted that Mark lied by saying he had been summoned to New York by telegram, but why should Celia have locked the door if she was expecting Mark to come upstairs and knew it must have been he who tried the handle? Celia goes so far as to admit that locking the door set the crisis off, then denies that her "childish prank"—as she calls it herself—could have been the cause. Such hesitation shows that Celia refuses to accept responsibility not only for her acts but also for her own words, which she disavows once she has said them. Her hypocrisy toward Mark is doubled by an excessive enthusiasm and affection. Shortly after the incident, she receives a letter from him asking her to join him at Lavender Falls, the home of the Lampheres, Mark's family. Celia is delighted: the letter proves she was wrong to mistrust him. But the letter proves no such thing: Mark could have sent it without having received a telegram, without having gone to New York. Celia's sudden and extreme change of attitude shows that she is willing to accept what Mark writes but not what he *says,* a willingness that is of the greatest importance for understanding Celia.

So Celia goes to Lavender Falls and becomes suspicious again when she learns from Mark's sister that she is his second wife, his first wife, Eleanor, having died young. "How did Eleanor die?" she asks herself repeatedly. The question can be interpreted in two fashions, which keep the two projects of the film going. It suggests that keeping something from someone is a sign of dishonesty—after all, Celia is Mark's wife— but also implies the attitude of Celia: nothing in the film indicates that she has told Mark of *her* past. She has talked of it as a voice-off and therefore to us, the spectators. It is here that we can see how dishonest she is being. She asks Mark not to keep her out of his life, but that is what she was doing by locking the door on him.

Mark keeps Celia in the dark in a very special way by refusing to let her see what is inside Room 7, part of his collection. So she steals the key, while he is taking a shower, in order to make a copy. The place occupied by the camera during her little subterfuge places the spectator clearly: Celia hides, she keeps silent when Mark asks if someone is there (just as she refused to open the door when he tried the handle). We *see* her hiding, we *see* him unaware of what is going on behind his back. We deceive him along with Celia, as if we were her accomplices, which we are without realizing it thanks to our status as recipients of Celia's thoughts via the voice-off. It is always from Mark that things are being hidden when we are also involved, which forces us to adopt a different point of view when contemplating his deceit toward Celia.

What is consistent about Celia's remarks is the presuppositions they convey and their attribution to Mark of any manifestation of neurotic behavior. Let us look more closely at the following observations:

1. "I lay awake for hours, or so it seemed to me. Over and over and over and over, the one thought: why doesn't he love me any more?"

2. "It was the way you immersed yourself in those stories, as if you were happy about their deaths."

3. "What goes on in this mind that he can change so suddenly? He keeps it locked like this door. I must open them both—for his sake."

Observation 1 is linked to the business with the telegram; observation 2 concerns Mark's collection of rooms; observation 3 precedes the scene where Celia steals the key to Room 7.

Observation 1 contains a discursive element that questions the truth of the statement and hence the status of the enunciator: "or so it seemed to me." Observation 2 contains a similar element, except that it is the person being addressed who is being questioned in this way: "as if you were happy about their deaths." A certain hesitation is introduced that concerns the enunciator rather than the person addressed. This is reinforced by the repetition of the word *over,* which overdetermines what Celia herself admits: the obsessive repetition of the same question, as if she were unsure of what she was saying, hence of what she thinks about Mark and hence of her own reasons for thinking such things.

Celia assumes that Mark does not love her any more because he has lied to her. The presupposition at work here functions to enable her not to *question* her own status in relation to what she says by passing off as obvious something that therefore cannot possibly be doubted. This is necessary in order that the logic inherent to Celia's discourse should not reveal itself to her, for it is she who is responsible for the logic (Ducrot 1972, 94). Were Celia talking to Mark, he would be forced to reply according to *her* logic, to inscribe himself into her discourse and forsake his own subject position, positioned by hers as the discourse of the other. However, Mark is not present, except as a "third-person pronoun," which, as Benveniste has pointed out, is a "non-person" (Benveniste 1966a,c). The spectators, on the other hand, are well and truly present, thanks to the position accorded them by Celia's voice-off discourse, and thus they interpret the logic of her remarks in "their own way," that is, according to the logic of Celia's desire. If Celia's is the discourse of the other for the spectator, both are now the effect of the discourse of the Other, given the dimension of desire and the unconscious introduced.

Unfortunately for the conscious project of the film, succeeding in passing Mark off as mad in the eyes of the spectators means the collapse of its project: if to lie equals no longer to love, then Celia no longer loves Mark *and must be mad too.* This is underpinned by observation 3, where Celia wonders why Mark keeps changing all the time. But it is she who keeps changing, she who moves from suspicion—she accuses him of lying—to euphoria—she is mistaken about him. The lack of consistency on her part shows a split subject position that merits a closer look as to its signification.

The psychoanalyst Luce Irigaray has made a number of observations on the enunciative strategies deployed by hysterics and obsessional neurotics that can apply to various remarks by Celia (Irigaray 1967). What are the characteristics of Celia's discourse? Having stated something, she then proceeds to question it by the form of her discourse; she is in a permanent state of doubt; she oscillates constantly between accusations and suspicion on the one hand and euphoria and reconciliation on the other; she displaces all blame and responsibility onto Mark without his ever having the chance to defend himself, either because he is absent or because he is caught up in the presuppositions of Celia's discourse. For Irigaray, it is just this that sets apart the formulations enunciated by obsessional neurotics (106).

Irigaray stresses the way in which certain enunciative strategies introduce doubt into the statements made, because the person experiences the need to keep the discourse going (106). This element tallies with Celia's constantly returning to the subject of Mark, which we can interpret as both an attempt to understand him (the conscious project of Celia's discourse) and an attempt to understand herself, an unconscious awareness of her real status as subject of desire. Irigaray's reference to the substitution of *as if* for *because* as part of these enunciative strategies is illuminating if one takes Celia's remark to Mark about his collections.

> It was the way you immersed yourself in those stories, *AS IF* you were happy about their deaths.

What Celia meant to say can be rewritten as

> It was the way you immersed yourself in those stories, *BECAUSE* you were happy about their deaths.

To the extent that Celia reverses the roles and puts herself discursively in the place she has reserved for Mark, and to the extent that she also speaks to herself in the film (thus allowing the spectator to become her privileged and imaginary interlocutor), it is clear that *I* can be put in the place of *you* and that the real significance of the statement can be considered a product of Celia's unconscious directed at herself as she really is, not as she presents herself. That Celia is unconsciously aware of the death instinct in herself can be judged from the use of the word *immersed,* which is a reference to her remarks on death by drowning.

Celia's search for truth thus provides another example of what I analyzed when discussing Gruber in *Hangmen Also Die* and Garrett in

Beyond a Reasonable Doubt (see chapter 3, sections 2, 4). She, of course, passes this search off as altruistic in the literal sense of the word: a concern for the other *(autrui)*. We have already seen that she talks to an absent interlocutor by referring to Mark in the third person, which annihilates his identity by turning him into a nonperson and allows the spectators to represent themselves in this absence as an imaginary presence on the level of the enounced. As Todorov has pointed out, the implicit interlocutor can be modeled only on the image of the speaker (Todorov 1970, 8), which means that the spectators, by "accepting" the position within the enounced, are constituted by Celia's discourse and are therefore spoken by her, with all that means for the status of the spectators, given that they are now identifying with someone who is unbalanced.[3] So it is the very institution of the cinema that is at stake, as I shall now demonstrate through the analysis of a certain number of codes, both specific and nonspecific.

A useful starting point is an observation by Paul Jensen on lighting. "Early in the film, on her wedding day, Celia enters the scene from a shadow that at first blocks out the top half of her body; this effective image makes visual the idea that only part of a person is visible at first glance" (Jensen 1969, 165). The remark is accurate, but quite inadequate. By insisting on the lighting as a pure symbol, it reduces it to its most mechanical level and creates a fixed signified that will henceforth move unchanged throughout the film, repressing the code's real status as *signifier.* The reduction of signifier to signified is part and parcel of the metonymy of desire, in which a fixed, unproblematic meaning moves from shot to shot and sequence to sequence, in endless pursuit of an imaginary closure that retroactively makes everything fit neatly into place. The spectators can thus repress their status as the locus of a series of shifting subject positions, a tactic that has been at work since the outset with the notion that elements of dreams mean one thing: the signifier is defused by being turned into a symbol.

In the sequence mentioned by Jensen, which takes place in church, we are informed of what is happening by Celia's voice-off. We see Mark from behind and in the shadows. Cut to a shot of Celia entering the church (on the right of the screen), then stopping, her face in shadow. Cut to Mark, who turns around and advances so that his face is clearly visible. Cut to Celia, who also moves forward so as to become visible. Thus the two characters are linked by a lighting technique that shows that Celia has as much to hide as Mark. The same technique is used soon after in a flashback sequence telling how they met. Mark approaches

Celia: he is on the right of the screen and moves out of the shadows. That he occupies the same space as Celia and is presented in an identical way means that the enunciation is saying that Celia equals Mark.

In two later sequences, Celia is filmed in the shadows in a way that reinforces the link with Mark. The first sequence takes place in the Mexican hacienda after Mark's sudden departure for New York (the telegram sequence). Alone in her room, Celia paces up and down, repeating the same question, "Why did he lie to me?" The second sequence relates the theft of the key. The two sequences are complementary, given Celia's ambiguous behavior and her dishonesty toward Mark.

Let us take the first sequence. Celia opens the bedroom door she has locked and steps out into the corridor. Only the end, in the background, is lit, a use of light and dark, overdetermined by identical framing, that is repeated just before the second sequence in question. Because we know that Celia is intending to have a copy of the key cut so as to penetrate into the forbidden chamber (of horrors?), the lighting links the sequence to the preceding one: refusing Mark entry into the bridal room triggers in him abnormal behavior that finds its double in that of Celia. Moreover. as Lotte Eisner points out (1976, 278), we see the corridor from Celia's point of view, which can only reinforce audience identification at a crucial moment of suspense and ambiguity (Celia is not being frank with Mark).

Likewise, when she descends the staircase to open Room 7, everything is in darkness. A single ray of light comes in through the window and plays the same role as the faint light at the end of the corridor. These enunciative devices can be naturalized by the spectator because both scenes take place at night, so the light of, say, the moon becomes what is in reality a studio light (as in *House by the River;* see chapter 6). The use of the lighting as signifier thus goes far beyond that of someone having something to hide to the point of informing the whole textual system, and it sets up not a simple opposition, as the conscious project of the text demands (Celia as opposed to Mark) but a totally different and unconscious project in which both Celia and Mark are implied and neither functions without the other.

The enunciation forbids a reading that tries to make of Celia a normal, objective person inasmuch as she is insistently represented in a way that assimilates her to Mark, the neurotic of the text's conscious project. Let us return to the shots where we see Mark from behind and in the shadows.

Shot 1: Mark in the church, with a brief track forward that stresses that he has his back turned. Celia enters, her face in the shadows.

Shot 2: After the scene where Celia locks the bedroom door: she goes downstairs, and Mark tells her he has received a telegram. He does not face her (equals dishonesty).

These shots find their equivalents where Celia is filmed in identical fashion.

Shot 3: Following Mark's departure for New York, Celia indulges in her secret thoughts, with her back turned to the camera. She does not face us (equals dishonesty).

Shot 4: Toward the end of the film, Celia, shot from behind, is looking through a window when Mark enters, his face in the shadows. (This repeats in a reversed form the first scene in the church: Mark seen from behind and Celia who enters, her face in the shadows.)

The textual system does not stop there, however, but introduces the character of Miss Robey, Mark's secretary. She wears a scarf that covers one side of her face, burned during a fire when she saved Mark's son, David. Since we learn later that there is really no scar at all, then she too has "something to hide" of a decidedly psychological nature. When Celia meets her for the first time, Miss Robey is shot from behind and in the shadows. In a later sequence where Celia is questioning herself about the death of Eleanor, Celia is shot from behind and in the shadows. When she turns around, her face is clearly visible, just as Miss Robey's was when she turned around to greet Celia. Thus the two women are linked by both framing and lighting. Instead of dismissing such elements as mere "stylistic effects" that burden the film to the point of collapse (Lambert 1955, 96; Burch and Dana 1974), it is surely much more logical to see them as the "semantic substance" of the film in keeping with *film noir* conventions (Harvey 1978), which Lang exploits here against a simplistic reading.

The multiplication of subject positions for Celia through the textual intervention of Miss Robey is pursued elsewhere in the context of a point of view imposing on the spectator a certain relation to diegetic space. The first sequence shows us Celia and her sister-in-law driving up to Mark's family home.

Shot 1: General shot of a house; sound of a car approaching.

Shot 2: Shot of a woman looking out from behind the curtains of an upper-story window.

Shot 3: Shot of the car arriving from the point of view of the woman.

Shot 4: Cut to a shot outside the house; the two women alight from the car. Celia looks around her, then raises her eyes to the window. The woman lets the curtain fall back into place and disappears.

In the second sequence it is Mark who drives up to his home.

Shot 1: Shot of Celia at the upper-story window spying on him from behind the curtain as he alights.

Shot 2: Shot from outside the house of Celia looking.

If the two sequences are not identical as far as the number of shots are concerned, they are with regard to what is essential: point of view. The woman at the window and Celia are assimilated, as are Celia and Mark inasmuch as both of them are spied on. The woman is, of course, Miss Robey. If Celia "replaces" her in the second sequence, that means that she is making Mark an object of her scopophilia and that she has something to hide.[4] Her behavior here is assimilated to her behavior when stealing the key and can be assimilated to the overall behavior of Miss Robey, who hides having nothing to hide in order to maintain her control over Mark, which is just what Celia is doing. There is no way of analyzing Celia without Mark and/or Miss Robey, as the articulation of a specific code (editing) and a nonspecific code (dialogue) shows.

Mark and Celia invite guests to their home at Lavender Falls and, in the course of the evening, Celia tells Bob about Mark's theories concerning the rooms he collects. "He has a theory . . ." Cut to Mark saying, "that a room affects, indeed determines, the actions of the person who lives in it." Given the narrative code used, it is clear that the beginning of Mark's remark is "I have a theory," and that Celia will continue her remark by using the same words as Mark. A classical example of the suturing of time and space? Yes, but far more than that. That Celia and Mark should say the same thing at the same time indicates that they have something in common, at least within the logic set up by the textual system as a whole, which is the only logic worth considering. At one and the same time the enunciation draws attention to itself, not to stimulate disavowal, but to underline the failure of the conscious project of the film. Discussing Hitchcock's *Suspicion* (1941), Pascal Kané has stressed the importance within classical cinema of rendering the characters "transparent" in order to facilitate the task of encouraging the spectator to look "innocently" at the diegetic world and the way Hitchcock leads the characters to "shift" in relation to what is expected (Kané 1971, 57). A particular nonspecific code will allow me to take the search farther.

The code in question is nonspecific because it is not peculiar to filmic narrative as such. It is, however, intimately linked to the specific code of lighting that is inscribed into the Langian textual system in general: its role has already been analyzed in chapters 5 and 6, and it will return in a different way in chapter 8 in the discussion of *Scarlet Street*. The element of interest here is, simply, the candle. When she locks the bedroom door on Mark, Celia is sitting brushing her hair before a mirror, which is flanked by candles, one on each side.[5] Such candles will be insisted on in due course and are here assimilated to Celia at the moment when she precipitates on Mark's part a crisis the responsibility for which she refuses to assume.

The second instance of the candles occurs on Celia's arrival at Mark's family home. The entrance to the house is a black rentangular hole flanked by twin lamps that function as substitute candles: it is their function and not their referential status that matters. As the house is his, Mark is inscribed metonymically into the text by the house, which represents danger, the unknown, shadows. However, by its form, the rectangular hole corresponds to Celia's mirror. What lies on the other side of the door is not therefore a symbol of the danger Celia is courting. Rather, what lies beyond the mirror image Celia wants to give (to herself) of herself is death in the guise of truth.

Analyzing such a blank, which he calls a "blind spot," in the films of Jacques Tourneur (and there are striking parallels between Lang and Tourneur, particularly the dimension of hesitation and ambiguity questioning the codes of representation and subject positions), Paul Willemen refers to its use in the *film noir* and horror films as "a potential threat,"[6] adding:

> It involves a denaturalisation of the spectacle in that the designated presence of absence breaks the illusion of a continuous unity and foregrounds what aesthetics would call composition, but which in fact is the emergence of the order of the signifier, and the consequent emphasis on the fact that the spectacle is in no way "natural" and transparent, but an organised arrangement of signifying elements. It introduces the presence of the symbolic into the imaginary mirror relation, not so much destroying identification as dramatising a break in the process of primary narcissistic identification into

which other modes of filmic writing attempt to lure the subject. The combination of these two points, the dramatisation of the structure of phantasy plus the introduction of the founding lack which marks the entry into the symbolic produces a text which appears to be the dramatisation of desire itself, the tracing of desire over/in the body of the text. (Willemen 1975, 24–25)[7]

At one point, Mark's sister is talking to Celia of the late Eleanor, saying that she is happy Celia is not jealous. Celia replies that it would be silly to be jealous, at which moment she is reflected in a mirror. The next shot frames her alone, flanked by two candles, suggesting that the image she is presenting of herself is purely imaginary, which in turn suggests a link between locking the door on Mark and what she denies with relation to Eleanor. The denial is of a sexual nature: no need to insist on the significance of locking doors so that Mark cannot penetrate. More interesting, however, is the aftermath, in which Celia is alone in bed after Mark's departure for New York. She seems to be asleep, but her slumbers are clearly being disturbed by dreams, and she is breathing heavily. Her real fear is of *jouissance,* and it is revealing that what obsesses her in the case of Eleanor is *how she died.* The unconscious links between death and orgasm are well known, and, for Celia, to discover the secret beyond the door is to discover the secret of life, namely death. Mark keeps the door of Room 7 closed because he blames his mother for locking him in his bedroom when he was a child. It was his elder sister who did so, which furnishes a further link with Celia, who cannot rid herself of her incestuous attraction for her elder brother. The Oedipal nature of Mark's and Celia's concern with origins stresses the link between knowledge, sexuality, and death.

Like Celia, the spectator wants to know all and flirts with death at the same time as she does, a flirtation that the conscious project displaces by having Celia threatened by Mark, the supposed fixed locus of madness. A frequent criticism leveled at Lang was that his characters were not credible, that they lacked "depth." It is rather a question of saying they are "too deep," inasmuch as no character is without other characters: the critical accusation is an unconscious way of admitting the opposite, namely the multiplicity of subject positions in the Langian textual system, which tends to heterogenize the material and lead to situations that are hardly plausible for the *doxa,* with its desire for neat solutions and immediately recognizable values.

Hence the interest of the endings in Lang. An ending being necessary, it becomes a sort of end in itself where everything is concentrated in the methods used, hence in the enunciation. The logic of the ending either shows itself to be artificial or else draws attention to another textual logic that dare not speak its name openly. I have pointed out the "fate" suffered by *The Woman in the Window*—the dream as ploy to solve a problem—and *The Blue Gardenia*—the murderess whose importance had not been stressed. In the case of *Beyond a Reasonable Doubt,* the constant shifting within the diegesis produces a text in which the spectators cannot "fix" themselves, then, when everything seems settled, the system starts up again by insisting on the yawning gap between desire and Truth, a gap closed only at death.

Another ending that poses a problem for any literal-minded reading is that of *The Ministry of Fear.* Inspector Prentice emerges onto the roof. Fade. Cut to Neale and Clara driving along a cliff-top. They are happy and it is broad daylight. She speaks of their impending marriage and mentions the need to have a cake. Faced with this word, Neale panics. The break between the previous scene and the final one is considerable: we are not treated to the usual scene where Prentice might have reassured the couple. The lack of a linking shot is, I would suggest, overdetermined by the complete lack of verisimilitude shown in the film since the opening. Neale exerts absolutely no control over the events, which take place according to a logic that escapes both him and us: things just happen without any respect for the usual cause and effect devices. Just as Dr. Mabuse succeeds through hypnosis in getting the theater audience in the film of 1922 to believe anything, so *The Ministry of Fear* forces us to believe what we see, while at the same time leaving us with the feeling that something is wrong.[8]

It is as if the last shot of *The Ministry of Fear* were the spectator waking up, along with Neale, after a series of more or less incomprehensible events that were imposed on him, emerging not from a dream but from a session of hypnosis. The relief felt that it is all over—like the relief when one wakes from a nightmare only to realize it was only a dream—is at once compromised by the word *cake,* a signifier destined to summon up a state that causes unpleasure, where, quite simply, *one does not know who one is.* The sudden change of mood that accompanies the cut from the roof*top* to the cliff-*top* (is this spatial link really due to chance?) is, for the spectators, the realization, however fleeting, that such a change mirrors their own shifting subject positions.

Such repetition plays its role at the end of *Secret beyond the Door,* in the very last shot of the film. Mark and Celia are back in Mexico: they want to have their honeymoon all over again, to start their marriage off "properly." Everything in the shot—the place, the decor, the framing—sums up their original meeting and decision to marry. Mark says, "I have a long way to go," to which Celia replies, "*We* . . ." The happy end introduces the very element the conscious project of the film had so long strived to repress: Celia equals Mark. When Celia does penetrate Room 7, she finds it is an exact replica of the bedroom she shares with Mark, so it is *she* who is the intended murder victim. And, indeed, Mark penetrates the room and tries to strangle her. In this way the two projects of the textual system converge: Mark is mad, and Celia's search for the "origins" (of his madness) is a metaphor for her/our search for absolute knowledge, which cannot but take the form of death.

At the same time as the enunciation subverts the enounced, however, another order is reinscribed into the film: phallocentrism. By recognizing that she has problems too, Celia now admits that it is through contact with Mark that she will rid herself of them. But the literal project of the film was opposed to this sexist ideology by making of a woman the stronger character on whom a man can count in order to be cured (leaving aside the dubious way the "cure" has been represented). The split subject position manifested by Celia through the voice-off was there all along to show that a woman cannot occupy such an active role. The film allows Mark to be made a weakling in order to force Celia-as-woman into the "correct" mold: she cannot possibly be stronger than he.

The last shot of the film also enables the story to come full circle, suturing difference and conflict in order to present the necessary and desired "happy end." This element is just as rife in Lang as elsewhere: were it not, he quite simply would not have made the films he did, and when he went too far, as in *Beyond a Reasonable Doubt,* he paid the penalty, artistic death. Although the various suturing devices never prevented the Langian textual system from failing to function properly in the eyes of the *doxa*—which has been the concern of this entire book—it does not mean they do not exist. The purpose of suture is to reinforce self-identity through a story and identification so as to counterbalance the subject positions involved in discourse. It is time now to turn to some of the devices deployed to attempt to re-constitute the subject as a self reassured by its own plenitude.

8 SutureSelf

The term *suture* has been hovering in the wings—hesitating between offscreen and onscreen—throughout this book. It is now time to let it perform, even if some of what follows will, to a certain extent, give the impression of being a rerun.

Suture is a term that comes from the unlikely source of surgery—*points de suture*, "stitches"—and was given its psychoanalytical meaning in a paper delivered in Lacan's seminar in 1965 by the future editor of the official version of the seminars, Jacques-Alain Miller. Miller, of course, was concerned exclusively with suture in the context of a linguistic discourse, "the relation of the subject to the chain of its discourse," a relation founded in "miscognition," itself "constituted not as a forgetting, but as a repression" (Miller 1977, 25). For Miller suture is part of an ideology "which makes of the subject the producer of fictions, short of recognising it as the product of its product" (27), which I take as meaning that the speaking subject sees itself as source and origin of what it says (and means), whereas in reality the subject is an effect of language and is constituted by the signifier. As Miller points out, within logical discourse—which one can perhaps designate not only as the discourse of the logician (Frege, Russell) but also as the discourse of "common sense"—anything that is in a position of "non-identity with itself" cannot but be rejected as "contradictory to the very dimension of truth" (29). For logical discourse, such an anomaly is an "impossible object," one "which it summons and rejects, wanting to know nothing of it" (32), in other words: the subject, locus of contradiction and the unconscious, of desire and the Other. (One must remember Miller was elaborating suture in the context of Lacanian theory.)

An excellent example is the parapraxis cited by Freud (SE 15:35) and mentioned in chapter 1: a woman, talking of her husband's diet, says at the end of her remark "what *I* want" instead of "what *he* wants." The lady in question thus "desutures" her discourse by revealing that it is her unconscious that is speaking her(e), insisting at the very moment when she wants to have nothing to do with it, "thereby making manifest the *division* of the subject which is the other name for its *alienation*" (Miller 1977, 34).

The "consistently planned programme" referred to by Freud in his observations on this case of parapraxis is the discourse of the Other expressing itself through the logic of the signifier, which logic is that of the Freudian "other scene" or, as Freud puts it in the same passage, the "other side." This "other side" can, by extension, be assimilated to the "absent field" evoked by Jean-Pierre Oudart in his discussion of cinematic suture. "Every filmic field is echoed by an absent field, the place of a character who is put there by the viewer's imaginary, and which we shall call the Absent One" (Oudart 1977, 36). Oudart, of course, was writing exclusively of the shot–reverse shot, by which a lack—the offscreen—is represented *for* and *by* the spectators in the Imaginary so that a full presence can allow them to misrecognize their real status as effects of the cinematic discourse. When the suturing system breaks down, even if only for a few moments, the Truth returns to dis-place the audience, to re-place it in relation to its own look as subject of desire. Hence the momentary panic—panic of the character and, crucially, of the spectator—of the shot in *The Ministry of Fear* where Clara looks horrified offscreen, only to realize Neale is present beside her, but not the object of her *original* look (see chapter 2, section 3). The fact that "the appearance of a lack perceived as a Some One (the Absent One) is followed by its abolition by someone (or something) placed within the same field" (Oudart 1977, 37) may ultimately suture the shot and the filmic field, "yet the haunting presence of the other field and of the Absent One remains" (41).

In the light of Oudart's remark, already quoted, to the effect that "every filmic field is echoed by an absent field" and his limiting of his theoretical intervention to the specificity of the shot–reverse shot, it is worthwhile noting Stephen Heath's comment that "the articulation of the signifying chain of images, of the chain of images as signifying chain, works not from image to image but from image to image through the absence that the subject constitutes" (Heath 1977b, 58). To this needs to be added, for reasons of clarity, an observation made elsewhere. "The narrative elision of the image flow, the screening of point of view as the ground of the image, the totalising of image and space in the frame of field/reverse field—these are some of the procedures that have been described in terms of *suture*" (Heath 1976b, 261).

"Some of the procedures," note. Suture is not to be reduced to the dimension of the shot–reverse shot and the present and absent fields constituted, but it must be grasped as functioning in any and every enunciative strategy partaking "in a perpetual retotalisation of the imaginary" for the spectator (Heath 1976b, 257). Inasmuch as Freud has taught us that the unconscious forgets nothing, then it becomes clear that, at any moment, an image can evoke not only all images past but also all images *possible* within the logic of the textual system so that the desired totality can always be represented. Lacan in turn remarks that, in order for something to pass into our memories, it must first be eliminated from perception, which assumes a never-ending process of the articulation of absence and presence, a process of the subject as effect of the signifier (Lacan 1973, 46).

I have demonstrated in the preceding chapters how the logic of the signifier can introduce gaps, hesitations, and contradictions into the apparently smooth flow of the images. It is—or should be—clear that too many such elements would prevent a film from functioning as a "good object," which was Lang's fate with *Beyond a Reasonable Doubt:* he made no more films in Hollywood. Any director can wittingly or unwittingly commit suicide in this way, as Orson Welles and Erich von Stroheim learned to their cost (and ours), but in the vast majority of cases, a film submits itself to a certain number of constraints, various manifestations of which must now be analyzed.[1]

Already in his first American film, *Fury,* Lang had assimilated the major narrative codes.[2] I am thinking in particular of elements of the story that are nonspecific codes but function as aspects of narrative within the textual system: the peanuts that Joe Wilson adores and that tie him in with the kidnappers; the word *mementum,* which he uses for *memento,* thus putting Katherine on his track; the blue thread she uses to mend his raincoat, the same raincoat she spots his brother wearing after Joe is supposed to have died in the fire. Such devices are classical to the point of banality: countless films function in this way, and to enumerate more would add nothing to what is already known about Hollywood. Rather than indulge in such an enumeration, I shall concentrate on specific codes: the fade out and fade in, the wipe, and the cut.

At the beginning of *Fury,* Joe and Katherine are walking in the street; it is night, they are alone, and it is their last evening together for some time. This is important for the psychology of the characters *and* of the spectator, who must not have anything else to think of. They walk slowly along a street. There now follows a fade where the shot of street A makes way for a shot of street B. As always, given the nature of the code, the two streets coexist momentarily on the screen. A new element is introduced into shot B, a lighted lamppost.[3] Since the two shots are both present for a moment, the lamppost also gives the appearance of existing in the shot of street A. It functions therefore as a condensatory signifier. On the level of the enounced, it denotes night and connotes the continuation of the walk. On the level of the enunciation it reinforces the fade, thus suturing the spatiotemporal coordinates at the same time as it highlights (as in *The Woman in the Window:* see chapter 1) the activity of the text.[4]

It is striking indeed to note the way the desire for unity and plenitude is inscribed "naturally" into the text by a signifier that can so easily be taken for a sign, given its banal referential status. This way, the rupture on the level of the enunciation "fades" into the psychic background and masks the spatial rupture on the level of the enounced. What Metz has called elsewhere "the internal cohesion of a segment" is thus maintained (1972, 120). At the beginning of *The Ministry of Fear,* the hero leaves a building of which we know nothing. He is accompanied to the gate by a man who remains anonymous. Following his departure, the camera tracks in to a plaque destined to furnish us with a considerable amount of (unsaid) information: LEMBRIDGE ASYLUM.

A fade introduces a new element: a railroad station. The words *Lembridge Asylum* are present in the two shots, which encourages us to assume that the station is not far from the asylum and that only a short time has elapsed since the hero's leaving the place. The plaque bearing the name of the asylum is more important than the lamppost in *Fury* because it is present at a key moment for generating not only what follows but an overall atmosphere that will be strengthened from sequence to sequence, indeed from shot to shot.

It is most instructive to note how the sequence asylum/station continues. Neale is looking for information on train times when his attention is drawn by voices and music emanating from a garden party, and he goes to take a look. There now follows the sequence introducing the cake. When Neale leaves, there intervenes not a fade but a wipe: the garden party makes way for the station. Why a wipe and not a fade? I would suggest that it is a case of the difference in nature between the departure from the asylum for the station and the return from the garden party to the station. The asylum and the station are linked diegetically: it is "natural" that Neale, having been released, should want to find a station. Such is not the case with the garden party. The station and the garden party constitute not two subsegments of a single segment, as in the case of the asylum and the station, but two separate segments. The dimension of "chance" is far stronger in the case of the diegetic role of the garden party. The introduction of the role of the cake and the idea that something decidedly bizarre is going on behind the apparently innocent surface of the garden party means that the "natural" link between asylum and station cannot be seen as natural in the same way as the return to the station from the garden party.

It is, however, necessary to link the garden party and the station and not resort to a cut—far too brutal—for a diegetic link does exist: the "blind" man who climbs into Neale's compartment in order to steal the cake. Although the reasons—the cake contains microfilm and is destined for a Nazi spy, Mr. Cost, the tailor—are unknown for the time being because what is important is the vagueness that creates suspense and unease (very considerable in this film), it is necessary to set up certain links so that, in retrospect, all will become obvious and hence naturalized. The wipe enables the textual system to link the garden party and the station from the point of view of the enunciation, while giving the impression that it is only the spatial and temporal coordinates of the enounced that are concerned. In this way the enunciation can function and mask itself at the same time, thanks to the way memory enables the spectator to reconstitute and represent everything that has gone before.

The material aspect of the wipe resembles the turning of the pages of a novel: Hollywood's frequent adaptations of novels and the occasional use in such cases of the actual turning of pages to connote the passing of time and so forth is part and parcel of the need to link phantasmatically (on the level of the enounced) what is in reality an intervention of the enunciation. The spectators must be shown that they are elsewhere, spatially and/or temporally, but nevertheless it is all part of the same "world." The wipe exists to attenuate the cut and trigger disavowal, whereas the fade exists to neutralize the cut and trigger repression. It is perfectly in keeping with the overall project of the text that *The Woman in the Window* should resort so carefully to the fade in the shot where Wanley asks the waiter to waken him at 10:30 P.M. because everything that takes place as from the fade that now ensues—the waiter wakes Wanley up—is part of the dream. It is a perfect example of the way the Langian textual system can subvert classical narrative by turning it against itself. The cut tends to create two separate segments, but the fact that they do not have to be completely separate and that links are permitted to exist between them can be exploited in particular ways.[5]

The ideology that the cut-as-suture buttresses can be overdetermined by an ideology peculiar to a given film so that both can function properly. In *Hangmen Also Die,* Gruber and members of the Gestapo are interrogating the Novotny family: father, mother, sister, brother, aunt. From the point of view of the enounced, the procedure is classic: one of the Nazis puts a question to one member of the family (they are, of course, interrogated separately). The enunciation proceeds in a special fashion: instead of creating five separate segments of a single sequence, the textual system passes from one member of the family to another at the moment the question is put. If one representative of the Gestapo puts a particular question to, say, Mrs. Novotny, we are treated to a cut that presents us with a shot of, say, the brother answering the same question in a separate room in the presence of a different representative of the Gestapo. In this way we notice that each member of the family is being asked the same questions. The device is very economical because it removes the necessity of repeating the same question several times and so introduces more questions and gives an indication of the Gestapo's line of thought. Moreover, it creates links of solidarity between the various members of the family in the face of the common enemy, on the level both of the enounced (the ideology of the film) and of the enunciation (the ideology of the spectator). The work of the enunciation is perfectly visible, but, since it removes most of the effort as far as the spectators are concerned—they know what is happening, where, when and why, given their interiorization of the codes—it ceases to exist as work, and the diegetic world is fetishized as pure presence and plenitude.

Paradoxically, it is when the film resorts to the cut in the most literal and banal way possible that the system fails to work properly. In *Fury,* Joe and Katherine are separated for several months while he can earn enough money to enable them to get married. He sends her regular letters telling of his progress. We see Katherine at home and, every now and then, she reads a segment of a letter aloud. Her reading enables us to know how Joe is getting on, but the film does not stop there (perfectly sufficient though this verbal information may be). It cuts each time to a shot summing up the news read out to us. "He's bought a car" becomes an image of a car. "He's bought a garage" becomes an image of a garage. "His dog is really a bitch" becomes a shot of pups, and so on. There is here a literal linking of word to image that can only lead the spectators to wonder whether they are not being taken for complete idiots. Oudart has spoken of Lang's "terrorism" in such a literal application of the *doxa* when it is totally unnecessary (Oudart 1977), and the redundancy of the shots only serves to show that they show nothing except themselves.

Even here, however, audience laughter at such banal literal-minded-ness can be a form of displacement in order not to face up to its real subject position. At the beginning of this chapter, I approached the question of lighting via lampposts, which is a dimension of lighting in which the Langian textual system has subverted many expectations on our part. The textual system, however, can function to displace its own activity onto something safer, as can be seen from *Scarlet Street.*

The first shot of the film is the first shot of the credits and presents us with a drawing of the upper part of a lamppost on a grey background. The names of the film's stars, Edward G. Robinson and Joan Bennett, then appear, followed by a crane shot down to the title of the film, presented as a street sign that is part of the lamppost. The next shot gives the names of the other actors, then the technicians; the lamppost is now absent. The first shot of the film "proper" is one of a street with passers-by. It is intended as the "first" shot of the film in the current sense of the word, which forgets that *everything* counts for the spectator and therefore that nothing is forgotten. That the title of the film—a street name—appears in the credits in the form of a street sign assimi-lates the film to everyday reality, which is reinforced by the very first shot of the film.

That the first shot of what is generally accepted as "the film" seems to flow "naturally" from the first shot of the credits—which are also part of the film—will tend to hide the activity of the text. However, it will be necessary for other factors to be put into place for such disavowal to be able to function. The drawing of a lamppost figuring so prominently in the credits accentuates at once the nonnaturalistic nature of the matters of expression. Furthermore, as Tom Conley has pointed out, "the com-bination of bars and the titled framing evokes the presence of clappers that begin shots in the production of a film" (Conley 1983, 1103). The artificiality that is rife in the Langian textual system as a whole is therefore present from the outset in *Scarlet Street*. Let us now see how the role of the lamppost sets about masking this textual activity.

The lamppost is there not only to light the street but also to allow people to see which street it is. The first function—to light up—is not present yet but will be represented unconsciously in the light (as the saying goes) of social coding. This function and the second function—indicating the name of the street—will therefore overdetermine each other. Moreover, the lamppost's assimilation to the street sign by spatial contiguity will lead it to be assimilated to the film metonymically through the name of the film figuring on the street sign. The lamppost is therefore a signifier condensing the referential (the everyday world we can recognize from the film because we know it by heart) and the discursive (the narrative and representational devices that allow us to see and understand the diegetic world). And, as if by chance, we have a lamppost in the very first shot—and lit, at that.

Tom Conley has rightly insisted on the artificiality of the name Scarlet Street to designate a street meant to exist in New York City, and I have shown in chapter 1 the play of the signifier at work via this title. I would suggest, however, that it is precisely the intertextuality involved that will tend to mask such artificiality, hide it behind our memories of other films and the expectations of the genre. The same goes for Duryea's apparently anachronistic hat, as I have tried to show in chapter 5. The lamppost will tend to give to the film a certain density, which will be referential, with all that entails for the spectator.

Returning home from the office party thrown to celebrate his twenty-five years with the firm, Chris Cross loses his way because he has drunk too much. He asks a policeman to set him in the right direction, which he does. The shot includes a lamppost, although it is not the same street as in the first shot of the film. Immediately afterward he saves Kitty from being beaten up by her pimp, Johnny.

To the criticism that it is perfectly natural to have streets lit at night by lampposts—that is what they are there for—I would reply as I have done on prior occasions: it is a question not of the referential but of the discursive, where any and every element signifies first and foremost in relation to every other element, present or absent. The logic of the text has been in place since the first shot of the credits: the film did not have to begin in that way, but it did, and that now determines everything that follows, in one way or another. Here, again, intertextuality rushes to the rescue of suture: the same world as in *The Woman in the Window* is presented to us, the world of New York as determined by *film noir*. There is nothing that is not motivated, even if the motivation is not evident until much later, which is precisely the role of suture: retrospective coherence, both textual and psychic.

When Kitty realizes Chris is madly in love with her, she and Johnny decide to exploit him. At one point she starts to write him a letter. A fade becomes a high-angle shot of a small square, and the camera cranes down to where Chris and Kitty are having a drink, a camera movement that repeats exactly—except that it cranes down farther—the crane shot contained within the credits. The second crane shot is superfluous from a purely diegetic point of view: there are other ways of introducing us to two characters in a café in a square. To adopt such an approach, however, would be to neglect the logic of the signifier, which is there to suture all elements of the textual activity: as the camera cranes down, we can see, in the background, a lamppost that would have remained hidden without this particular camera movement. The logic of the unconscious project of the text must henceforth be to justify constantly an element introduced to emphasize the text as *activity*, which the text at once sets out to disavow.

What is striking about the textual activity of *Scarlet Street* is that the lamppost is an enunciative device that the enunciation strives to naturalize, along with its own activity. It is the enunciation that dictates the presence of the lamppost, not its importance for one or other of the main characters. Take, for instance, a shot of one of Chris's paintings: it shows us a young woman standing under a lamppost that is lit. The painting predates Chris's meeting with Kitty, which eliminates any interpretation based on his desire for her. Such would be the solution that tends to give a fixed symbolic meaning to an element of a text that is promptly called upon to have a meaning on the level of the enounced rather than to function as part of an overall enunciative strategy. Thus, when Chris tells Kitty that he would like to paint her, he is shown standing beside a painting representing two lampposts.

Though Chris's work tends to be highly stylized, he talks of it in a very special way: he puts on canvas what he thinks and feels, which (con)fuses art and life in favor of a style that represents the artist as individual. Despite moments when the idea of work is insisted upon—the famous shot where the camera pans from a miserable, wilting flower to a beautiful flower consigned to canvas—it is always approached from the standpoint of the artist as someone-having-something-to-say. The film eschews any structured theoretical approach to what art "is."[6]

A final observation here, inasmuch as the film seems to present points in common with both *The Woman in the Window* and *House by the River* beyond those of genre. The reader will have noticed that I referred above to a painting of *two* lampposts and that the lampposts one finds everywhere have an equivalent—a sort of "double"—in the lights present as the decor of homes. Although I stand to be proved wrong, I do not see the double as functioning in the same way as in the two films mentioned, where it was an integral part of a textual activity concerning repetition as a metaphor for the place of the spectator as subject of desire and the whole question of the need to fetishize absence in the form of presence in order to disavow castration. As I have already pointed out, the lampposts have a double function within the text, but this is precisely to disavow the activity that the text does not want to contemplate. As a result the two lampposts within the painting will tend to overdetermine the disavowal and to suture the diegetic world so that the enunciation will be passed off as the enounced.

What is principally at stake is the maintenance of verisimilitude, whereby the heterogeneous elements that occur at various points throughout the text will be naturalized retrospectively, just as they are there to naturalize other elements that have already appeared. Two examples will suffice to show this. When Chris leaves his colleagues at the party, he does so in the company of his old friend Charlie. It is raining and only Chris has an umbrella. The first street scene we have seen—right after the credits—does not include rain: if it had, Charlie would have been armed with an umbrella too. Thus Chris has an umbrella not because it is raining (equals the enounced) but because of the need to motivate the meeting with Kitty (equals the enunciation). Chris accompanies Charlie home because he has an umbrella, then manages to get lost in the labyrinth of streets, which all look alike, as he says to the policeman. Since Kitty lives in a part of town that a solid, upright citizen like Chris would hardly be likely to frequent, he cannot just "happen" on her like that. Therefore the enunciation has to work very hard in order to allow us to take the events "as they come," as if we were dealing with the everyday.

Similar observations can be made about the murder of Kitty: it is far too important a part of the diegesis to occur without motivation as far as the weapon is concerned. So Johnny has already borrowed the ice pick from a restaurant, which ensures it a safe place in the apartment. Even that is not enough: Chris must, in a moment of anger, knock the object from a table to the ground, which enables him to pick it up, which enables him, beside himself (a delightful everyday expression for a multiple subject position), to use it.

Motivation seems to function only as far as the story goes, but it is the enunciation that has taken things in hand. Here, however, the unconscious of the text is also at work, inasmuch as there is a psychic motivation at work. As I have already pointed out, that Chris has more or less openly threatened his wife with scissors when she has threatened to throw out his paintings prepares the murder of Kitty with the ice pick. What is naturalized is the diegetic dimension, but the real psychic dimension is present, albeit repressed. "The objects to which men give most preference, their ideals, proceed from the same perceptions and experiences as the objects which they most abhor" (Freud, SE 14:150). Kitty is assimilated to Chris's wife as her mirror image or double, a subversion of the ideology of the family that is frequent in *film noir* (Harvey 1978). The true status of the enunciation as posing problems for stable subject positions returns momentarily to work against the strategy of motivation-as-suture but is easily recuperated by this device, much more systematically worked out in the text.

The overall force of a text can often be judged by its ability to encourage such strong identification that illogical or impossible elements within the story line can be passed over without difficulty by the spectator. An example in *Scarlet Street* is the way the film motivates the meeting between Kitty and the art critic Janeway: it quite simply does not motivate it, although that is anything but apparent. Aware that Chris has talent, Johnny shows his pictures—unknown to Chris, of course—to a Greenwich Village artist. They are spotted by Janeway, who buys them and decides he must meet the artist. Johnny serves as a go-between, and the next thing we know, Janeway is discussing "her" work with Kitty. All perfectly logical and natural, except for one thing: Johnny did not give Janeway Kitty's name and address but said he would drop in and see him again later. So it is quite impossible for the critic to go to see Kitty off his own bat. Impossible, but in keeping with the laws of verisimilitude, which are there to hide the way the intrigue is put into place in favor of an immediate and apparently nonmediated identification with the elements of the intrigue, first of which are the characters.

The intrigue moves toward closure in the best tradition, and readers will not be surprised if I point out that a lamppost plays a central role in the concluding scenes of the film. The fade is also present. Chris, who has lost his job for embezzling, is now reduced to the life of a tramp, wretched, miserable, and burdened with guilt at having sent Johnny to the electric chair for Kitty's murder.[7] He makes his way painfully along 57th Street among people doing their Christmas shopping; it is night, which takes up and repeats the first shot of the film. A fade shows Chris still moving along the street, except that it is now empty. If it is meant to underline his loneliness, more important is the theme of time passing, for time is central to the diegesis.

The passage of time is present essentially in the concept of getting old without achieving anything, neatly summed up by Chris's sole reward for his twenty-five years of loyal service—a watch. During the party, Chris's boss says, "I'm having the time of my life—and speaking of time . . . ," a remark that prompts him to hand over the watch. It is not the literal meaning of the word that stimulates his memory but a purely figurative meaning in the context of an idiomatic expression. *Time* therefore functions as a signifier.

At one point in the film, Chris tells Charlie that he paints to "kill time." The purpose is quickly clear: to enable the spectator to attach a fixed metaphysical connotation to the word, whatever the context: a wasted life. It does not mean that the word does not change meaning from one context to another. Johnny says he is "wasting his time" with Kitty because she is not bringing him in enough money, and the film certainly does not invite us to approach Johnny on a metaphysical level. However, the theme of waste is there to be linked to the other level of the text, a link ensured by the presence of the word *time,* which functions as a signifier but tends to be reduced to the overall conscious project of how Chris could have added up to something. The repetition of the word is taken up by Chris's imagining Kitty and Johnny repeating their names lovingly to each other from beyond the grave, a repetition that is present through the lamppost in the film's very last sequence. In this way the doubling and repetition that undermined the conscious project of *The Woman in the Window* and *House by the River* by stressing spectatorial desire in order to question it function here rather as elements of suture, given the way in which the lamppost is used throughout the text: its presence brings the other examples of repetition within the same framework of homogenization.

In this way the spectator can be offered an ending in the form of "knowledge": look at what happens when one wastes one's life and does not make the right decision when the "time" is ripe (as Homer, the first husband, did). The ending, presented as inevitable by both the story line and that enunciative ploy that is the lamppost, now becomes the "truth" of the film, that ending which was expected and desired and which rewards the spectator for having waited for it (Barthes 1970, 82). The true psychic signification of an ending in which all is resolved— death—is therefore comfortably transformed into a meaning suffi- ciently credible and acceptable—the criterion of the *vraisemblable*—to be seen as that toward which the film was heading all along.

Conclusion

Concluding is always a difficult and artificial process, a domain where the Symbolic is forced to recognize the Imaginary while at the same time striving to maintain the open-endedness of hesitation in face of the desire for closure. An analysis of *Moonfleet* will, I hope, enable the reader to put in perspective the contradictory strategies at work in the Langian textual system and suggest the significance of its overall thrust.

Moonfleet is one of Lang's rare color films, and it is an aspect of the text's use of color that I want to approach first: gold-tinted fades. Every time one occurs—not all the fades are gold tinted—the image takes on a golden hue at the moment of the fade-out, and this hue is present in the first image of the fade-in. It lasts for a few seconds only, then the image returns to its "natural" color. Given that color is already a technical intervention and an ideological way of representing the world, such tinted fades can hardly be passed off as due to chance or to a technical "mistake." Several normal fades take place at the beginning of the film, and the first manifestation of the gold-tinted fades is when Jeremy Fox receives John Mohune at his home, having thought he had got rid of the boy. The fade links John (first shot) and Fox (second shot). The action takes place at the ancestral home of the Mohunes, which now belongs to Fox, who tries desperately to relive through his memories his love for John's mother, Olivia.

Since the film encourages us to conclude that Fox may be the father of John, I would suggest that we can interpret the fades as an enunciative ploy to underline the force of the links between man and boy: we must remember that the fade sets up an imaginary relationship between two images that corresponds to the need on the part of the spectator to fantasize, to suture heterogeneity and transform it into order, unity, and continuity, which here could be called filiation. John is looking for a father figure and Fox for something to fill the void of the empty mansion. Everything that flows from the phantasm of paternal plenitude—the names Fox and Mohune, the mansion, and the diamond—must bear its mark in some form.

Starting from the reunion between Fox and John at Mohune Manor, the film concerns itself with the relationship between the two. The fades are all gold-tinted, including those that seem to have no link with the two central characters. A look at two instances of the subcode under discussion will show that the system is at work and coherent to its own unconscious logic. Lord and Lady Ashwood are at the center of the first sequence, Fox's mistress at the center of the second. The Ashwoods are part of a crucial decision on Fox's part: he intends to go abroad with the couple to make a fortune and get rid of both John and his mistress by shipping them off to the colonies. Every time he tries to behave like a free man, Fox fails: he just cannot let the boy fend for himself, which suggests an unconscious paternal link, given his unscrupulous behavior elsewhere. We only have to contemplate the gold-tinted interior of the Ashwoods' coach to see the system functioning, for Fox changes his mind in the coach, and that costs him his life. Moreover, Fox wears a gold vest and gold breeches in three scenes: when he appears in the smugglers' lair where John is hiding (see below); when he fights with a smuggler to defend the boy after stating that he, Fox, is responsible for him; and when John, who is trapped in the lair, calls out to Fox to help him in a sequence that, precisely, links the two with a fade from John to Fox, who is on his way to the Ashwoods'. Fox is the center of John's world, and the color gold, whether it be present in a fade or through other aspects of the text such as clothes, functions as the textual system's master signifier, from the first meeting to the final fade-out to the credits at the end, where John says with insistence that Fox will return (we know he is dead) because "He's my friend."

Moonfleet is also particularly rigorous in its use of point of view to place the spectator. After a shot establishing the scene, we see John, who is making his way across the moors of Dorsetshire in England, stop and look offscreen left, his eyes raised. The camera gives us a high-angle shot at this point. Cut to a road sign indicating the way and distance to Moonfleet, shot from a low angle. Once we have been led to see who the character is, we then adopt his point of view and continue to do so in the next shots. John stops at one point to remove his shoe. A noise is heard and he turns to look offscreen right. Cut to a low-angle shot of a statue, which therefore seems to "threaten" us too because we see it from John's point of view. Now we see John's look shift to fix something lower down. Cut to a hand emerging from a tombstone at the foot of the statue, a shot that is important for introducing, in the form of a classical enigma, the smugglers and their lair, which is under the ground around the statue. It also serves to inscribe the spectator into the play of looks within the film. Every cut presents us with a shot of the absent image that drew the attention of the boy, and which we see as he does, given the camera angles employed.

Later in the film, John discovers that the statue hides a secret path to the smugglers' lair and is forced to hide when they suddenly arrive. He climbs up into a little niche in the wall and observes their arrival; he is looking offscreen left. Cut to a long shot of the men entering the cave. They are filmed slightly from above, which corresponds to John's physical position. Thus we find again the same procedure as in the opening shots: an overdetermination of camera angles and point of view. Then the voice of Fox is heard, and we see John's gaze shift again—he has been following the movements of the smugglers within the cave—to the entrance of the lair. Fox enters in a replay of the earlier shot where, from John's point of view, we had seen the smugglers arrive; the organization of the spatial coordinates and the way of seeing them are identical.

In what follows, however, the textual system is obliged to change tactics. Fox has a long discussion with the other smugglers, who follow his orders. There is a clash between ideologies at work here. Fox is the other main character in the film; if the camera stayed with John to maintain a coherent point of view for the spectators, then they would run the risk of finding the sequence boring. Moreover, Fox would remain in the background, which would reduce his "stature" from every point of view. The film must therefore reframe within the point of view set in place in order to enable us to identify with Fox. What is striking about this tactic is that the textual system keeps the two points of view going, each reinforcing the other. It is necessary to cut back to John from time to time, given the importance of his role. So we see him looking, and, every time such a cut occurs, the following shot shows us the smugglers from his point of view. No break is allowed in the functioning of the text. I would suggest that it is here that we can see the logic of the gold-tinted fades at work. They function, as I have shown, to indicate that nothing in the film is outside the logic of the relationship between John and Fox—the logic of the enounced—and that logic now returns on the level of the enunciation: our identification with Fox passes through John's point of view.

Another enunciative device intervenes to strengthen what is already in place, but in such a way that it can be passed off as part of the diegetic world: sounds-off. It was the grating of the tombstone that drew John's attention to the hand emerging from the tomb, and it was Fox's voice that set off the pattern of looks and point of view in the cave. When the smugglers come across John early in the film, they find on him a letter from his mother and are intrigued by the presence in it of the name Jeremy Fox. Suddenly there is heard the sound of a door opening, and all heads turn and look offscreen right. Cut to a man alone, framed in the open door: it is Fox, as if summoned up by his name. The camera tracks back to show us the smugglers staring at him, and we realize that, for a moment, we have seen Fox from their point of view.

The use of "natural" sounds gives a referential density to the diegetic world, with all that implies for the correct functioning of the text. What I have just mentioned in the preceding paragraph about the arrival of Fox shows, however, that we do not identify with this fictional world exclusively through the looks of John Mohune. What is at stake is an enunciative ploy that articulates two shots and the absence that sutures them, placing the spectators in a position of imaginary plenitude and mastery. However, to cut back constantly in a given sequence to the point of view of one character (John) runs the risk of decentering the spectator when other points of view are necessary elsewhere in the film. Let us consider another sequence.

At one point, John goes to Mohune Manor in search of Fox. He opens the great iron gate and walks in awe into the garden. Cut. A slow track forward imitates a person advancing slowly and, because we no longer see John, we are clearly meant to identify with his measured tread, which is crucial for what follows. Gypsy music can be heard as we watch John moving around the garden looking for the source, which is immediately revealed to him and to us: drunken men and dancing gypsy women can be seen in a huge room. Cut to John gazing through the window, his nose pressed against the pane. He is looking offscreen right. Cut to Fox and a gypsy woman who obviously attracts him sexually. But we do not see them from John's point of view, for we are "in" the room and in relative proximity to the couple. The shot is not therefore a simple retake of the shot in the cave, for we are being given information here that is beyond the comprehension of a small boy whose innocence is stressed by the vulgar laughter that follows his remark about "the ladies present" once Fox has admitted him to the room.

The break in one logic of the text has its meaning: Fox thinks he has got rid of the boy, and the film must show him from another point of view in order to set up the hesitation that exists concerning Fox's behavior. This hesitation on the story level is also one on the far more important level of the enunciation, inasmuch as there is a conflict between the need to suture looks and point of view in order to safeguard spectatorial unity and the need to encourage us to interpret the nature of the relationship between the man and the boy. The use of gold-tinted fades means that the only coherent way of carrying out such an act of interpretation is through the various enunciative ploys put in place. Again and again, then, the logic of suture is forced to show its hand so as to ensure its own disavowal.

Let us return to the question of John's purity and innocence, for it is their diegetic importance that has forced the enunciation to accept a gap in its functioning. At the end of the film, Fox, fatally wounded because he has tried to save John and his heritage from Lord Ashwood, manages to hide his wound from the boy and pretends he is leaving temporarily: hence John's conviction in the film's last sequence that Fox will return. Fox and John are together in a hut on the beach where they are hiding. Fox takes his leave and sets off in a rowing boat clearly destined to be his last resting place. Cut to a shot of John inside the hut, looking offscreen right and smiling. The framing is identical to that used when he observes Fox and the gypsy woman, all the more so because we see John looking through the window of the hut. Cut to Fox drifting away. This time, however, he is seen in long shot, clearly from John's point of view. I would suggest that the reason is that John does not know Fox is dying or that the man tried to steal the diamond from him.

This point of view condenses the projects of the textual system and their incoherence and incompatibility. Up till now we have adopted the point of view of a character when we have seen what he sees and interpreted it in the same way. Such is not the case here: we see from John's point of view, but we know full well that Fox will never return, and we therefore enjoy knowledge that the boy cannot grasp. The whole question of identification is thus highlighted as a delusion, a snare—in the fullest Lacanian sense of the *leurre*—to hold us within the classical system of suture while at the same time pretending we are free to see and interpret as we will. We cannot have the same point of view as John on the level of the enounced, but we can on the level of the enunciation, thanks to the *camera*. The great repressed therefore returns, but it has not always been absent except on the mode of disavowal.

When the smugglers realize that John knows all about them, they shut him in a room at the back of their tavern and decide what to do with him: kill him there and then or else tell Fox. Suddenly the local magistrate arrives to search the premises. He moves around, then sweeps to one side the curtain that shuts the tavern off from the small room where John is being kept. John is seated at a table with Ratsey, one of the smugglers. The magistrate expresses surprise that the boy should frequent such individuals, to which Ratsey replies that the boy sees beyond the surface and understands they have kind hearts. The spectator is not duped, but the observation about "seeing below the surface" must be taken as an invitation to reflect on the nature of the image. At the moment when the magistrate speaks, the camera is placed behind him, which means that we see John and Ratsey at the table from a point of view similar to his. When Ratsey replies, the camera is placed behind the table, and we can see that he is holding a knife in the small of John's back. The magistrate can see nothing, and neither could we and the camera, until the point of view changed. Then we can see the magistrate looking without seeing the essential: we see him not seeing. If we see what is going on, it is thanks to the interdependent articulation of the look, the camera, and the point of view.

Thus *Moonfleet,* in a classical way pushed to its logical conclusion, has the spectator adopt now the point of view of a character, now the point of view of the camera without fully succeeding in hiding from the spectators that the former point of view is impossible except through the presence of the latter. This presence is at once hidden and admitted, as the sequence just analyzed shows, a disavowal that enables the spectators to function according to the primary logic of the system: the masking of the enunciation. Let us go back to the sequence where John waves goodbye to Fox on the beach, thinking he is leaving only to return for him later. The spectators both share John's point of view within the film (thus becoming subject of the *énoncé*) and stand outside his point of view because they know the dying Fox will not return, and so they become subjects of the *énonciation*. Hence they attain a subject position in keeping both with the true situation in the film and with their real status as spectators. But the latter dimension will be repressed in turn, because they will reduce the question of point of view as structured by the enunciation to a question of point of view as structured by the enounced. They will understand why John is led astray, but they will fail to understand what ploy is functioning to enable them to grasp their true subject position. Truth will be grasped as a dimension of the diegetic world, allowing the truth as being determined by the enunciation—by desire and the unconscious—to be elided.

The situation can be seen as a *mise en abyme* of the spectatorial quest for the "good object," the maintaining of the right balance between belief and knowledge, which is the purpose of the pleasure principle. The "good object" is found in the "body" of the text, which is a displacement, for the "good object" sought—and, by the very nature of things, never recovered—is the mother's body. The articulation of belief and knowledge involved in every such instance, filmic or other, is also the articulation of desire and the Law. If the Law in the case of the mother's body is the taboo on incest, as Lacan claims (1986, 82–83), then the "good object" can be attained only at the moment of birth. As Freud has shown, to be born is to be on the road to death, by the very nature of every living organism. The attaining of the "good object" is thus also the moment of death, the "death" of the narrative, the resolution of all problems, conflicts, and enigmas in the film's ending, happy or not.

The spectators know Fox will not return, but nevertheless something in them believes he will, that "something" which leads them to identify with John, to believe that Fox will return, and to believe that the story will continue after "The End" *despite* knowledge to the contrary. If the Langian textual system ultimately functions this way, it is because it had no choice, and the exceptional merit of the system is to have shown the unpleasure that ensues when the balance I have so often mentioned is jeopardized. If *Beyond a Reasonable Doubt* signed Lang's death warrant as far as Hollywood was concerned, it was because the film refused to play the game, showing explicitly what would await the main character we have identified with if the film were to continue: death, which is precisely what any narrative exists to avoid and to placate. The objective "to avoid and to placate" sums up disavowal, inasmuch as one need not placate something that one has avoided, except on the level of *knowing* that one has to placate what one *believes* one has avoided. The realism of Lang's cinema is beyond any reality that spectators can contemplate. They would like Fox to return to the very place they left him and he left John, but that desire can never be satisfied. The spectators carry on looking with every new film, but, like the sack Stephen pursues in *House by the River,* what they are looking for is never at the "right" place and what they do find is not what they were looking for.

Lacan's reading of Freud led him to claim that the belief that the object was lost arises *after the event* (after "finding" it) to justify the search being undertaken in the first place. This would seem to indicate that imaginary possession of the filmic text can never lead to the satisfaction of desire, because what is being possessed does not necessarily correspond to anything lost. Going to the cinema is a manifestation of a psychic structure articulated around loss or absence, which loss or absence determines every human act that is a striving for plenitude. Not finding what one expected or was looking for or coming across something else in its place can be seen everywhere in Lang, even if only fleetingly: here a mistaken identity, there a look offscreen that reveals nothing; here a front-page headline that is revealed as an unwitting lie at the very moment the truth seemed absolute; there a newsreel that reveals something that is not there. Each and every one of such textual manifestations of hesitation is a metaphor for an unconscious awareness that the object sought is a *leurre* or delusion, with all that implies for the ideologies of plenitude, fixed subject positions and self-knowledge.

Commenting on Louis Lumière's remark that "the film subjects I choose are the proof that I only wished to reproduce life," Stephen Heath has said that "one has the right to demand to know where this 'life' comes from" and has pointed out that the images in question are "a reproduction of the image of life" (Heath 1976b, 253–54). It means quite simply that to train the camera on X rather than on Y is not chance but a decision ideologically determined by the social role of X or Y, that the subject of the enunciation is already coded to see the subject matter in a certain way—in other words, has unconsciously received an image of it from elsewhere, hence from the Other, ideology being the unconscious representation of the discourse of the Other.

Film is thus the *representation of a representation.* Lacan, commenting on the pleasure principle, has stated that it is the hallucinatory representation of a need that has already found a hallucinatory satisfaction (Lacan 1986, 164). This, I would suggest, helps one to understand the repetition compulsion involved in film-going and the search for plenitude through identification and narrative resolution (equals satisfaction of desire). The image represents for the spectator the realization of a need (for plenitude, to find the "lost" object) that has already been satisfied. The spectator wishes to live out endlessly the repetition of this satisfaction. The constant manifestations of "disappointment"—to avoid a more loaded term—on the part of critics, faced with the systematic refusal by the Langian textual system to apply transparently, according to received ideology, the codes of representation, must be seen in this light.[1] Ultimately it means that director, spectator, and critic are to be approached as a "function" of the text rather than its "foundation" (Weber 1987, xix).

If Lang's American films are "about" something, then it is that.

Filmography

This filmography includes all Lang's American films, but only those discussed are followed by credits and a summary. I have used the filmographies in Eisner 1976 and Jensen 1969.

Fury (1936)

Screenplay: Bartlett Cormack and Fritz Lang, based on a story by Norman Krasna. Photography: Joseph Ruttenberg. Art Directors: Cedric Gibbons, William Horning, and Edwin Willis. Editor: Frank Sullivan. Music: Franz Waxman. Producer: Joseph L. Mankiewicz. An M.G.M. production. 90 minutes.

Players: Spencer Tracy (Joe Wilson), Sylvia Sidney (Katherine Grant), Walter Abel (district attorney), Bruce Cabot (Kirby Dawson), Edward Ellis (sheriff), Walter Brennan ("Bugs" Meyer, the deputy), George Walcott (Tom Wilson), Frank Albertson (Charlie Wilson), Arthur Stone (Durkin), Howard Hickman (governor), Jonathan Hale (defense attorney), Leila Bennett (Edna Hooper).

Joe Wilson is wrongly accused of belonging to a gang of kidnappers and is locked up in the jail of a small town. Rabble-rousers encourage the townspeople to demand that Wilson be handed over to them. When the sheriff refuses, the crowd, out of control, sets fire to the prison. Unknown to everyone except his brothers, Joe escapes from the flames and decides to get his revenge by keeping silent when the state charges twenty-two citizens with murder. They are all condemned, but Joe's fiancée, Katherine, has discovered he is alive and convinces him of the need to appear in court and save the citizens from being executed.

You Only Live Once (1937)

Screenplay: Graham Baker, based on a story by Gene Towne. Photography: Leon Shamroy. Art Director: Alexander Toluboff. Editor: Daniel Mandell. Music: Alfred Newman. Producer: Walter Wanger. A Walter–United Artists production. 85 minutes.

Players: Henry Fonda (Eddie Taylor), Sylvia Sidney (Joan Graham), Barton MacLane (Stephen Whitney), Jean Dixon (Bonnie Graham), William Gargan (Father Dolan), Jerome Cowan (Dr. Hill), Warren Hymer (Muggsy), John Wray (warden), Jonathan Hale (district attorney), Ward Bond (guard), Wade Boteler (policeman).

When he leaves prison, Eddie Taylor cannot find work, despite all his efforts; nobody will let him forget his criminal past. Circumstantial evidence links him to a bank robbery during which a murder was committed. He gives himself up, but when he realizes he cannot clear himself, he escapes from prison, killing a priest in the process. He and his fiancée, Joan, now on the run, are forced to steal to survive until they are both shot down by the police.

You and Me (1938)

Screenplay: Virginia Van Upp, based on a story by Norman Krasna. Photography: Charles Lang, Jr. Art Directors: Hans Dreier and Ernst Fegté. Editor: Paul Weatherwax. Music: Kurt Weill. Lyrics: Sam Coslow. Producer: Fritz Lang. A Paramount production. 90 minutes.

Players: Sylvia Sidney (Helen), George Raft (Joe Dennis), Robert Cummings (Jim), Roscoe Karns (Cuffy), Barton MacLane (Mickey), Harry Carey (Mr. Morris), Warren Hymer (Gimpy), Guinn Williams (Taxi), Cecilia Cunningham (Mrs. Morris).

The managing director of a large New York department store, Mr. Morris, has hired a number of former criminals in order to give them a second chance in life. Among them are Helen and Joe, who fall in love and marry. Joe contacts his old gang when he learns that his wife too has a criminal past, and the gang decides to rob the store. Helen tips off Mr. Morris and manages to convince the men that crime does not pay. Joe returns home and soon after a child is born.

The Return of Frank James (1940)

Western Union (1941)

Man Hunt (1941)

Screenplay: Dudley Nichols, based on the novel *Rogue Male* by Geoffrey Household. Photography: Arthur Miller. Art Directors: Richard Day and Wiard Ihnen. Editor: Allen McNeil. Music: Alfred Newman. Associate Producer: Kenneth MacGowan. A 20th Century Fox production. 102 minutes.

Players: Walter Pidgeon (Captain Alan Thorndike), George Sanders (Quive-Smith), Joan Bennett (Jerry), John Carradine (Mr. Jones), Roddy McDowall (Vaner), Ludwig Stossel (doctor), Heather Thatcher (Lady Risborough), Frederick Worlock (Lord Risborough), Eily Malyon (postmistress).

Captain Thorndike is arrested by the Gestapo, who think he was trying to assassinate Hitler, which he denies. They want Thorndike to admit he was working for the British government, but he refuses, even under torture, and manages to escape back to England, where he is tracked down by Quive-Smith and his henchmen. Cornered, Thorndike succeeds in killing Quive-Smith and returns to Germany with the firm intention of killing Hitler.

Hangmen Also Die (1943)

Screenplay: John Wexley, based on an original story by Bertolt Brecht and Fritz Lang. Photography: James Wong Howe. Art Director:

William Darling. Editor: Gene Fowler, Jr. Music: Hanns Eisler. Producers: Fritz Lang and Arnold Pressburger. A United Artists–Arnold production. 130 minutes (for the print available).

Players: Brian Donlevy (Dr. Svoboda), Walter Brennan (Professor Novotny), Anne Lee (Mascha Novotny), Alexander Granach (Gruber), Gene Lockhart (Czaka), Dennis O'Keefe (fiancé), Nana Bryant (Mrs. Novotny), Billy Roy (brother), Margaret Wycherly (aunt), Hans von Twardowsky (Heydrich), Jonathan Hale (Debic), Lionel Stander (cabby), Sarah Padden (Mrs. Dvorak), George Irving (Necval), Ludwig Donath, Tonio Selwart, and Reinhold Schünzel (Gestapo).

The assassination of Heydrich by the Czech Resistance triggers a wave of repression on the part of the Nazis. The person responsible for the killing, Dr. Svoboda, manages to persuade Miss Novotny, who knows he is the assassin, to help him and the Resistance by pretending to be his mistress. Inspector Gruber, who is working with the Nazis, does not believe their story and finally unmasks the whole plot. But Svoboda and a colleague kill him, and the Resistance manages to convince the Gestapo that the double agent Czaka assassinated Heydrich. Czaka is shot down by the Gestapo, and the Resistance against the Nazis continues.

The Ministry of Fear (1943)

Screenplay: Seton Miller, based on the novel of the same title by Graham Greene. Photography: Henry Sharp. Art Directors: Hans Dreier and Hal Pereira. Editor: Archie Marshek. Music: Victor Young. Producer: Seton Miller. A Paramount production. 84 minutes.

Players: Ray Milland (Stephen Neale), Marjorie Reynolds (Carla), Carl Esmond (Willi), Dan Duryea (Cost), Hillary Brooke (Mrs. Bellane), Percy Waram (Inspector Prentice), Alan Napier (Dr. Forrester), Erskine Sanford (private detective), Eustace Wyatt (blind man), Mary Field (Mrs. Penteel), Byron Foulger (Newby).

Stephen Neale is released from an asylum where he had been incarcerated for helping his dying wife to commit suicide. By accident, he wins at a garden party a cake containing important microfilm destined for a member of a Nazi spy ring. Framed for a murder by the Nazis, he finds himself on the run and is helped by a young refugee, Carla. They are finally caught by Inspector Prentice, who explains what is happening and gets them to help him break up the ring, controlled by Dr. Forrester, who works for the British government. Cornered by Forrester and his henchmen, Neale and Clara are rescued by Prentice.

The Woman in the Window (1944)

Screenplay: Nunnally Johnson, based on the novel *Once off Guard* by J. H. Wallis. Photography: Milton Krasner. Art Director: Duncan Cramer. Editors: Marjorie Johnson and Gene Fowler, Jr. Music: Arthur Lang. Producer: Nunnally Johnson. An International Pictures and Christie production. 99 minutes.

Players: Edward G. Robinson (Professor Wanley), Joan Bennett (Alice Reed), Raymond Massey (district attorney), Dan Duryea (bodyguard), Edmund Breon (Dr. Barkstone), Arthur Loft (Mazard), Thomas E. Jackson (police inspector), Dorothy Peterson (Mrs. Wanley).

See chapter 5 for a summary of the film.

Scarlet Street (1945)

Screenplay: Dudley Nichols, based on the novel *La Chienne* by Georges de la Fouchardière. Photography: Milton Krasner. Art Directors: Alexander Golitzen and John Goodman. Editor: Arthur Hilton. Paintings by John Decker. Music: Hans Salter. Producer: Fritz Lang. A Universal-Diana production. 103 minutes.

Players: Edward G. Robinson (Christopher Cross), Joan Bennett (Kitty March), Dan Duryea (Johnny), Vladimir Sokoloff (artist), Rosalind Ivan (Adele Cross), Jess Barker (Janeway), Charles Kemper (Homer).

Christopher Cross, an accountant with a New York firm, paints in his spare time to escape the monotony of his work. His wife's hostility to his painting and her nostalgia for her former husband, Homer, lead Cross to start an affair with a young prostitute he has met by chance. Her pimp and lover, Johnny, encourages her to exploit Cross by passing his paintings off as hers, since an art critic has shown admiration for them. When Cross discovers what is going on, he murders Kitty, and Johnny is executed for the crime. Fired for embezzling, Cross becomes a tramp while his paintings, still considered to be Kitty's, sell for ever-larger sums.

Cloak and Dagger (1946)

Screenplay: Albert Maltz, Ring Lardner, Jr., based on an original story by Boris Ingster and John Larkin. Photography: Sol Polito. Art Director: Max Parker. Editor: Christian Nyby. Producer: Milton Sperling. A Warner Brothers–United States Pictures production. 105 minutes.

Players: Gary Cooper (Alvah Jasper), Lilli Palmer (Gina), Robert Alda (Pinkie), Vladimir Sokoloff (Dr. Polda), J. Edward Bromberg (Trenk), Dan Seymour (Marsoli), Marc Lawrence (Luigi).

Professor Jasper is asked by the U.S. government to go to Europe to find out whether certain important scientists who have disappeared are helping the Nazis to build an atomic bomb. In Italy, Jasper works with the Resistance, which helps him get Dr. Polda, one of the scientists concerned, out of the country and over to the United States.

Secret beyond the Door (1947)

Screenplay: Sylvia Richards, based on the story "Museum Piece No. 13" by Rufus King. Photography: Stanley Cortez. Production Designer: Max Parker. Editor: Arthur Hilton. Music: Miklos Rozsa. Producers: Fritz Lang and Walter Wanger. A Universal-Diana production. 98 minutes.

Players: Michael Redgrave (Mark Lamphere), Joan Bennett (Celia), Ann Revere (Caroline Lamphere), Barbara O'Neill (Miss Robey), Paul Cavanagh (Rick), James Seay (Bob), Mark Dennis (David).

Following the death of her elder brother, Celia Barrett goes to Mexico, where she meets, falls in love with, and marries Mark Lamphere, an architect. On the first night of the honeymoon she locks the door of their bedroom and is increasingly frightened at the effect this has on Mark. They return to the States and go to live at the Lamphere family home, where Celia makes the acquaintance of Mark's sister, his son, and the boy's tutor, Miss Robey. Celia becomes increasingly suspicious of Mark as he hides things from her, especially the contents of Room 7: his hobby is collecting rooms where acts of violence and passion have taken place. Celia manages to gain access to the room and realizes she is to be the victim of Mark's madness. However, she stops him by revealing the secret of his fear of locked doors, and the couple return to Mexico to take up where they had left off.

House by the River (1949)

Screenplay: Mel Dinelli, based on the novel of the same title by A. P. Herbert. Photography: Edward Cronjager. Art Director: Boris Leven. Editor: Arthur Hilton. Music: George Antheil. Producer: Howard Welsch. A Republic Pictures production. 88 minutes.

Players: Louis Hayward (Stephen Byrne), Jane Wyatt (Marjorie), Lee Bowman (John), Dorothy Patrick (Emily), Ann Shoemaker (Mrs. Ambrose), Howland Chamberlain (district attorney), Will Wright (police inspector).

For a summary of the film, see chapter 6.

An American Guerrilla in the Philippines (1950)

Rancho Notorious (1952)

Screenplay: Daniel Taradash, based on the novel *Gunsight Whitman* by Sylvia Richards. Photography (Technicolor): Hal Mohr. Editor: Otto Ludwig. Music: Emil Newman. Songs: Ken Darby. Producer: Howard Welsch. A Fidelity-RKO production. 89 minutes.

Players: Marlene Dietrich (Altar Keane), Arthur Kennedy (Vern Haskell), Mel Ferrer (Frenchy Fairmont), Gloria Henry (Beth Haskell), John Raven (Chuck-a-luck dealer), Jack Elam (Geary), George Reeves (Wilson), Frank Ferguson (Preacher), Francis MacDonald (Harbin), Dan Seymour (Comanche Paul), John Doucette (Whitey), Stuart Randall (Starr).

Vern Haskell, a farmer, goes in search of the outlaws who have raped and murdered his wife. He finally discovers they are part of a band led by Altar Keane. Haskell's obsession with revenge and the fact that he cannot be sure of the identity of the killers lead to the death of everyone. At the end, Haskell and Fairmont, Altar Keane's lover, ride away for the final showdown.

Clash by Night (1952)

The Blue Gardenia (1953)

Screenplay: Charles Hoffman, based on a story by Vera Caspary. Photography: Nicholas Musuraca. Art Director: Daniel Hall. Editor: Edward Mann. Music: Raoul Kraushaar. Song: Bob Russell and Lester Lee. Arranged by Nelson Riddle. Producer: Alex Gottlieb. A Warner Brothers–Blue Gardenia production. 90 minutes.

Players: Anne Baxter (Norah Larkin), Richard Conte (Casey Mayo), Ann Sothern (Crystal), Raymond Burr (Harry Prebble), Jeff Donnell (Sally), Ruth Storey (Rose Miller), George Reeves (Police Captain Haynes), Nat "King" Cole (himself).

Norah, a young switchboard operator, is one of the women pursued by a local Don Juan, Harry Prebble. He takes her back to his apartment after dinner and tries to take advantage of her drunken state to seduce her. She defends herself with a poker but remembers nothing of the incident the next day. Learning that Prebble has been murdered, she thinks she is the murderess. An unscrupulous journalist, Casey Mayo, collaborates with the police to find the killer by writing open letters to her in his paper. Norah falls into the trap, but the real murderess is discovered: a woman who was trying to force Prebble to marry her.

The Big Heat (1953)

Screenplay: Sydney Boehm, based on the novel of the same title by William McGivern. Photography: Charles Lang, Jr. Art Director: Robert Peterson. Editor: Charles Nelson. Music: Daniele Amfitheatrof. Producer: Robert Arthur. A Columbia production. 89 minutes.

Players: Glenn Ford (Dave Bannion), Gloria Grahame (Debby Marsh), Jocelyn Brando (Katie Bannion), Alexander Scourby (Mike Lagana), Lee Marvin (Vince Stone), Jeanette Nolan (Bertha Duncan),

Peter Whitney (Tierney), Willis Bouchey (Lieutenant Wilkes), Adam Williams (Larry Gordon), Howard Wendell (Commissioner Higgins), Dorothy Green (Lucy Chapman).

Dave Bannion, a policeman, is prevented from taking the necessary measures against organized crime because of the close links between gangsters, politicians, and members of the police force. His constant clashes with his superiors and his stubborn attempts to bring Mike Lagana, a gangster, to justice lead to an attempt on his life that kills his wife instead. Bannion resigns and wages war on the gangsters with the help of Debby, mistress of Vince Stone, Lagana's chief henchman. Thanks to her, Bannion finds the evidence necessary to convict Lagana and returns triumphantly to the force as a hero.

Human Desire (1954)

Moonfleet (1955)

Screenplay: Jan Lustig and Margaret Fitts, based on the novel of the same title by J. Meade Falkner. Photography (Eastmancolor and Cinemascope): Robert Planck. Art Directors: Cedric Gibbons and Hans Peters. Editor: Albert Akst. Music: Miklos Rozsa. Producer: John Houseman. An M.G.M. production. 87 minutes.

Players: Stewart Granger (Jeremy Fox), George Sanders (Lord Ashwood), Joan Greenwood (Lady Ashwood), Viveca Lindfors (Mrs. Minton), Jon Whiteley (John Mohune), Liliane Montevecchi (gypsy dancer), Melville Cooper (Ratsey), Sean McClory (Elzevir Block), Alan Napier (Parson Glennie), John Hoyt (Magistrate Maskew), Donna Corcoran (Grace), Jack Elam (Damen), Dan Seymour (Hull), Ian Wolfe (Tewkesbury), Lester Matthews (Major Hennishaw), Frank Ferguson (coachman).

Young John Mohune goes to Moonfleet in search of Jeremy Fox bearing a letter from his dead mother, Olivia, Fox's former mistress. Fox, a rich and cynical man, lives off smuggling. Despite himself, he is drawn to the boy and decides to look after him. By chance, Fox and John stumble on the hiding place of an enormous diamond that had belonged to John's ancestors. At this point, Fox decides to steal it and get rid of the boy.

However, he changes his mind and is fatally wounded in a fight with his partner in crime, Lord Ashwood. Fox sails away to his death, leaving behind John, convinced that the man will return for him soon.

While the City Sleeps (1956)

Screenplay: Casey Robinson, based on the novel *The Bloody Spur* by Charles Einstein. Photography: Ernest Laszlo. Art Director: Carroll Clark. Editor: Gene Fowler, Jr. Music: Herschel Burke Gilbert. Producer: Bert Friedlob. An RKO production. 100 minutes.

Players: Dana Andrews (Edward Mobley), Ida Lupino (Mildred Donner), Rhonda Fleming (Dorothy Kyne), George Sanders (Mark Loving), Vincent Price (Walter Kyne), Thomas Mitchell (John Day Griffith), Howard Duff (Lieutenant Kaufman), Sally Forrest (Nancy Liggett), James Craig (Harry Kritzer), John Drew Barrymore (Robert Manners), Mae Marsh (Mrs. Manners), Vladimir Sokoloff (George Pilski), Robert Warwick (Amos Kyne).

A murderer is terrorizing New York by killing young women and leaving messages in lipstick in their apartments. The owner of the *New York Sentinel* takes a personal interest in the affair, but, after his sudden death, his weak and unscrupulous son uses the murders as a form of bait for his top journalists: the person who solves the killings will become manager of the newspaper. One of the interested parties, Ed Mobley, goes as far as to use his own fiancée, Sally, to trap the killer, a disturbed adolescent. The youth is apprehended, but Mobley prefers to resign and get married rather than continue to work for Kyne.

Beyond a Reasonable Doubt (1956)

Screenplay: Douglas Morrow, based on his original story. Photography: William Snyder. Art Director: Carroll Clark. Editor: Gene Fowler, Jr. Music: Herschel Burke Gilbert. Producer: Bert Friedlob. An RKO production. 80 minutes.

Players: Dana Andrews (Tom Garrett), Joan Fontaine (Susan Spencer), Sidney Blackmer (Austin Spencer), Philip Bourneuf (district attorney), Barbara Nichols (Dolly), Shepperd Strudwick (Wilson), Arthur Franz

(Hale), Edward Binns (Lieutenant Kennedy), Dan Seymour (Greco), Rusty Lane (judge).

Austin Spencer, a newspaper proprietor, uses his paper to wage a campaign against capital punishment. To prove his case, he persuades his future son-in-law, Tom Garrett, to allow himself to be framed for the murder of a dancer that is making headlines. Garrett is duly tried, convicted, and sentenced to death. On his way to hand over the evidence to the police in order to show that Garrett is innocent, Spencer is killed in an automobile accident. Just before the execution, the district attorney discovers in Spencer's papers proof that Garrett was deliberately framed in order to show that the law can make a mistake. At the same time, Garrett makes a slip of the tongue that proves he knew the dancer long before—they were married—and that he is in fact the killer. About to be reprieved, Garrett now returns to his cell to await execution.

Notes

Preface

1. For an excellent historical survey and analysis of the problems involved in attempting to articulate Marxism and psychoanalysis, see Eagleton 1985.

2. As Frank Lentricchia has put it, "to proceed with the illusion of purity is to situate oneself on the margin of history, as the possessor of a unique truth disengaged from history's flow" (Lentricchia 1983, 36). He follows this up (37) with a remarkable observation by Kenneth Burke (in 1935!) about the propagandist. "As a propagandizer, it is not his work to convince the convinced, but to plead with the unconvinced, which requires him to use their vocabulary, their values, their symbols, insofar as this is possible." Could not we today see this as an invitation to challenge from within the dominant codes of representation structuring Hollywood?

3. Another film is plagiarized by *Young Dillinger,* Don Siegel's *Baby-Face Nelson* (1957). Here it is a question of reshooting a sequence, the one where Nelson ambushes rivals on a staircase and shoots them down. The idea is there, but nothing else: what was brilliantly staged by Siegel through judicious placing of the camera and rapid cutting is just another botched collection of images in Morse's hands.

4. For an analysis of the sequence in question, see chap. 2, section 1.

5. In an attempt to avoid unnecessary ambiguity, I should add that Lang's concern with other matters does not necessarily exclude a point of view on the apparent subject matter of a given film. The anti-Nazi films are a case in point. The sequence in *Hangmen Also Die* where the Gestapo man tortures the crippled and arthritic Mrs. Dvorak by forcing her to bend down and pick up the back of the broken chair she leans on is one of the most chilling and effective

denunciations of the totalitarian personality one could hope to find. Lang's camera fixes Mrs. Dvorak and forces us to contemplate her suffering. The point of view is unambiguous: we either consume images or we take a stance. There is more to social comment than wringing one's hands over the kitchen sink.

6. See Stephen Heath's analysis of a sequence in *Suspicion* (1976a, 68–72).

1 Preliminaries and Polemics

1. Richard Lester's film *The Bed-Sitting Room* (1969) provides a similar example. A character who is moving house is asked by a moving man carrying a picture where he wants it to be hung. The owner points to an empty wall, "Hang it there." The moving man promptly hangs the picture on the outstretched finger. Which reminds me of a Chinese proverb: "When a man points to the moon, an idiot looks at his finger." The place of the idiot is occupied by those film critics who take the sign for the referent.

2. One of Lacan's seminars deals extensively with this problem, the starting point being the memoirs of President Schreber (Lacan 1981).

3. "The Wolfman" case is recorded in SE 17:7–122.

4. This notion is constantly stressed in a filmic context by Christian Metz. See in particular Metz 1977b, 220–29.

5. A caricature of this desire—in a mode of deliberate parody—is the sequence in *Bedazzled* (Stanley Donen, 1967) where the Devil subjects readers to a fate worse than death (as the revealing expression has it): tearing from all copies of Agatha Christie novels the final page containing the identity of the murderer and the resolution of all enigmas. The ultimate unpleasure.

6. Like Lentricchia, I use *Truth* to designate something that is taken for granted, "goes without saying" (the ideological thrust of this expression cannot be too much insisted on). Like Lacan, I use *Truth* to designate those (rare) moments when the subject is brought face to face with its real status (see below, chapter 5, for a discussion of Wanley's sudden realization of this Truth through his parapraxes).

7. A pleasure due in large part to the dimension of repetition inherent to genre. As Lacan has said, we are always happy to find again what has already been represented, and he adds that, for Freud, this is how we create our world of objects (Lacan 1981, 121).

8. I owe this observation to Sam Weber. The texts for such an undertaking are ready and waiting: Hector Babenco's *Kiss of the Spider Woman,* Martin Scorsese's *After Hours,* and, especially, David Lynch's *Blue Velvet.* The last film, which I would suggest should be seen as a sort of remake of *Vertigo,* is all but incomprehensible if one takes it simply as an example of the *fantastique* instead of paying attention to the psychic and ideological functions of the Isabella Rossellini character and the hero's girl friend. The two young women represent the realization of two "scripts" for the hero, played off against each other in a reflection on desire, representation, and closure, both narrative and ideological (think of the final sequence, where the totally unrealistic presence of Rossellini challenges the *Peyton Place* yearnings of the hero). A profoundly political film,

Blue Velvet can show the way to an opening-out of narrative studies in the 1980s, and those who would reduce narrative to its sole "deconstructive" aspects and swear only by Jean-Luc Godard, Straub and Huillet, and Michael Snow are doomed to be by-passed by History. A displacement of the center of interest is necessary, together with, at the same time, care not to neglect the gains of the 1970s.

9. See Kaplan 1978.

10. See my comments on *The Woman in the Window* (chapter 5) and *Scarlet Street* (chapter 8) for the roles of hats and lampposts respectively.

11. Given the social elements present in Lang's first three films, one could perhaps see them as belonging to a tradition represented by such works as *20,000 Years in Sing Sing* (Michael Curtiz, 1932) and *I Am a Fugitive from a Chain Gang* (Mervyn LeRoy, 1932).

12. Blake Edwards's extraordinary *Darling Lili* (1969) met with the same hostile incomprehension.

13. I am anticipating here by referring to the double, a question I analyze in detail in chapter 5.

14. If one applied Jensen's criteria generally, the worst Hollywood director would be Josef von Sternberg. No comment.

15. Arguably, Losey's most far-reaching analysis of the relations among class, sex, and money in British society was *The Go-Between* (1971). Why did this film go down so well? Firstly, Losey had become (generally to his artistic detriment) the darling of the smart set (he was Giscard's favorite director, not something easy to live down and something no self-respecting artist would want to live up to). Secondly, the style adopted in the 1960s fitted in, superficially, with the dominant notions of what cinema, especially art-house cinema, was. Thirdly, the onslaught of the *Movie* team, notably the work of Robin Wood, had made it more difficult to continue to ignore certain directors and to trumpet so loudly the merits of philistinism.

16. Clearly, the killing of Kitty with an ice pick is a displaced murder of Cross's wife, whom he had earlier threatened with scissors.

17. Another example is *The Blue Gardenia*. For an admirable analysis and defense of this film, see Kaplan 1978.

18. The crucial changes in point of view imposed on the spectator within shot 4 were missing from the print of the film, apparently the most complete available, shown at the Edinburgh Film Festival in 1975.

19. Francis Courtade, who has also committed an appalling book on Lang, denounces the way Lang evokes the streets of Prague in a studio (Courtade 1963, 64). Doubtless he would have been happier if Lang and his crew had gone to film in the heart of war-torn Europe.

20. It is for this reason that I would take issue with Robin Wood over his otherwise fine presentation of Lang. He sees the logic of the text as being the logic of the creator (Wood 1980, 603), thus centering the argument on Lang rather than on the signifier. Despite his admirable insistence on framing, off-screen, and point of view, Wood ultimately sees this as a conscious choice on Lang's part, which, I would maintain, avoids the real issue.

2 Aspects of Looking: On with the Show

1. I have analyzed the implications of Powell's film elsewhere: see Humphries 1979.

2. In *Scarlet Street* a close-up of a hat is followed by a track to the left, which reveals the hat's owner, lying on a bed.

3. That the hat is a signifier can be seen from the way verbal and visual elements overdetermine each other. Thus Taylor's refusal to return to a life of crime elicits the following jibe from a fellow prisoner: "Lay off the high hat, Taylor—you're still one of the boys."

4. Just how complex this issue can become is evident from the articulation of looks around the portrait in *The Woman in the Window* (see chapter 5).

5. A perfect example in Lang: the way the spectator spies on the maid Emily in *House by the River* (see chapter 6).

6. In very special cases, spectators are informed of such manipulation, but it is done to make it seem exceptional and to encourage them to be fascinated by it, which just keeps the machine going. An obvious example is journalistic discourse surrounding Hitchcock's films and the director's remarkable exploitation of it.

7. For a full discussion of suture and the writing on it, see chapter 8.

8. This could be seen as a working out of an element ideologically reversed in *The Woman in the Window,* in which it is the "dangerous" and "enigmatic" female who makes the first advances, thus becoming responsible on the conscious level of the text for the unconscious of the text: that it is male desire that triggers everything, as the textual system reveals perfectly (see chapter 5). Despite recuperation elsewhere, *The Blue Gardenia* is a most interesting film from a feminist standpoint, as E. Ann Kaplan has shown in detail (1978).

9. André Bazin reacted this way to a shot in *Les Enfants Terribles,* as Stephen Heath has pointed out (1977a, 11).

10. *Cat People, I Walked with a Zombie, The Leopard Man,* all made in the period 1942–43.

11. Perhaps the most remarkable use of a portrait in a Hollywood film is that of the patriarch of the Hadley family in Douglas Sirk's *Written on the Wind* (1956), inasmuch as it condenses family, sex, money, capitalism, and an entire ideology of representation. Since Lang was not interested in the family and had a negative view of humanity, it would be foolish to expect to find such a portrait in his work. What makes Sirk's use of the portrait exceptional is the articulation of a Freudian analysis of the family and a Marxist analysis of capitalism, unique (?) in a Hollywood movie. As Thomas Elsaesser has nicely put it, the articulation shows us "where Freud left his Marx in the American home" (Elsaesser 1972, 11).

12. A quick check list of the most obvious examples: Huston's *Maltese Falcon,* Preminger's *Laura, Fallen Angel,* and *Angel Face,* John Stahl's *Leave Her to Heaven,* John Brahm's *Locket, The Killers* (both the Robert Siodmak and the Don Siegel versions), Jacques Tourneur's *Out of the Past,* Welles's *Lady from Shanghai.* I propose an analysis of *Mildred Pierce* in my opening remarks of chapter 3 and a reading of the portrait in *Laura* when discussing *The Woman in*

the Window in chapter 5. The Oedipal dimension of *The Big Heat* is to be compared with that presented extensively in Raoul Walsh's *White Heat* and Robert Aldrich's *Grissom Gang.*

13. Chris is unable to explain what he is doing with his paintings, and his desire to paint could be attributed to having a tyrannical wife: it is the only way he can assert himself. An artist says of his work that it has "a certain . . . something," a remark hardly conducive to analysis. An art critic admires his work, which makes it respectable.

3 Belief, Knowledge, Truth: The Case of the Unwary Investigator

1. Only the spectators know that Wilson is innocent and that the suspicions of the sheriff have been aroused by a simple coincidence.

2. I analyze the very special "realistic" nature of the images in the film in chapter 5.

3. The "logic" of this argument is owed to Georges Allembert (1957).

4. We are told that the killer was wearing "a dark brown hat." In an earlier draft of my book, I used my own eyes in a very special way by stating that the district attorney wears "a dark brown hat" when ordering Garrett's arrest. What is wrong with that? Simply that the film is in black and white, which means that I "passed through" the image (the enunciation) in order to reach the "truth" of the dialogue (the enounced).

5. I have referred to the editor as the subject of the enunciation, which he is when taking the photographs, but this status is *within the enounced.* He thus presents himself as existing at one and the same time on the two levels, which, as I have shown, constitutes the imaginary subject position *par excellence.* Given the film's realism, the enunciation disappears in favor of the enounced, already reinforced by the *doxa* as concerns the nature of the image.

6. "Snare" is one way of translating Lacan's term *leurre,* where the subject is led or leads itself astray as to its real position. In other contexts one could translate by "delusion."

7. The attitude of the fiancée stresses the very nature of Truth. Garrett is in fact lying so that his fiancée will know nothing about the scheme thought up by her father, the editor, but by lying he is in fact telling the truth inasmuch as the "research" does exist. The *énonciation* is thus true, the *énoncé* a lie, a situation complicated by the fact that, within this *énonciation,* Garrett's real subject position is also that of a liar.

8. It is worthwhile stressing how such an insistence of the letter can determine a textual activity irrespective of the conscious project of the text. Preminger's *Thirteenth Letter* (1951) provides a striking example. The film tells of the impact on a small Canadian community of a series of poison-pen letters, where what starts as an apparently isolated piece of malicious gossip builds up into a veritable plot to turn neighbor against neighbor and cultivate the worst form of baseless suspicion. The power behind rumors of a purely anonymous kind leads one of the characters to make observations that can clearly be in-

terpreted as a denunciation of a very special kind of rumor enjoying currency at the time: accusations of Communism and the resulting witch hunts. What needs to be stressed in *The Thirteenth Letter* is that at no time is there an attempt to count the number of letters: there is the first, then the second, but after that the accent is put on their existence, not on their number. The text's logic invites us to see the title of the film differently: the "thirteenth letter" is literally that, the thirteenth letter *of the alphabet,* namely *M* for McCarthy. Q.E.D. (or quite elementary deduction).

9. I attempt in chapter 5 to draw together a few threads as to the place of hats in the Langian textual system as a whole.

4 Identity and Identification: Seeing is Believing

1. Referring to this passage in *The Legend of Freud,* Samuel Weber points out that Freud uses the word *Trieb* ("drive") to designate the desire to see or know. I have, as usual, substituted *drive* for *instinct.* On this question see chapter 6 n. 1.

2. Lacan makes a similar point (1978, 202).

3. Paul Jensen has rightly compared the film to *The Most Dangerous Game* (Ernest B. Schoedsack and Irving Pichel, 1932), but he refrains from asking who plays the villain Zaroff: Thorndike the hunter or Quive-Smith the Nazi? Apparently Count Zaroff on his island equals Quive-Smith, and Rainsford, who is captured by him, equals Thorndike. Rainsford hunts animals, Zaroff humans. But the film quickly sets up comparisons between the two activities to show that the two men are not so different (the film introduces a most interesting sexual element that is absent from the original story and that highlights the link between *jouissance* and death). That Rainsford kills Zaroff with an arrow indicates the extent to which *Man Hunt* is a remake of the earlier film. One must not forget that it is Thorndike who is first presented as the hunter. Thus the role of the double prevents any clear-cut answer to the question I put in Jensen's place.

4. See my discussion of doubling via the function of the champagne bottles in *The Woman in the Window* (chapter 5).

5. Another intertextual reference: Zaroff is always dressed in black.

6. Intentional or not, this is a subtle reference to the sympathy shown by the British ruling class for Hitler.

7. Part of the hunt takes place in the Underground, which looks forward to the ending of *While the City Sleeps* and Fuller's *Pickup on South Street,* thus underlining the way the Langian textual system condenses apparently separate genres.

8. When Thorndike jumps from the plane, his bodily position recalls the one when he was dumped over the cliff by Quive-Smith, a resemblance that ties up the various narrative strands, while also functioning as a doubling of signifiers.

9. Her father is arrested, like many others, and is threatened with execution if the assassin is not found. He does not appear at the end of the film, and his fate is not evoked. It would seem likely that the complete original version of the film

included some information on this; certainly a still I came across in an issue (1962) of the now defunct British film magazine *Motion* indicated that the film did indeed include shots of hostages being executed, which are now missing from all prints of the film I have seen, including the—apparently—most complete one available shown at the Edinburgh Film Festival in 1975.

10. A contemporary anti-Nazi film, Leo MacCarey's *Once upon a Honeymoon* (1942), makes a contribution to this theme in a remarkable sequence that sums up much of what is being discussed here (like *To Be or Not to Be,* it is a comedy). The Cary Grant character is forced to make a speech over Nazi radio calling on Americans to see Nazi Germany as their true friend and ally. The Nazis have allowed him to write the talk himself to lend it spontaneity and verisimilitude, but they have three translators standing by for the trial run, just in case. Grant adopts the tactic of trying to create a discourse whose enounced will convince the Nazis, but whose enunciation will reveal his true subject position: as an anti-Nazi under pressure warning Americans of the danger. Thus he begins, "Hitler's love for American knows no bounds." The translators immediately start waving their arms and shouting, "Nein!" Says Grant, "OK, bounds equals boundaries," thereby emphasizing for the spectator the play of conflicting subject positions through language, where the meaning of what is said is determined by the position of the enunciator and not by a preordained message. Except for Gruber, the Nazis of *Hangmen Also Die* are less astute than the translators in *Once upon a Honeymoon.*

11. If Gruber the Nazi is likable and sympathetic in certain ways, so Inspector Prentice, the English policeman in *The Ministry of Fear,* is taken by the hero for a Nazi. Like Gruber, he wears a bowler hat (see below).

12. He is played by Dan Duryea, who was to figure prominently in Lang's next two films. For a discussion of his roles, see chapter 5.

5 *The Woman in the Window:* Home Sweet Home

1. As Stephen Neale has pointed out, "the process of desire in melodrama interrupts or problematises precisely the order the discourse and actions of the law have established in the face of 'lawlessness' and social disorder" (Neale 1980, 22).

2. The whole question, to which he gives the name of "motivation," has been analyzed in detail by Gérard Genette (1969).

3. And scissors "return" in *Scarlet Street:* Cross almost "cuts" his wife with them.

4. As Wanley and the woman plan how best to dispose of the corpse, he insists on something important: "We mustn't overlook any detail." This, of course, is impossible, as that alert snooper, the blackmailing bodyguard, shows. Only the unconscious is in the position never to overlook a detail, and Wanley's slips are very eloquent.

5. The word *key* takes on a new dimension in the context of *Secret beyond the Door,* a title that condenses the various meanings of *heimlich* and *unheimlich* and plays systematically on the importance of keys and doors (see chapter 7).

6. Quoted by Luc Moullet (1963, 167). My translation.

7. From such a point of view, the simultaneous presence of Laura and her portrait is also *unheimlich*.

8. Needless to say—but I will say it anyway—the film cannot be too explicit about homosexuality and must proceed by carefully chosen codes: Lydecker has a high voice, has a "pretentious" way of speaking, is fastidious about his clothes, and eats in a "prim" manner. In other words, he is "really" a woman. Needless to say (see above), such codes are never innocent.

9. *Angel Face* can be seen as a more radical and extreme remake of *Laura*. The emphasis from beginning to end on the death wish component of the later film helps explain its increased misogyny (see above, Introduction).

10. I say "horror," but one could use the word *surprise* in the Lacanian sense: that feeling in which the subject realizes there is something beyond the self, finding at one and the same time more than was expected (Lacan 1973, 27). The "surprise" is displaced by the spectator and becomes "frustration" (that is, critical rejection). The fate of the ego is, after all, to be dispossessed by its own reflection of all it strives to attain (Lacan 1978, 308).

6 *House by the River:* Pinups and Hang-ups

1. I am adopting, after Lacan, the word *drive* to translate *Trieb,* the official SE term *instinct* being hopelessly confusing and a mistranslation of major proportions. See chapter 4, n. 1.

2. Willemen is presumably thinking of the observation in Freud, SE 14:130.

3. The word *figures* figures as a signifier: John is interested in numerical ones, Stephen in female ones. Which figures.

4. It is therefore interesting to note that, as soon as the police find the sack, they bring it to Stephen, although they know it belongs to John. This fact is naturalized on the level of the *énoncé* by their wish to question Stephen, but its real significance lies on the level of the *énonciation:* it is Emily—and what she represents for the spectator, via Stephen—who returns metonymically as the sack.

5. John is also put in Stephen's place by being accused of the murder. By saying nothing in order to avoid being suspected and by playing on his elder brother's sense of (paternal) duty, Stephen is, as it were, framing him.

6. I deliberately take up here, in the very structure of my sentence, the English equivalent—*nevertheless*—of the formula used by Octave Mannoni (1969) to define the structure and function of disavowal: "Je sais bien, mais quand même . . ."

7. The word *limp* can be taken here as a noun or an adjective.

8. Except for Emily, who has been strangled and who must remain the scapegoat for male desire; and Stephen, who must be punished and dies from a combination of strangulation and falling (a Christian ending?).

9. See chapter 2, n. 1.

7 *Secret beyond the Door:* Romance in a Low Key

1. I use the dubious terms *guide* and *labyrinth* deliberately because the conscious project of the text—which finds itself reinforced at the end—functions within a framework that is a travesty of Freudian psychoanalysis (which the script claims to be applying) but reinforces ego psychology.

2. It can be said therefore that this function of the voice-off recalls that of the particular use made of the newsreel in *Fury* (see chapter 2, section 1). In both cases the place of the enunciator disappears behind a would-be transparent message.

3. It is, however, necessary for Celia to have someone within the diegetic world to talk to, and this person is Bob, her lawyer, who, being in love with her, is an ideal interlocutor: he will listen and believe. At one point, Celia says to him, "Mark would not lie to me." The word *lie* being too strong in the context, it heralds the return of Celia's central obsession and, especially, a desire to accuse her husband. Her statement must be interpreted as its opposite inasmuch as it is Celia's unconscious that is talking. She thus succeeds in planting doubt in Bob's mind and getting him on her side, as she does with the spectator.

4. This can be compared with the bathroom sequence in *House by the River,* where the spectator spied on Emily through Stephen and the scopophilia could be disavowed because of the way Emily was represented by the textual system. Again, an unconscious drive is turned into its opposite thanks to secondary revision, shored up by disavowal.

5. Readers will remember my observations on the twin lights that flank bathroom mirrors on two occasions in *The Woman in the Window.*

6. The overall mood and the use of lighting to create the unknown is persistent in Lang and brings him close indeed to Tourneur, whose horror films of the 1940s are a high spot in the evolution of the genre.

7. Willemen's reading of the voice-off in such Tourneur films as *Experiment Perilous* and *Out of the Past* (Willemen 1975, 26–29) raises questions similar to those I am broaching here.

8. Raymond Bellour insisted on the link between hypnosis and Lang's films during a talk in the context of Christian Metz's seminar.

8 SutureSelf

1. As I pointed out in chapter 1, I wish to indicate certain elements only in the present chapter, as suture is not the major concern of this book, the enunciative devices it entails being common to all classical films or films of fiction. To reject suture is to reject Hollywood, which some have decided to do.

2. Present massively in a German film such as *M.*

3. This is no accident, given the dimension of lighting in Lang, already discussed in detail. I shall return to the question of lampposts below when analyzing *Scarlet Street.*

4. This disavowal has been referred to by Christian Metz (1977b, 344–45).

He points out that the hesitation invites us to pay attention to the way the film constructs itself as an activity (equals enunciation) and that the link created between two shots reinforces the ideology of cause and effect within a recognizable diegetic world (equals enounced).

5. I would add, in the case of the wipe, that discursive contiguity is displaced, seemingly, onto referential *non*contiguity. In reality, the technique of the wipe favors the metonymy of desire by avoiding a sharp cut, too abrupt a jump: there is a sense of continuity that gratifies the ego's need for images that throw back a unified self.

6. There is a logic of the signifier that takes no account of the referential dimension of the text: a linguistic one showing that Lacan's "instance de la lettre" is to be taken literally. See Conley (1983) for a detailed analysis.

7. This is the one aspect of the film that is decidedly inferior to the Renoir of which it is a remake, *La Chienne* (1931). In the earlier film, the Michel Simon character (the French version of Chris) not only is indifferent to the death of the pimp (moreover, a far less vicious character than Johnny) but positively enjoys being a tramp because it rids him once and for all of his wife. The ending of *La Chienne* is amoral and anarchistic, that of *Scarlet Street* ideologically conventional: Chris must be punished, one way or another.

Conclusion

1. A fact that Godard had clearly grasped when making *Sympathy for the Devil/One + One* (1968). His refusal to film the entire, complete recording of the Rolling Stones' song was part of a desire not to give the audience that plenitude sought.

References

Allembert, Georges. 1957. *Image et Son* 106:13.

Barthes, Roland. 1964. "Rhétorique de l'image." *Communications* 4:40–51.

————. 1970. *S/Z*. Paris: Editions du Seuil.

Bellour, Raymond. 1979. "Psychosis, Neurosis, Perversion." *Camera Obscura* 3/4:105–35.

————. 1981. "On Fritz Lang." In Jenkins, Stephen, 26–37. Originally published in *Critique* 226 (March 1966).

Benveniste, Emile. 1966a. "Structures des relations de personnes dans le verbe." In his *Problèmes de linguistique générale*. Paris: Editions Gallimard, 1:225–36.

————. 1966b. "Les Relations de temps dans le verbe français." In his *Problèmes de linguistique générale*. Paris: Editions Gallimard, 1:237–50.

————. 1966c. "La nature des pronoms." In his *Problèmes de linguistique générale*. Paris: Editions Gallimard, 1:251–57.

Bergala, Alain. 1976. "La Pendule." *Cahiers du Cinéma* 268/69:40–46.

Bogdanovich, Peter. 1967. *Fritz Lang in America*. London: Studio Vista.

Bonitzer, Pascal. 1971a. "Le Gros Orteil." *Cahiers du Cinéma* 232:14–23.

————. 1971b. "Hors-champ." *Cahiers du Cinéma* 234/35:15–26.

————. 1977. "Les Deux Regards." *Cahiers du Cinéma* 275:41–46.

Brooks, Peter. 1977. "Freud's Masterplot: Questions of Narrative." *Literature and Psychoanalysis. The Question of Reading: Otherwise,* special issue of *Yale French Studies* 55/56:280–300.

————. 1979. "Fictions of the Wolfman: Freud and Narrative Understanding." *Topology of Freud,* special issue of *Diacritics* (1):72–83.

Burch, Noël. 1969. *Praxis du cinéma*. Paris: Editions Gallimard.

————. 1980. "Fritz Lang: German Period." In Roud, Richard, ed., *Cinema: A Critical Dictionary.* London: Martin Secker and Warburg, 583–99.

———— and Dana, Jorge. 1974. "Propositions." *Afterimage* (London) 5 (Spring):40–66.

Comolli, Jean-Louis, and Géré, François. 1981. "Two Fictions Concerning Hate." In Jenkins, Stephen, 125–146. Originally published in *Cahiers du Cinéma* 286 (1976).

Conley, Tom. 1983. "Writing Scarlet Street." *Modern Language Notes* 98 (December):1085–1109.

Cook, Pam. 1978. "Duplicity in *Mildred Pierce.*" In Kaplan, Ann, 68–81.

Courtade, Francis. 1963. *Fritz Lang.* Paris: Le Terrain Vague.

Demonsablon, Phillipe. 1981. "The Imperious Dialectic of Fritz Lang." In Jenkins, Stephen, 18–25. Originally published in *Cahiers du Cinéma* 99 (1959).

Descombes, Vincent. 1977. *L'Inconscient malgré lui.* Paris: Editions de Minuit.

Douchet, Jean. 1981. "Dix-sept Plans." In Bellour, R., ed. *Le Cinéma américain. Analyses de films.* Paris: Editions Flammarion, 200–232.

Ducrot, Oswald. 1972. *Dire et ne pas dire.* Paris: Editions Hermann.

Eagleton, Terry. 1985. "Marxism, Structuralism, and Post-Structuralism." *Marx after Derrida,* special issue of *Diacritics* 15(4):2–12.

Eisner, Lotte. 1947. "Notes sur le style de Fritz Lang." *Revue du Cinéma* 5 (février):3.

————. 1976. *Fritz Lang.* London: Martin Secker and Warburg.

Elsaesser, Thomas. 1971. "Why Hollywood." *Monogram* (London) 1:4–10.

————. 1972. "Tales of Sound and Fury." *Monogram* (London) 4:2–15.

Freud, Sigmund. *The Standard Edition of the Complete Psychological Works.* London: Hogarth Press, 24 vols. References in the text are abbreviated as follows:

SE 4:1–338. *The Interpretation of Dreams.*

SE 5:339–627. *The Interpretation of Dreams.*

SE 7:130–243. *Three Essays on the Theory of Sexuality.*

SE 12:147–56. "Remembering, Repeating and Working-Through."

SE 12:218–26. "Formulations on the Two Principles of Mental Functioning."

SE 14:117–40. "Instincts and Their Vicissitudes."

SE 14:146–58. "Repression."

SE 14:222–35. "A Metapsychological Supplement to the Theory of Dreams."

SE 15:15–79. "Parapraxes." *Introductory Lectures on Psychoanalysis.*

SE 17:7–122. "From the History of an Infantile Neurosis."

SE 17:217–52. "The Uncanny."

SE 18:7–64. "Beyond the Pleasure Principle."

SE 20:87–172. "Inhibitions, Symptoms, Anxiety."

Genette, Gérard. 1969. "Vraisemblance et motivation." In his *Figures II.* Paris: Editions du Seuil, 71–99.

Harvey, Sylvia. 1978. "Woman's Place: The Absent Family of *Film Noir.*" In Kaplan, Ann, 22–34.

Heath, Stephen. 1976a. "Narrative Space." *Screen* 17, no. 3 (Autumn):68–112.

———. 1976b. "On Screen, in Frame: Film and Ideology." *Quarterly Review of Film Studies,* August, 251–65.

———. 1976c. "Screen Images, Film Memory." *Edinburgh 76 Magazine,* no. 1, 33–42.

———. 1977a. "Film Performance." *Cinetracts* 2:7–17.

———. 1977b. "Notes on Suture." *Screen* 18(4):48–76.

Humphries, Reynold. 1979. *"Peeping Tom:* Voyeurism, the Camera and the Spectator." *Film Reader* (Northwestern University) 4:193–200.

———. 1982. *Fritz Lang cinéaste américain.* Paris: Editions Albatros.

Irigaray, Luce. 1967. "Approche d'une grammaire d'énonciation de l'hystérique et de l'obsessionnel." *Langages* 5:99–109.

Jakobson, Roman. 1956. "Two Aspects of Language and Two Types of Aphasic Disturbances." In his *Fundamentals of Language.* The Hague: Mouton, 69–96.

Jameson, Fredric. 1977. "Imaginary and Symbolic in Lacan: Marxism, Psychoanalytic Criticism and the Problem of the Subject." *Literature and Psychoanalysis. The Question of Reading: Otherwise,* special issue of *Yale French Studies* 55/56:338–95.

———. 1981. *The Political Unconscious. Narrative as a Socially Symbolic Act.* Ithaca: Cornell University Press.

Jenkins, Stephen. 1981. "Lang: Fear and Desire." In Jenkins, Stephen, ed., *Fritz Lang. The Image and the Look.* London: British Film Institute, 38–124.

Jensen, Paul M. 1969. *The Cinema of Fritz Lang.* New York: Barnes.

Kané, Pascal. 1971. "Soupçons." *Cahiers du Cinéma* 228:56–57.

Kaplan, Ann. 1978. "The Place of Women in Fritz Lang's *The Blue Gardenia.*" In Kaplan, Ann, ed., *Women in Film Noir.* London: British Film Institute, 83–90.

Kitses, Jim. 1969. *Horizons West.* London: Thames and Hudson and British Film Institute.

Lacan, Jacques. 1973. *Les Quatre Concepts fondamentaux de la psychanalyse.* Vol. 11 of Le Séminaire (1963–64). Paris: Editions du Seuil.

———. 1975. *Les Ecrits techniques de Freud.* Vol. 1 of Le Séminaire (1953–54). Paris: Editions du Seuil.

———. 1978. *Le Moi dans la théorie de Freud et dans la technique de la psychanalyse.* Vol. 2 of Le Séminaire (1954–55). Paris: Editions du Seuil.

———. 1981. *Les Psychoses.* Vol. 3 of Le Séminaire (1955–56). Paris: Editions du Seuil.

———. 1986. *L'Ethique de la psychanalyse.* Vol. 7 of Le Séminaire (1959–60). Paris: Editions du Seuil.

Lambert, Gavin. 1955. "Fritz Lang's America: 2." *Sight and Sound* (London), Autumn, 96.

Lentricchia, Frank. 1983. *Criticism and Social Change.* Chicago: Chicago University Press.

McArthur, Colin. 1972. *Underworld USA.* London: Secker and Warburg and British Film Institute.

Mannoni, Octave. 1969. "Je sais bien . . . mais quand même . . ." In his *Clefs pour l'Imaginaire ou l'Autre Scène.* Paris: Editions du Seuil, 9–33.

Méraud, Michel. 1956. *Image et Son* 95/96:16.

Metz, Christian. 1972. *Essais sur la signification au cinéma.* Vol. 2. Paris: Editions Klincksieck.

———. 1977a. "Le Perçu et le Nommé." In his *Essais sémiotiques.* Paris: Editions Klincksieck, 130–62.

———. 1977b. *Le Signifiant imaginaire.* Paris: Union Générale d'Editions, 10/18. This volume contains the following articles:
"Le Signifiant imaginaire," 7–109.
"Histoire/Discours: Note sur deux voyeurismes," 111–20.
"Le Film de fiction et son spectateur: Etude métapsychologique," 121–75.
"Métaphore/Métonymie, ou le référent imaginaire," 177–371.

Miller, Jacques-Alain. 1977. "Suture: Elements of the Logic of the Signifier." *Screen* 18 (4):24–34.

Mitry, Jean. 1963. *Esthétique et psychologie du cinéma.* Vol. 1. Paris: Editions Universitaires.

Moulet, Luc. 1963. *Fritz Lang.* Paris: Editions Seghers.

Mourlet, Michel. 1981. "Fritz Lang's Trajectory." In Jenkins, Stephen, 12–17. Originally published in *Cahiers du Cinéma* 99 (1959).

Neale, Stephen. 1980. *Genre.* London: British Film Institute.

Oudart, Jean-Pierre. 1970. "Travail, lecture, jouissance." *Cahiers du Cinéma* 222:43–50.

———. 1977. "Cinema and Suture." *Screen* 18 (4):35–47. Originally published in *Cahiers du Cinéma* 211 and 212, (1969).

Récanati, François. 1979. *La Transparence et l'énonciation: Pour introduire à la pragmatique.* Paris: Editions du Seuil.

Smith, Henry Nash. 1950. *Virgin Land. The American West as Symbol and Myth.* Cambridge, Mass.: Harvard University Press.

Todorov, Tzvetan. 1970. "Problèmes de l'énonciation." *Langages* 17:3–11.

———. 1971. "Introduction au vraisemblable." In his *Poétique de la prose.* Paris: Editions du Seuil, 92–99.

Tyler, Parker. 1947. *Magic and Myth of the Movies.* London: Secker and Warburg (published in this edition in 1971).

Vernet, Marc. 1976. "Espace (Structuration de l')." In his *Lectures du film.* Paris: Editions Albatros, 86–95.

Weber, Samuel. 1982. *The Legend of Freud.* Minneapolis: University of Minnesota Press.

———. 1987. *Institution and Interpretation.* Minneapolis: University of Minnesota Press.

Willemen, Paul. 1975. "Notes toward the Construction of Readings of Tourneur." In Johnston, Claire, and Willemen, Paul, eds., *Jacques Tourneur.* Edinburgh: Edinburgh Film Festival Publications, 16–34.

———. 1976. "Voyeurism, the Look and Dwoskin." *Afterimage* (London) 6:40–50.

Wollen, Peter. 1969. *Signs and Meaning in the Cinema.* London: Thames and Hudson and British Film Institute.

Wood, Robin. 1980. "Fritz Lang. 1936–1960." In Roud, Richard, ed., *Cinema: A Critical Dictionary.* London: Martin Secker and Warburg, 599–609.

Index

Fritz Lang

Designed by Chris L. Smith
Composed by the Composing Room of Michigan in Simoncini Garamond with display
lines in Simoncini Garamond and Futura Bold.
Printed by the Maple Press on S. D. Warren's 50-lb. Sebago Eggshell Cream
Offset paper and bound in Joanna's Arrestox A and stamped in black.